D0477696

A NAME ON A WALL

'*A Name on a Wall* is one of the finest and most moving books I have read in a long time. It is calm and understated, and yet it is written with great emotional intensity. The contrasting stories of two men, a generation apart, in wars fought on widely different moral bases, is extraordinarily powerful. I found it hard to think about anything else for days after I finished reading it. I can't recommend it too highly.'

John Simpson, BBC World Affairs Editor

'We gaze at the names on war memorials and wonder, and now I know the reason why. This book is meticulous in its research, compelling in its structure. A marvellous book.'

Sir Michael Parkinson, broadcaster, journalist, author

'It is, quite simply, a beautiful book. It is a meditation on war, chance, honour and duty, but more importantly it's about grief, love and the ties that bind us as families. Mark Byford has a curious nature and a tender heart, and his detective work gives new life to one soldier who died in Vietnam nearly fifty years ago. I shall never look at a war memorial again without wondering who was the young man whose name is on a wall.'

Dame Jenni Murray, award-winning author and broadcaster; presenter of *Woman's Hour*, Radio 4

'A remarkable story that skilfully knits together heroic family history and the broader historic sweep of the tragedy of the Vietnam war. So moving and thoughtful, there has been no history of that conflict remotely like this one.'

Andrew Marr, award-winning author, journalist and broadcaster

'A compelling read, with thoughtful reflections on the futility or otherwise of wars. A raw but sensitively drawn cameo, the result of extraordinary research driven by a compulsive sense of mission and pilgrimage ignited by the name on a memorial wall of a soldier killed in action.'

Admiral The Lord Boyce
Chief of the Defence Staff 2001–03

'A tour de force: unique, gripping and both intimate and sweeping at the same time. In this remarkable book, Mark Byford finds in the life of a single soldier a compelling and timeless story – a story of heroism and duty, of leadership and inspiration, and of making sense of a tragic loss. Along the way he teaches us about the parallels – and differences – among all wars and between the United States and his own United Kingdom. This is such a powerful and profound read that speaks to all of us who have watched the best of our young men and women march off to combat, whether in the European battlefields of the Second World War, the hamlets and caves of Vietnam, or the desert and cities of Iraq.'

David Westin, president ABC News 1997–2010

'A thoroughly absorbing story, written with great compassion. It is a sincere and captivating exploration of family, friendship and duty, told with real humanity. Mark Byford shows a detective's zeal in following up the flimsiest of leads and developing it into a gripping and moving narrative. For the reader who wants an insight into the Vietnam War, and the kind of Americans who fought in it, this book is the ideal starting point. An enormously ambitious project, pulled off with great style, it's a remarkable achievement.'

Tony Maddox, executive vice-president and managing director, CNN International

'An absolutely fascinating and original story. It can be read in so many different ways in terms of biography, human emotions and war, spirituality and human destiny. It captures so many insights about human nature and human dilemmas. A name on a wall has become rich in identity.'

The Very Reverend James Atwell, Dean of Winchester Cathedral

'An extraordinary and emotional journey described in vivid terms. Vietnam is a war which many would like to forget, but for those who mourn the deaths of their sons, husbands and fathers it can never be far from their minds. Mark Byford provides a compelling illustration of the human cost of conflict.'

Rt Hon. Sir Menzies Campbell MP,
politician and commentator on international affairs

'Extraordinary – the word appears innumerable times throughout this exceptional book, and it serves as the most appropriate one-word summary of its power and impact. Mark Byford's unbiased, objective-observer role, coupled with his dogged determination to research, interview and travel to the ends of the earth to follow every lead to "get it right", have, in my view, created a masterpiece worthy at minimum of the mandatory reading for every military and political professional. While the author says: "The ordinariness [of the story] was to be at the heart of the matter", that "ordinariness" is precisely what makes this such an "extraordinary" piece of work.'

Robert (Bob) Brace II, Colonel, Infantry, USA, retired
C Company Commander 2nd/5th 1st Cavalry Division, Vietnam 1970;
USMA Class of 1968

'Mark Byford's terrific, thoughtful book shows the power of great storytelling in contributing to a clearer understanding of both the Vietnam War and the realities of war for present and future generations. Following his providential experience at the Vietnam Veterans Memorial, he dedicates himself to telling the inspirational story of one Vietnam veteran through dogged investigation, careful documentation and moving and meaningful accounts from those who loved and served with him. In return, he is rewarded with new insights and revelations about the life of his own father, a veteran of the Second World War. Since 2000, the Library of Congress Veterans History Project has been collecting, preserving and making accessible the wartime stories of America's veterans. I envision that *A Name on a Wall* will encourage more Vietnam veterans to come forward and tell their own stories to provide instruction, information and education about such an important time in America's war history.'

Bob Patrick, director of the Veterans History Project, American Folklife Center, Library of Congress, Washington DC

'A masterpiece. A page-turner. A deeply moving, unfolding drama from an evocative storyteller on a remarkable and uplifting quest. First and foremost, it is a powerful and provoking reflection of the tragic legacy of the Vietnam war. But it offers so much more: inspiring personal stories, challenging and poetic pictures, and, most compellingly, a profound expression of the underlying theme of loss. After being immersed in the grief of such tragedy, the book emphasises a need for hope: that our troubled, contemporary world has more beams of sunshine like the one that shone on Larry's name; more examples of how grief from loss can be channelled constructively; and hope that all the positive emotional energy we can muster can keep fuelling our motivation to find alternatives to war.'

Gael Lindenfield, psychotherapist, author and leading expert on healing and recovery

'I will be honest. Part of me wanted to read it and part of me didn't – I guess the part not knowing and afraid to know. The research is awesome. It's kinda strange how Mark Byford came into our lives and wanted to do this. But I'm glad he did. Now Larry's journey is complete – thanks to him.'

Debbie Sitton, Larry Byford's sister

A NAME ON A WALL

TWO MEN, TWO WARS, TWO DESTINIES

MARK BYFORD

with HILARY BLEIKER

EDINBURGH AND LONDON

First published in Great Britain in 2013 by
MAINSTREAM PUBLISHING COMPANY
(EDINBURGH) LTD
7 Albany Street
Edinburgh EH1 3UG

ISBN 9781780576619

In June 1967, Mark Byford celebrated his ninth birthday. Living in Huddersfield in Yorkshire, he was a football-mad schoolboy and had no connection with the Vietnam War.

In 1979, he graduated in Law from the University of Leeds and joined the BBC as a researcher. An award-winning journalist and editor, he worked at the BBC for 32 years. From 2004 to 2011, he was Deputy Director General and Head of Journalism, responsible for all the BBC's news and current-affairs output across the UK and around the world.

Hilary Bleiker was eight years old in June 1967, living in Hempstead in Kent.

In 1980, she graduated in English from the University of Leeds and for three decades taught English and Media Studies in a number of schools in England.

They married in 1980, have five children and live in Winchester.

For Larry and Lawry Byford
Heroes to their families
Both called up
Both did their duty
One paid the price
The ultimate sacrifice
A name on a wall
Never to be forgotten

. . . war is always the same. It is young men dying in the fullness of their promise. It is trying to kill a man that you do not even know well enough to hate. Therefore, to know war is to know there is still madness in the world.

President Lyndon B. Johnson
State of the Union address
12 January 1966

CONTENTS

FOREWORD

A deeply religious friend of mine swears that everything happens for a reason. That every birth, death, close call, flat tyre, fire and tornado is being choreographed by a Supreme Being who keeps track of it all – and each of us – as we are being tossed about by His events. It seems far-fetched, but one cannot really disprove this any more than one can disprove that God – or Gods – do or do not exist.

When you read this book, one begins to wonder if we do live in a world composed of something beyond just random events. Maybe some events come to pass for a reason. Certain events surely do trigger responses that can be profound.

I was 19 in Vietnam. I was wounded and really should have died. I can tell you that the best metaphor for war is the game of Russian roulette. You are spinning the cylinder on a loaded gun by entering a combat zone. You are there because of world events far beyond your control.

Both Lawry and Larry Byford could have shared the same fate – decades apart – in the random madness of war. Both men felt a sense of duty. After all, a citizen owes something to his country. Lawry Byford would probably never, due to his social class and lack of opportunity, have risen much further than a coal miner or the tradesman that he was training to be as war engulfed Europe. Yet Lawry blossomed as a 19 year old in war when his abilities to take down codes and send messages were discovered by the British and American armies. Lawry went on to a brilliant career and was knighted by Her Majesty The Queen. So what future might have unfolded for Larry? Would he have had horses and a private plane with a big Texan cowboy hat painted on the fuselage? Larry Byford met his fate in Vietnam in a futile, courageous mission trying to save a wounded man, a talented graduate of the US Military Academy. Larry remains at rest, forever young, in a Texas cemetery.

This entire book takes you on a journey. You will learn a great deal. A journey that unfolded as a mission. An extraordinary experience like nothing ever done before in America that I know of. I could relate to the personal drive, to something which others will just have to wait to understand. The story is important. It matters. That is why Mark Byford wrote it. That is why he saw Larry Byford's name.

From an odd coincidence at the crack of dawn on a spring morning by the shiny granite of the Vietnam Veterans Memorial, he ends up travelling the world. In his quest to make sense of a tragedy in South-East Asia, he links up with a still-grieving family in rural Texas, American veterans who were present at Larry's death, former members of the Viet Cong as well as leading academics and historians. At the same time, he comes to terms with the war tale of his own father.

Those fellow veterans who remembered Larry are still in psychic and spiritual pain when recounting the circumstances of a sad, chilling, fateful day, long ago. The reader will see the agony of the Vietnam War for its survivors and for American society. And, as we see the most recent wars coming to a close in Iraq and Afghanistan, the book leaves the reader much to ponder.

The Wall is a place where the living and the dead commune. It is here that I met Mark Byford. His story was fascinating to hear as we sat near much activity of volunteers lining up to read the names of the American War Dead on the 30th anniversary of The Wall. He read the name of Larry Byford. His journey had reached its conclusion where it had begun – at a 492-ft-long memorial in Washington DC.

This book is amazing and relevant for a worldwide audience. It touches so many issues. People need to do things that matter.

Foreword

I believe we all have a calling in our life. This was part of Mark Byford's. To tell the story. To touch others. To inspire.

Jan C. Scruggs

Jan C. Scruggs is the founder and president of the Vietnam Veterans Memorial Fund. He conceived the idea of building the Vietnam Veterans Memorial, the most visited war memorial in the United States, as a tribute to the more than 58,000 dead who served during America's longest and most divisive war of the twentieth century, and to help 'heal a nation'. The memorial was built and dedicated in 1982.

CHAPTER 1

PANEL 22E LINE 52

I woke around 5 a.m., showered quickly and headed off down 17th Street in search of The Wall. Walking briskly through the gradually fading darkness, I passed the home of the most powerful man in the world. The city felt eerily quiet and empty. Still asleep. Unoccupied.

As I crossed Constitution Avenue, a couple of taxis whisked past me, taking what I presumed were early-morning government workers to their desks. The road returned to silence. In front of me, the world's tallest stone structure, the Washington Monument, dominated the scene. I cast my eyes to its highest point, 550 feet up, and as I did so I became aware, through the breaking clouds, of the faint stirrings of the upcoming dawn. I turned right into Constitution Gardens. Ahead, the floodlit, gleaming white stone of the Lincoln Memorial looked magnificent, its colonnaded facade shimmering in the reflection pool ahead. I stopped in my tracks, trying to get my bearings. I knew that my destination must be very close.

The sun had started to peek tentatively over the horizon. Cloaked in muted shades of orange and red, it turned the sky a murky grey and cast a feeble light on the surroundings. I peered hard into the grainy gloom, squinting, trying to find what I was looking for.

There, about a hundred metres away, it stood. Unlit, it was difficult to decipher. Sunk into the ground, shaped like a long, thin arrowhead, it blended into its surroundings. In contrast to the gleaming white of the Lincoln and Washington, this memorial was black, which struck me as painfully appropriate. The closer I got, the more its power and presence struck me. I realised that I was actually looking at two walls made up of a series of shiny black-granite panels that came together at an oblique angle to form a chevron. Each wall started out at just eight inches high and gradually built to a height of more than ten feet.

Then I remembered what I'd read the night before in the guidebook I had found in my hotel bedroom. How its young creator, Maya Ying Lin, had said that she wanted it to appear as: '*a rift emerging from and receding into the earth*' and to create the sensation of walking down to the depths only to come out again. '*The names,*' she declared, '*seemingly infinite in number, convey the sense of overwhelming numbers, while unifying these individuals into a whole.*' Slowly, I walked down the path towards the point where the walls met, the panels increasing in size with every step. And as I descended, I saw myself reflected in the sheen of The Wall's surface, my face pixellating into the mass of names. I had arrived at The Wall. The Vietnam Veterans Memorial. Built:

> in honour of the men and women of the armed forces of The United States who served in the Vietnam War. The names of those who gave their lives and of those who remain missing inscribed in the order they were taken from us.

Fifty-eight thousand two hundred and eighty-two names. Almost five hundred feet long, the list seemed to go on for ever. Each name clearly and cleanly carved, together forming a sea of sacrifice and courage. A hundred and forty panels of polished black-gabbro rock etched with the name of each American killed or missing in action from the country's longest war. In chronological order, the first casualty in 1959, the last in 1975. The power was its simplicity. The beauty was its boldness. The effect was overwhelming.

I stood facing one panel and cast my eyes slowly down the names. Row after row after row. Each and every soldier had made the ultimate sacrifice. No statements. No explanations. No rank or status. No faces. The only marker being a name set amongst comrades.

I continued walking alongside The Wall. Instinctively, I genuflected in reverence in front of a panel and offered a silent prayer. I realised that I was completely alone, surrounded by silence, apart from an occasional bird call from the nearby trees.

The rising sun, fully robed now in vibrant orange, was starting to reveal itself in all its glory as it lit up the brand-new day. I stood up slowly, reflecting on the lives of so many lost. I felt a sense of bewilderment, horror and despondency. But then, something extraordinary happened.

As I straightened, a bold, yellow finger of light flashed directly over my right shoulder. My gaze followed its course as I saw it hit The Wall and illuminate the panel directly in front of me. It underlined the engraved lettering with ruler-like precision and caused reflections to bounce off the polished stone. The light thrown out was blindingly intense, but as I looked I became acutely aware of one particular name. On the right-hand side, almost halfway up, it appeared to shine out, the light focusing in such a way that it appeared to project out from The Wall itself.

PANEL 22E LINE 52

I looked again and took a deep breath. I followed every letter from left to right, devouring each one with my eyes, then scanning the name as a whole:

L A R R Y S B Y F O R D

Larry Byford. I breathed in deeply. Byford . . . my own surname, but more than that . . . a similar name to that of my own father, Lawry Byford. Larry and Lawry. Both names variations on the theme of Lawrence. I felt a shiver run through my body. A burst of adrenalin straight to the heart.

Lawry Byford, my father, had also been attached to the US Army, but that was many years earlier, during the Second World War. He had been in France, Belgium and Germany. But why had he, a Brit, served with the American Army? I realised then that I hadn't a clue. I thanked God that his name was not on a wall somewhere. I looked again at the name, and as my own reflection stared back at me I was aware of a tear trickling down my face. I thought of those army songs my dad used to sing with such humour when I was a child in the back of the car. Then, the mood had been joyful. But this was the true face of war: stark and cold. I found myself thinking: what if my father had been killed in conflict? What if he had been the one robbed of living life to the full, like Larry Byford, whose name had just been highlighted so dramatically? And who was this Larry Byford? Where did he come from? What had happened to him? Why did he have to die?

An elderly man in uniform approached, clearly seeing that I was emotional. He was the only other person in the vicinity.

'You a relative?' he enquired.

'No, I'm sorry. I'm British,' I replied lamely. 'I've no military background at all. And I don't have any connection with the Vietnam War. I've seen some of the films.'

'Don't take any notice of them damn Hollywood lies. They're not the truth,' he snarled. 'Hey, why are you tearful, buddy?'

'You see that name up there, Larry S Byford?' I pointed. 'That one with the light hitting it? Well, that's the same name as my own father, except he spells his with a "w". And even though he's British, he served with the American Army in the Second

World War. I've never understood why, but he did. He's now in his 80s. So it all feels a bit strange and a bit emotional. I didn't expect to see that name here.'

I was talking to myself as much as to the man beside me. He came close and put his hand on my shoulder.

'You see that stepladder over there? Bring it across. Here, take this pencil and paper. Put the paper against The Wall. Get up on that ladder if you need to. And make a rubbing of his name. Your poppa was lucky. He came back. But that Larry Byford didn't. Your poppa would want to have it,' he said in a deep, gravelly voice.

I didn't need the ladder; at 6 ft 3 in. I could reach it easily. I touched each letter lightly, feeling its shape and tracing the grooves. I covered it with the paper, started rubbing the pencil over it and watched the letters emerge. As I was doing this, I noticed that printed on the paper were two dates: 1959 in the top right-hand corner and 1975 in the bottom left, together with the words: '*Our nation honors the courage, sacrifice and devotion to duty and country of its Vietnam Veterans.*'

I looked at the name on the paper. I kissed it, folded it carefully then tucked it into my jacket pocket. What was going on here? My heart was beating fast as the old man led me down to the end of The Wall where a directory of names – a huge book – sat inside a protective glass case.

'They're all in alphabetical order,' he explained. 'Take a look. Find out who he was and when he was killed.' I noticed then that his cap had the word 'Vietnam' on the side and a regimental emblem stamped on the front: a yellow shield with a horse's head in the top right-hand corner. At that time, I didn't know its significance.

I opened the book and turned the pages. Name upon name, just like a telephone directory. I put a finger down the Bs. There were thousands. Page after page. Butlers. Butterfields. Then to the Bys until I got to Byfords. To two entries. Gary D Byford. And then there he was. Larry S Byford. I started to read:

> BYFORD LARRY STEPHEN PFC AR 01 MAY 45 23 JUN 67 CENTER TX 22E 52

That was it. Stark, cold, emotionless and brief. Just 22 years of age. A Private First Class in the army. A Texan. June 1967. I was just nine years old when he had died. I thought about that very time in my life. Living in Huddersfield. Attending St Patrick's primary school. Football mad. I remembered I'd come second in the sack race at the school sports day that month. For me, it was a time of innocence, a time of fun.

'Farewell, buddy, and you do what I told you now. Make me a promise. Go take that rubbing to your poppa.'

I looked up. The old man was making his way back along The Wall with a limp and a crook in his back. I waved my goodbye.

I returned again to that 22nd panel on the east side of The Wall and made my way down through all the names. He was right. There would be no Mike Vronsky or Nick Chevotarevich from *The Deer Hunter*. No Walter Kurtz or No Benjamin Willard from *Apocalypse Now* on this wall. This wasn't Hollywood make-believe. This was the real thing. The real war. The pain of real loss. *Martin L Plotkin. James P Schueller. Wayne S Fielden. Bobby L Murphy. Charles L Cronkrite. Stephen C Hass. Carlin M Campbell JR. Vins R Hooper. George Patton.* I paused at that last one, George Patton – I wondered if he was related in any way to the legendary Second World War General, George 'blood and guts' Patton, who, at the end of that war, I recalled, had famously declared: *'It is foolish and wrong to mourn the men who died. Rather we should thank God that such men lived.'* Wrong to mourn the death of all these guys? Well, I was mourning right now and I had no direct connection with any of these lost souls. My eyes zigzagged across the panel, scanning each line. The names just went on . . . *Johnson A Steidler. Edward J Williams. Alexander C Zsigo Jr* . . . until there he was again. Just as the directory had highlighted: on Panel 22E Line 52.

I stood before the name in silence. Taking the paper out from my jacket, I looked at the rubbing again and held it close. June 1967. Four decades ago. The past right there in the present. A dead soldier. A name on a wall. I checked my watch and spontaneously decided to stand for two minutes in silence – in respect to Larry and all those thousands of names and lost lives before me.

Within an hour of arriving, I found myself leaving The Wall and heading back to the hotel to get ready for the day ahead filled, as ever, with business meetings and appointments. What had all that been about? I felt deeply touched, angered at the magnitude of such loss, but dazed and inspired, all at the same time. As I walked up the slope, the panels became smaller and smaller but still more names floated past me. I thought about the founding figure behind The Wall's construction, the Vet Jan Scruggs, and his original vision: never to forget; to heal a nation. I looked back as The Wall faded from sight. A 'black gash of shame' is how one Vet had chastised the design at its unveiling nearly thirty years ago. But shame was not the feeling I'd experienced. The Wall had impacted profoundly on me. Seeing Larry Byford's name singled out from thousands of others by the rays of the early-morning sun had been a strange experience. And yet one of the most moving and most memorable. A very private event that, as it would turn out, I'd be unable to forget.

And that's how it all began. If I hadn't made that early-morning visit, the whole journey of discovery that was to follow would never have happened. A journey that would take me to my father's roots in Normanton; to Larry's childhood home in Texas; to the Rockpile; to a Vets reunion in Georgia; and back to The Wall again.

CHAPTER 2

BEHIND EVERY NAME

Upon my return to England, I didn't tell my father about my experience in Washington immediately, nor did I take the rubbing to show him. I can't explain why. Maybe I was nervous. Maybe I was concerned that such a powerful, intensely personal moment wouldn't mean anything to him. So, although I knew I would never forget it, I tucked away the memory in the recesses of my mind and kept the rubbing in the top drawer of my study desk at home. Every so often I'd open the drawer, take a peek, then hide it away again for safekeeping.

But some years after my return from that trip, something started to gnaw away at me, silently, unobtrusively. That something was indefinable at the time but undeniably present. It seemed to be urging me to act upon my unease, to explore matters further. Maybe it was time to learn more about my dad's war experiences; to find out why he had been with the Americans and discover what had happened in his war. Perhaps the time had come to fulfil the instruction of the man at The Wall: to show my dad the rubbing of Larry's name, to retrieve my own memories of that day and revisit that extraordinary experience which had lain dormant for so long. Or it could be that I just needed to try to understand why this seemingly random experience had affected me so deeply.

Before I knew it, I had set off to my parents' home in Yorkshire, some 250 miles away. I was anxious and apprehensive.

*

Today, my father is 88 years old. He enjoys a happy, contented retirement in the small, neat, picturesque village of Pannal, near Harrogate, in the north of England. Married to my mother, Muriel, for more than 60 years, he's lived a life full of adventure, responsibility, challenge and success. He is undeniably a lucky man: a stellar career in the British police, rising from the very bottom to the very top to become Chief Inspector of Constabulary; knighted by the Queen; a Doctor of Laws; a qualified barrister; a father of three; a grandpa to eight; a diamond wedding anniversary. There's no doubt about it, life has been kind to Sir Lawrence 'Lawry' Byford: a blessed and fortunate man.

As I pulled into the driveway, I marvelled at his prim, orderly front garden with its bright, colour-coordinated pansies planted in ranks, the dwarf conifers standing smartly to attention, and the lawn edges so perfect they appeared to have been sculpted with a sharp knife. Everything about the place spoke of order. There was the house plaque, 'Dalefield' – the housing estate where my dad had grown up as a child – fixed prominently onto the stone facade of the modest detached house. Demonstrably proud of his roots. Above the name was the crest of a white rose: the symbol of Yorkshire. 'God's own country' was how he, as a proud Tyke, used to describe England's largest and 'greatest' county when I was young. I spotted him through the bay window with that familiar ruddy face and silver hair. As ever, sitting in his favourite 'grandpa chair' in his tidy, compact home, surrounded by family pictures laid out on the windowsill. A scene of utter contentment. A lucky man, indeed.

My dad appreciates that he is probably in the final chapters of his life. And as he looks back now, more than he looks forward, fondly reminiscing over the events he's experienced and the people he's encountered along the way, he's keen to stress how his childhood and wartime experiences were such key shapers of the Lawry Byford of today. I was full of curiosity, aware that I had come to Pannal with a mission to understand more about those times before it was too late.

I knew he would be happy to oblige. I'd heard snippets of information over the years but had never been able to form a coherent, complete picture in my mind. This time, I'd brought a recorder with me so I could keep his memories for posterity. I felt that future generations of Byfords should hear about and understand this part of his life – the part that had happened before I was born; the part that no other family member would have had any experience of; the part that had shaped him and widened his horizons, awakening the realisation of his potential. I needed to know more. What had his childhood been like? Why had he joined up with the Americans? What impact had war made on him? And why did he go on to feel such an affinity with the United States throughout his life? He started to reminisce.

We began with his birth on 10 August 1925. At that time, his father, George, worked as a miner, digging for coal down a local pit near the town of Normanton, in the West Riding of Yorkshire. He'd come up north from London, looking for work, then met and married Monica Cairns, a local girl whose father was also involved with the collieries.

Lawrence Byford was destined to be an only child. He told me how the family started off living in rented rooms on Scarborough Row in Normanton, before moving to a small, newly built two-up two-down council house at Neville Street on the Dalefield estate. After several years, they secured a slightly bigger home nearby on Dalefield Avenue, with an extra room downstairs so my dad could do his homework, together with the luxury of a bathroom inside the house and a small garden.

A tight-knit, industrial, working-class community, Normanton was originally a small agricultural village that expanded rapidly in the second half of the nineteenth century. Its population grew from 750 to 17,000 in less than 30 years. The growth first focused around its role as an important railway junction, and at the time it boasted of having the world's longest station platform. Six hundred thousand rail passengers came through Normanton each year at its peak. A million and a half tons of freight were handled by the thousands of station wagons shunted around the spiderweb of railway sidings.

As the twentieth century arrived, coal began to dominate the area, with six pits surrounding the town. A tapestry of terraced houses, full of mining and railway families, weaved across the fields and woodlands, changing the landscape for ever. Thousands of men worked underground around the town. But then came the general strike of 1926 and the great recession of the 1930s. Both hit Normanton hard and unemployment soared. Those who did work received wages well below subsistence levels. Miners were laid off for long periods. My dad began recalling how, when he was a young child, his mum and dad and he would wait anxiously for the pit buzzer to go off every evening at eight o'clock precisely. One blast meant the pit would be open for work the next day. Silence meant it would be closed. Then, the next morning the streets would be quiet, devoid of men clattering along the cobbled streets in their steel-tipped clogs, heading for the pit. Most miners then were lucky to work two shifts a week. Poverty and ill health were endemic, with more than a hundred cases of tuberculosis recorded in the town in the year my dad was born.

Lawry Byford in 1935, and at the Whitsun procession in Normanton with his father

The Byfords were poor. It was often a real struggle to make ends meet. But the local Catholic Church formed a central part of their life and provided a strong belief in a higher order. As a boy, my dad had a prestigious role within his parish community: he served as head altar boy at St John the Baptist Church. I remember visiting my grandmother's house as a child and being given two grainy photographs of my dad as a young boy to hold. One showed him dressed in a red and white laced cassock, dutifully holding his prayer book. The other, again in altar-boy dress, showed him as a ten year old at the head of a long procession through the town. Proudly carrying an incense burner, he was walking next to his father as the local Catholic community marched to celebrate the feast day of Pentecost. Christianity and faith were then, as now, pivotal to his life.

Then he told me how he was an active member of the local youth club that met in the Parochial Hall, next to St John's Church. Indeed, his entire life was parochial at that time. Visiting the nearby town of Wakefield, just five miles away, would be a real treat, he said, to be undertaken by bus or on foot. To go to the city of Leeds, 11 miles away, would be a special annual excursion. When I later contacted his lifelong best friend, Bill Rodway, he described it thus: 'Normanton children had very limited horizons indeed. We never in our wildest dreams anticipated ever visiting the places shown in our geography and history books. You just never left the town.'

Throughout his childhood, my father was a happy lad. He loved football and cricket, and played endless games with Bill on the field off Newland Road. Like all boys then, he passed many hours entertaining himself, chalking out a hopscotch court, creating kaleidoscopes with his whipping top or digging out his bag of marbles. When dusk came, he recalled, it was time for 'Jack, Jack shine your light'. The family couldn't afford a radio and, of course, no one owned a television.

My dad paused, took a deep breath, and then began to reveal for the first time to me a key moment in his life when he reached 11. A bright, hard-working lad, he passed his 11-plus exam, which meant he would be going on to the local grammar school. He was thrilled. His parents were rightly proud and delighted. But his grandfather filled in the application form wrongly, mistakenly putting down his birth year as 1926 rather than 1925. The authorities made no allowance and stubbornly insisted that he couldn't go. He was shattered, confused and deeply hurt. He had to stay on at St John's primary school for a further two years.

The more he spoke, the more I realised how deeply scarred he had been by this cruel act of injustice and petty bureaucracy. I could feel his pain and frustration. He had been rejected, humiliated, his life put on hold for two years. That's a long time in the life of an 11 year old.

He shook his head as he recalled leaving school at St John's at 13 with no qualifications. I stopped him in his tracks. Did I hear that right? I had. He was just 13 years old. Having missed out on attending grammar school, he felt that his academic career had been effectively stunted. He moved on to a local technical college for two years, where he was given basic industrial training in metalwork, woodwork and electronics. At 15, without an exam certificate to his name, he began to work as an apprentice electrician at a nearby coal mine, Park Hill Colliery.

By now, the country was at war and shafts were being sunk everywhere to reach the rich coal seams. Ten thousand men were working underground in Normanton alone to meet the ever-increasing demand for the 'black stuff'.

In his late teens, the highlight of his week, he told me, was going to the Saturday-night dances at the local baths. In the winter months, a sprung wooden dance floor was laid out on top of the local swimming pool, and each Saturday evening the eight-piece Ernie Richardson Band would swing the night away. Another favourite activity was going to the pictures. There were three picture houses in the town at that time and films provided a great escape from mundane lives. As Bill Rodway again would later explain: 'Apart from revealing how people lived outside our very restricted world – even though many were obviously artificially contrived – it also showed us parts of the world that might as well have been on a different planet. I'd bet a pound to a penny that he never thought he'd one day go and see parts of the world which were then only in his dreams.'

My dad reached his 18th birthday in 1943, with both Britain and America deep in the toil of the Second World War. Food rationing had been in place for three years. Coal was a vital ingredient in fuelling the Allies' armies and the vital support industries. He told me how he found himself exempt from the draft, working in what was then called 'a protected industry'. However, he was determined to make as strong a contribution as possible to the war effort, and for him that meant joining up. So keen was he 'to do his duty', so desperate was he to become a soldier, that he decided he had to leave the pit and change jobs so that he could be called up. He switched from the mine to working in the nearby Blackburn aircraft factory simply to qualify for conscription.

'Well, it was my duty, Mark, wasn't it?' he said simply.

I made a note of that word. Duty. It kept cropping up in the conversation. Clearly, it was fundamentally important to him.

Eventually, he was called up on 3 August 1944 but, by chance, he didn't join the local regiment – the King's Own Yorkshire Light Infantry, the 'KOYLIS' – like so many others. Not for him the front line and the blood and guts of hand-to-hand combat. Instead, he found himself on his way south to Bletchley to join the Royal Signals Corp. Trained there for ten weeks to send and receive Morse Code messages, he achieved the highest marks in the class in the seven tests he faced and was seconded to the special communications unit within the Royal Signals. An innate intelligence and latent ability had been identified and recognised for the first time in his life and this was to be nurtured throughout the rest of his induction at Bletchley. He qualified as a wireless operator, learning to send and receive the 'Ultra' top-class, secret messages that would help enable British and American forces across the battlefields of Western Europe to communicate with one another and their bases.

I felt touched and rather proud as his story unfolded, relieved that the appalling snub he had experienced aged 11 was being rectified. I was fascinated by his account, incredulous that I had been unaware of these life-changing experiences before now, yet delighted that I was finally recording them for posterity.

December 1944. A new draftee, aged just 19, he suddenly found himself on board an American Liberty ship crossing the English Channel, attached to an American convoy. But he wasn't following the rest of the men on deck heading to the bloody battlefields of Western Europe. He was en route to a place he understood to be called 'Triumph'. On landing at Rouen, he was driven to the location just south of Paris. Little did he realise that he was making his way to SHAEF – the Supreme Headquarters of the Allied Expeditionary Force – which was led by the Supreme Commander of the Allied Forces, General Dwight D. Eisenhower. His final destination was to be Versailles.

Versailles: one of the most beautiful and opulent palaces in the world, with its spectacular and meticulously laid-out gardens. Built originally in the seventeenth century, it was designed to fulfil the ostentatious dreams of France's 'Sun King', Louis XIV, as he moved his court and seat of government out of Paris in 1682. With Paris just liberated from the Germans, the Allies had requisitioned some of the outer buildings of Versailles to serve as a temporary strategic nerve centre for the main military-planning headquarters of their campaign in Europe.

General Eisenhower was based in the grand Trianon Palace Hotel on the Versailles estate, looking out at the vast royal gardens, less than a mile from the palace. My dad, working in the command centre of the Allied operations as a wireless operator, was based in the Petite Écurie du Roi, the little stables opposite the Palace's main entrance. 'Little stables' was the ultimate understatement. The extraordinary Hardouin-Mansart-designed, horseshoe-shaped building was more than 300 metres wide at its front. Originally, these buildings, built in 1679, housed the coaches and carriage horses of King Louis XIV. The magnificent surroundings as well as the sheer scale of these buildings were like nothing my dad had ever seen. The view from his desk across to the Place d'Armes and on to the chateau's gilded facade was extraordinary; he found himself looking out on one of the most beautiful buildings in the world. And all this happened to him just months after D-Day; just weeks after the Allies had liberated France and were heading on to Germany; just days after leaving his training at Bletchley. He was safe. Away from the trenches, the tanks and the carnage. And yet at the very heart of the biggest military-planning operation ever undertaken. He had been transported to a completely new world. The young Limey with the Yanks. From Normanton, the grimy pit community, to the gilt and marble of Versailles. Was there anyone recently drafted in the war as lucky as him, I wondered? Hearing him speak with such energy and enthusiasm about his experience was making me realise for the first time what a pivotal moment this had been in his life. It was the beginning of an exciting, enthralling new chapter for him.

I suddenly thought about Larry Byford in Vietnam. His experience of war was probably the ultimate contrast. Drafted to his death in the jungle while looking for 'Charlie', the enemy. I wrote three words down on my notepad: 'lucky', 'unlucky' and 'chance'.

My dad then explained to me how, after only a month working at Versailles, he found himself being moved on. Once again, he was posted to extraordinarily extravagant surroundings: to the Chateau D'Ardenne in Belgium, where he joined up with Lieutenant General Leonard T. Gerow and his senior command team from the US 15th Army. Built to be the finest castle in Belgium in 1874 by King Leopold II, on the site of an old hunting lodge used by his father, the chateau was a beautiful, large stately home. Although on a smaller scale than Versailles, the Alphonse Balat design created an exquisite place steeped in high living and extravagance. Soon after being built, it was transformed into a luxury hotel, at King Leopold's request, in order to attract European royalty and the international elite to Belgium. Set deep in the dense forests of the Ardennes, it had been requisitioned earlier in the war by the invading Germans as they occupied Belgium.

Now, in January 1945, on the back of the D-Day invasion the previous June, and after the Allies had advanced successfully through France and Belgium, liberating both Paris and Brussels, this chateau had become a command centre for the Allies and the battle-hardened American, Lieutenant General Leonard Gerow. It was situated less than ten miles from the scene of one of the Second World War's most bloody and savage encounters, which had just drawn to its dramatic end: the Battle of the Bulge. Hitler's last throw of the dice, his final audacious gamble to turn back the Allied invasion of occupied Europe. Through extraordinary courage, determination and brilliant military tactics, the Allies had held out against a daring and surprise attack of massive force by advancing German Panzer divisions, ensuring that the 'bulge' in their lines did not break. Then they had overpowered the Germans in desperately ferocious combat over a three-week period in the most severe of Belgian winters. More than 600,000 American troops had been involved across the snow-bound hills and frozen forests of the Ardennes. Nineteen thousand of them were killed. Ninety thousand were casualties. No other battle in the war would cost so many American lives. Now the chateau had become Gerow's 'temporary retreat' as he and his senior command team paused briefly to help plan how the Allies would capitalise on their victory and make further advances into Germany itself.

Lawry Byford had arrived by army truck from Paris immediately after that battle, to work at the chateau assisting with signals communications. He recalled how he was based in the annexe to the side of the castle, looking out on to the manicured lawns, richly coloured, pristine flower beds and ornamental ponds that lay in front of the main building and its towering turrets. The place was a hive of activity and secrecy. His job there was to receive and dispatch messages to Bletchley, many of which would then go on to Bletchley Park, the nerve centre of the Allies decoding operations. In addition, he would listen, at specific times, for messages coming up the line from the battlefields and from 'ghost stations' behind enemy lines. He would take down the messages, he told me, not understanding their significance or their meaning. He remembered the occasion when Eisenhower came to the Chateau D'Ardenne to meet Gerow. I listened intently, hanging on his every word, as my dad described with great enthusiasm his excitement as he handed an urgent message to Gerow's staff officer for decoding, which he'd taken down personally. It was marked for the attention of General Eisenhower. My dad was just 19 years old. He was so caught up in the telling of this anecdote that he had left his chair and was pacing round the lounge.

Major General Leonard T. Gerow and
General Dwight D. Eisenhower, northern France, 1944

At that moment, my memory flashed back to our family holiday to Belgium back in 1971. I remembered how we'd left our relaxing spot on the Belgian coast to undertake a mammoth car journey to the Ardennes so my dad could see 'the chateau'. Amid much protest from the back of the car, as my brother, sister and I snarled in boredom, he drove at a snail's pace up endlessly winding, steep forest roads in search of his destination.

When we got there, we saw nothing. Just the charred remains of a building and small piles of brick rubble scattered across a desolate place hidden deep in the woods. I remembered that scene vividly, and how, for the very first time, I'd witnessed my dad shedding a tear but couldn't understand why. 'This is definitely the place. The chateau. It's gone,' he'd cried, as he wandered through the remains. When we asked if we could leave – it all seemed so tedious and irrelevant to us – he lost his temper and went for a walk alone.

Now I understood the significance. The chateau had been destroyed by fire three years earlier and the wrecked buildings had been razed to the ground just months before. He didn't know what he was going to discover that day. It had been a shock. The fabric of such an important place in his life wiped out forever.

What a six months it had been in the life of Lawry Byford. From pit village apprentice electrician to draftee wireless operator at the very heart of the Allies' top strategic military operation. Based with two of the Allies' greatest military leaders – the five star General 'Ike' Eisenhower and Lieutenant General 'Gee' Gerow – working next to two of Europe's most beautiful buildings. He was a few miles away from one of the most epic and brutal battles in military history but uninvolved himself in active combat. Lucky him, I thought again.

My dad's final war days in Europe in early 1945, he recalled, saw him moving on to Bad Neuenahr in Germany to the 15th US Army's HQ, then, finally, dispatched to Reims for the unconditional surrender. Lawry Byford, my dad, had been in the city of Reims on the day of one of the greatest moments in the history of the twentieth century . . . and I hadn't known it until that moment.

He insisted on writing down all the dates and precise locations on a card. It was as though he realised he wanted to pass it on as the definitive record. What an extraordinary war for him, I concluded, and what a fortunate one. I looked at my notepad again and read the words I'd jotted down in large letters during our conversation: 'lucky', 'unlucky', 'chance' and 'duty'.

Pulling a chair close as he nestled back in his comfortable armchair, I thanked him for reminiscing about his wartime experiences. I felt pleased that I understood for the first time how he came to be attached to the American Army, and that I was starting to learn how his childhood and wartime experiences had helped to make him the man he is today. Although I'd originally intended to stop after an hour, a strong instinct told me to keep the recorder running.

Then I explained that I had my own extraordinary story to tell of an unforgettable experience that had happened early one morning, some time ago, on the other side of the Atlantic. He listened intently. As I drew to a close, I took the rubbing carefully out of its envelope and passed it to him.

'Look, Dad, here's the name that's on that Wall. I made a rubbing of it on this paper. A Vet who was there at the time told me to bring it to you,' I explained. 'And here's a leaflet I picked up that same morning about the Vietnam Veterans Memorial,' I added, passing it to him. 'I thought you might be interested.'

Dressed, as ever, in jacket, collar and tie, with polished shoes and carefully groomed, slicked-back silver hair, he sat very still, holding the fragile piece of paper in his left hand and the leaflet in his right. He was sitting with his back angled towards the window, leaning slightly forward. Light streamed in through the small glass panes and over his left shoulder, spilling over his hair and clothing, illuminating both the rubbing and the leaflet. He stared at the thin block of grey shading, made from the lead pencil, some four inches wide, in the centre of the creased paper, the typeface of the letters Larry S Byford coming through.

Time ground to a halt. Silence hung in the air, suspended between us. First, he moved the rubbing of Larry's name closer to his eyes, then he read the information on the leaflet. I watched him carefully in an attempt to gauge his reaction. Finally, his eyes settled once again on Larry's name. After what seemed like an eternity, he shook his head slowly from side to side as if in disbelief, and sighed loudly. Then he began to reflect.

'That's rather moving, Mark,' he exclaimed. 'What a remarkable coincidence.'

He shook his head from side to side once more.

'Larry and me were pretty much the same age. Both involved in conflict. Both with the US Army. Lawry and Larry Byford . . . I was fortunate. That's for sure. But he wasn't. God bless him.'

He sniffed and took a sip of tea as he looked out through the bay window.

'Poor lad. Think of his relatives today,' he sighed. 'He was still a boy, really. Today, for most people, he's just a name on a wall. But to his family and friends he'll still mean everything. Think about his courage. A brave young soldier doing his duty, serving his country.'

That word 'duty' again.

Suddenly he became emotional – not a trait I associate regularly with my dad. Indeed, a rarity in such a controlled, dignified man. He heaved himself out of his chair and walked slowly towards his study. A few minutes later he returned, armed with a small tin containing a collection of photographs, postcards, medals and a key.

'Look, Mark, this is me at 19. A soldier.'

I'd never seen the photograph before. It showed a young man with slicked-back hair, in heavy army fatigues, a hopeful, optimistic expression in his wide eyes and a half-smile playing round his lips, which framed a set of slightly crooked teeth.

'Here's a postcard from Versailles and, look, there's another of the Chateau D'Ardenne. This is the very key to my room at the chateau. I worked just along the corridor from Lieutenant General Gerow. This is my French phrasebook, issued to me by the Americans and given to me on my arrival. And here are my medals.'

He picked them up, then, looking both pensive and proud, took the cloth kept in the case and started to clean them gently, one by one: his Knighthood awarded by the Queen; the Commander of the British Empire medal; the Deputy Lieutenant of North Yorkshire; the Queen's Police Medal for distinguished service; another awarded for long service and good conduct; the Office of St John insignia; and then, on the right, his three precious medals from the Second World War: his General Service medal; the France and Germany Star; and, finally, the Victory medal. He kissed them and held them next to his chest.

Lawry's war memorabilia and medals

'I'm sorry, Mark. I'm getting a bit emotional here, seeing that rubbing of Larry's name and thinking about my own time with the Yanks. You know, the seeds were sown there and then for my lifelong affection for the Americans. They were fantastic to me then. I'll never ever forget it.' He looked down at his medals and went on.

'I'd probably still be in that colliery town today. Probably have stayed in a very similar job. But once I was at SHAEF and then with the 15th Army . . . well, I'd tasted a different life. So the war did it for me, Mark. It caused so much sorrow to so many. But for me, it changed my whole outlook on life. I was suddenly in a whole new environment where I saw leaders at first hand. What they did. What motivated them. Guys like Gerow. Can you imagine how that felt for me? A three-star general who had played a major part in planning the invasion of Europe. The first corps commander ashore at D-Day. Who'd led the US Fifth Corps out of Omaha beach. The first American major general to enter Paris. And there he is walking past a young 19-year-old lad – me – saying, "Hiya, fella."'

I would later understand the significance of this recollection when I contacted my dad's army colleague, Norman Ashdown, who joined up with him on the very same day. He wrote: 'Yorky [my dad's nickname] was always going on about how good the Americans were. So much so, it got us a bit pissed off some times, even though he was a lovely chap.'

I'd never heard my father speak so deeply and affectingly before about his own war experience. He was now very emotional, handkerchief in hand, wiping away a tear from his cheek.

'You know what war taught me, Mark? Well, let me tell you. That the most important aspects of life are family, friendship and happiness. Remember that, and always to have a motivation towards the common good.'

He opened up the rubbing and looked at the name again. He sniffed and swallowed heavily.

'Poor Larry. His family. His friends. Their loss. Lives changed forever. Such unhappiness.'

Less than an hour later we'd arrived in his home town to visit what my dad would describe as the 'Normanton Wall'. Dressed in a warm winter coat, he was wearing a poppy in his left lapel. Purposefully, he got out of my car and headed down towards the entrance to a park. It was bitterly cold. All the trees around us were bare, stretching high to catch the limited light.

As he walked through the sorry-looking park gates, with green paint peeling off the rusting metal railings, he looked across to the old library building that he'd visited regularly as a child. Ahead lay the small lake he had played in as a young boy. In a scene that has been recreated time after time, we saw a young boy watching gleefully as his small boat drifted to the other side of the pond. We caught sight of the bandstand, now unused and neglected, still there up on the small hill. That was the place he'd watched local brass bands entertain big crowds on sunny Sunday afternoons. For him, this modest park had been a small oasis of calm, peace and green, set within the grime and gloom of the surrounding town.

He moved slowly towards a tall, thin column of stone, some 20 feet high, and before long, a blood-red carpet of poppy wreaths, left over from the last Remembrance Day service, came into view. We had arrived at the war memorial in Haw Hill Park, in the town of his birth. A place of nostalgia. A place of both pleasure and pain. He stopped and stood upright in silence, looking towards the monument. He could just make out the sunken crosses and the carved wreaths, weather worn now, within the stonework.

Silently, to himself, he slowly read the words chiselled on to the Cornish granite obelisk:

THIS MONUMENT
IS ERECTED
TO PERPETUATE
THE MEMORY OF
THE MEN
OF NORMANTON
WHO
IN THE GREAT WAR
1914–1919
FOUGHT THE GOOD FIGHT
DYING
IN THE CAUSE
OF HUMANITY
THAT HONOUR
MIGHT LIVE

He moved around the monument and looked up again to another side:

AT THE GOING DOWN
OF THE SUN AND IN
THE MORNING WE
WILL REMEMBER THEM

He closed his eyes. He then moved round the column further and glanced up again:

GREATER LOVE HATH
NO MAN
THAN THIS.
THAT A MAN
LAY DOWN
HIS LIFE
FOR HIS FRIENDS

The memorial was first unveiled in 1923, two years before he'd been born. It was financed by public subscription to remember those in the recent Great War who'd made the ultimate sacrifice. So that they would never be forgotten. Just like The Wall in Washington.

Leaving the obelisk, he walked a few yards away to what looked like a small wall built of sandstone.

'Come over here, Mark,' he said.

I made my way across as he stood to attention in front of a modest stone wall, no more than six feet high. A small marble plaque was built into the stonework, three feet by two. On it were the words:

1939 WORLD WAR 1945

THIS TABLET RECORDS THE NAMES OF THE MEN OF NORMANTON WHO MADE THE SUPREME SACRIFICE IN THE SERVICE OF THEIR COUNTRY, TO WHOSE MEMORY IT IS DEDICATED.

Below the wording was a list of names, blocked together in four columns. We scanned them – each and every one of them. Adams H.L., Chapman W., Hancox J.H., Parkes J.S. . . . down to Young L. There were 76 in total. I could see my dad's face superimposed onto the names, reflected in the marble sheen: a parallel image of my own face reflected on The Wall in Washington.

'You know, Mark, I can put a face to so many of these names here. I knew so many of them. I remember that lad there so well . . .' He pointed at one specific name. 'He was a lovely guy: inoffensive, quiet, black curly hair. The thought of him losing all those years. Aagh!' He shook his head and wiped away another tear.

'Names on walls they may be, Mark. But remember, behind every name there's always a story. There'll be a story about that Larry Byford, too, you know. That's what I want you to remember today.'

Two walls, three thousand miles apart. Fifty-eight thousand names on one of them. Seventy-six on the other.

As we left the memorial, he began to shiver with the cold. The only sound around us was the strengthening wind whistling through nearby leafless trees. We walked slowly towards the car in poignant yet companionable silence and my thoughts started to wander: was seeing Larry Byford's name in Washington a matter of pure coincidence or was something else at play? Since the moment his name had been highlighted, I had felt a stirring, an emotional connection that was troubling yet intriguing. Talking to my dad that day had somehow validated the original intensity of my response. In addition was the recognition that although the Vietnam War had clearly truncated Larry's life at an unbearably young age, in contrast the Second World War had given my dad opportunities in life that he would otherwise never have had. One deeply unlucky, robbed of life, who sacrificed all. In contrast, the other fortunate, whose life had taken off in war. Whose horizons were completely realigned. Two lads doing their duty with two very different outcomes.

Varied thought strands started to gather and strengthen, forming the root of an idea. I realised that this was gradually evolving into an unshakeable compulsion that I couldn't ignore.

To me personally, Larry Byford had become like the unknown soldier of the Vietnam War. The only difference was that he had a name. But I knew nothing more about him. Nor did nearly anyone else who'd be looking at those letters on the 22nd panel at line 52. Anonymous. The everyman. One name among more than fifty-eight thousand. A name on a wall. 'Never must he be forgotten,' I thought.

'You know, Dad, what I want to do? I want to find out the story of that Larry Byford. Who he was. Where he was from. What happened to him in Vietnam,' I gabbled. 'To do it for his family. For that Vet at The Wall. For you. And for me.'

My dad looked me straight in the eye. 'Well, you do that, Mark. Yes, you do that. And when you know what the story is, come back and let me know what you've discovered.'

I nodded and put my arm round his shoulder. We got back in the car and headed to Pannal, to the warm comfort of his home.

As we drove back, I realised this wasn't curiosity at play or a simple desire to learn more. I felt compelled to follow this story further. It was fast turning into a personal mission. I had to embark on this journey of discovery. And to begin it right away.

CHAPTER 3

THE SEARCH BEGINS

During the four-hour drive back home to Winchester, I reflected deeply on my visit to Yorkshire and my decision to find out more about Larry Byford. I was more than a little fired up about the direction I had decided to take. But at the same time puzzled. Why had the life of a total stranger captivated me with such force? Why did I have such a strong feeling about it? Perhaps the sighting of Larry's name had awakened in me a realisation of my own father's mortality. Perhaps their shared experience of war had triggered in me an awareness of the different types of impact a war can have on people's lives. Perhaps it had raised issues of chance, fate, godly intervention – call it what you will – that I needed to explore. I had been interested in the Vietnam War for many years but my only exposure to it had been through films. However, according to the veteran I spoke to at The Wall, those films are largely inaccurate. 'Lies,' he called them. So, perhaps I wanted to learn more about the true Vietnam War through Larry's own story. And to answer the nagging question that faced me that morning at The Wall – was it all worth it?

As soon as I arrived, I got down to work immediately and typed his name into the search engine. The web was the obvious place to start. First up came contact details for a few Larry Byfords alive in the UK today. I scrolled down the screen a little further. The first relevant entry was from a memorial site, 'findagrave.com'. The information was basic but every piece would now be essential to me. There was his birth date again and the date of his death as well as the place where he died – listed as 'Quang Binh'. A new revelation to me was that he died 'from small-arms fire' while serving in Vietnam. New information too about his parents. His father, listed as Fate Byford 1911–1987. His mother, Cecil Stephens Byford, 1911–1968. I noticed that she died very soon after Larry's death. He was buried at Mt Pleasant cemetery in Center, Shelby County, Texas. There was a small photograph of his grave. A simple, modest gravestone lying flat on the ground. Upon it was a rectangular metal plaque that stated the briefest of personal details: PFC Larry Byford PH. I knew the Purple Heart was awarded to all who were wounded in battle. A cross at the top of the plaque acknowledged his Christian background. The grave was framed by uncultivated, dry grass. All very plain and unassuming.

I carried on surfing, scanning all the search results. I wanted more information. I moved on to a Vietnam Veterans Memorial Fund site. Entering his name, I clicked the mouse and, suddenly, there on the screen, for the first time, his face appeared.

Larry Byford

My heart started to race. I studied the photograph with forensic precision, looking for any clue I could find about this young man. In front of me was a somewhat faded black-and-white photograph. My first impression was that he looked much older than the 22 years I knew him to be. He was well built and quite full in the face, with a blunted jawline that could be the precursor to a double chin in middle age. A soft, gentle, slightly tentative expression with a modest smile. The photograph appeared to have been produced by the military and must have been taken before the horrors of Vietnam had taken a grip. Dressed in full uniform, Larry sported a jacket, a pristine collar and tie, and a peaked cap with an unknown emblem on the front. I wondered exactly when it had been taken – after he took the draft, perhaps? Maybe at boot camp? Maybe at his passing-out parade?

I scrolled down the screen further. A little more information, each piece slowly but surely helping to build up a picture. 'Died in Binh Dinh province.'

And then, lower down, came possibly the most interesting revelations to date: three email postings of remembrance. Three messages that had been sent to the site over the past eight years. I clicked on each message and, with much anticipation, read each one slowly and carefully:

'YOU ARE NOT FORGOTTEN'
I think of you often and wish I had more memories of you. But I know we will meet again. Just know you and all the other fallen soldiers are not forgotten.'
Love Mel (niece) October 21st 2010.

'I LOVE YOU AND MISS YOU VERY MUCH'
Thanks. You are a hero to me and all your family and friends.'
Sister July 4th 2005.

'THE ROCK PILE'
'You tried to save the Major. We know your courage. Possom Trot TX can be proud. The lock of hair on your helmet was your statement.'
Don Jensen March 25th 2005.

Saving 'the Major'. Was he rescuing his Commanding Officer? Did he die performing some kind of heroic act? Who or what was Possom Trot TX? And what was the lock of hair on the helmet all about? Who was Don Jensen? Presumably a comrade of Larry's, probably a witness, there at the scene of his death. Was he still around? If so, where? I needed to track him down. These tantalising snippets of information whirled round in my head. Plenty of questions were being raised. Now I needed to find out exactly what had happened on that fateful day.

Soon after, I discovered a third website with another relevant entry. 'The Virtual Wall' highlighted more precisely his military background as 'C Company, 2nd Battalion, 5th Cavalry, 1st Cavalry Division.' I checked out the 1st Cavalry Division and soon discovered it to be one of the most-famous and most-decorated divisions in the US Army. Known as the 'First Team', it was the first full division to be deployed in the Vietnam War back in 1965 and the first-ever airmobile division. Before Larry had got there in 1967, the First Team had already spearheaded the Pleiku campaign, where soldiers fought to the death at the horrific Battle of Ia Drang Valley, the brutal events of which were dramatised later in the Hollywood blockbuster *We Were Soldiers*. The division carried out thirty-five days of non-stop continuous airmobile operations in late 1965, during which it completely destroyed two of the three regiments of a North Vietnamese Division. Awarded the very first Presidential Unit Citation of the war, these guys were brave. They knew the business.

After absorbing these facts, I returned to the Virtual Wall site, where I discovered that Larry's tour of duty began on 18 April 1967. So he was there for just 67 days before he fell. He died 'outright' due to 'gun or small-arms fire' and his body was 'recovered'. His religion status was noted as Baptist. More surfing. More facts.

I followed a link to a site called 'Tall Comanche'. I discovered that it was the specific site for Charlie Company of the 2nd Battalion 5th Cavalry 1st Cavalry Division (Airmobile). Larry's company. The website had been constructed as a historic, chronological record of the company's time in Vietnam from when it first arrived in 1965 through to when it left in 1972. A history of their missions, drawn up by the Vets themselves. This would be important. I typed in the words Larry Byford and waited. Up came a specific paragraph, describing the events of 23 June 1967:

> PFC Larry S Byford of 3rd Platoon is killed in action when he goes to the rescue of Major Edwin W. Martin. C 2/5 Cav was securing the area as Major Martin, a divisional Psychological Operations Officer, attempted to talk NVA soldiers out of their holes just east of the Nui Mieu mountains (co-ordinates CR055747 map 6937-3). Both men were killed and the medevac bird that came in for the wounded was shot up. [Source: Ken Burington]

From Tall Comanche, I followed a link to a special C company reunion site: a place for the Vets to come together for fellowship, news updates and to remember their colleagues who didn't come back. I sent off an email to the reunion coordinator, John McCorkle. I hoped he might be able to find Vets from Larry's time out there, still alive and still willing to remember.

Meanwhile, from an opening position of pretty much ignorance, I began to read widely about the Vietnam War – its history, its causes and the political and military context back in 1967. I began watching historical documentaries about the war. Vietnam and Larry Byford now dominated every day. Indeed, in less than a month since that visit to my father, the study in my house had been transformed into a 'war room', full of books, notes, maps and photographs. I'd left the BBC earlier that summer, so I had the opportunity to concentrate full time on this new project.

I set out to make initial contact with Vets I thought could well have been with Larry during his time in Vietnam. I left a note on the reunion site message board asking for help. I sent an email to every Vet I'd calculated might have served in the company in 1967. This was a long, painstaking task but I recognised that the work might well prove its worth.

The very same day, Don Jensen, the man who'd left the note about Possum Trot and the lock of hair, came back to me with a brief response:

> `Mark Byford. I was there when Larry was KIA [killed in action].`

Twenty-four hours later, a Richard Bratton replied:

> I was on the rock pile with Larry. He was killed trying to get the body of the Major in front of the cave entrance.

He attached a photograph, taken from inside a helicopter back in 1967. It was an aerial view of a strange-shaped black rock outcrop protruding into the sea next to a wide sandy beach on the South China Sea coast.

The next day another message arrived, this time from a Clinton Endres:

> Yes I knew Larry. He and I were good friends. Your message stirs up a lot of memories. That's all I can say for now.

I felt I was now embarking on a personal mission and I didn't know how or when it was going to end.

Ken Burington, the Vet who'd made the specific entry about Larry's death on 23 June 1967 on the Tall Comanche site, sent back an extract from a letter he'd written to his parents on the day that Larry died. It included these chilling details:

> Every day we corner a couple more and dig them out of a bunker. Right now we're sitting on top of a hill trying to dig six out. We cornered them two days ago and we think there's a radio down there too.

Tracked down, hunted and killed like animals. Well, this was war wasn't it? The harsh reality of it began to sink in.

But what about Larry's family, presumably still living in the Center area of Texas? Clearly I needed their cooperation and for them to be supportive of my search for Larry's story. Without them, I knew I could go no further.

I went through the local Shelby County registry records of births, marriages and deaths, line by line, scrupulously looking for Byfords and noting any relevant entries. I began to compile a rudimentary family-tree framework relating to Larry. By now, I knew the names of his parents, Fate and Cecil, when they were born and when they died. An older brother, Harold, had died in

2002. There were two more brothers, David and Hughie. David had moved to Baytown near Houston. Hughie had married a girl from Louisiana called Tommye. I surmised Larry had a sister called Patricia, the one who'd posted the message on that memorial site. And it appeared that two other sisters may have died in childbirth or at a very early age.

I thought I'd take a chance and see if I could find any of them on social network sites. I went to Facebook, where I noticed a Tommye Byford, living in Mansfield, Louisiana, just across the Texan border, some 35 miles from Larry's home town of Center. I clicked on her entry and focused on a family photograph clearly taken during recent Christmas festivities. In the centre of the family gathering was an older father figure dressed in blue-jean dungarees, identified as 'Huey'. I looked at his face, then immediately cross-referenced it with that of Larry. Even though there was an age difference of more than 50 years, they were the spitting image of each other: the same physique, rounded face, kind eyes and gentle facial expression. Surely the two were closely related. I scrolled down Tommye's 'wall' of recent messages and stopped abruptly when I saw one that had been posted seven months earlier:

> Honoring the memory of Larry Stephen Byford, brother-in-law, who lost his life in Vietnam trying to save a critically wounded Major. A HERO indeed.

I sought advice from a recently retired senior British Royal Navy officer, well versed, I suspected, in dealing with bereaved families. He told me to write a handwritten letter, preferably using a fountain pen, on good-quality writing paper, as a mark of respect. Another piece of advice was to remember to enclose a US stamped addressed envelope and to tell them a little about myself. He made it clear that I needed to convey both my own integrity and also my respect for their family.

I heeded his advice and constructed a carefully worded, handwritten letter, explaining what had happened to me at The Wall: how Larry's name had shone out at me; how he had a similar name to my father, who had also served with the US Army in the Second World War; how I now felt compelled to embark upon a journey of discovery about their own Larry Byford. Then, I waited.

Twelve days later, an email popped up in my inbox:

> I am Hughie's wife, Tommye, and I am writing to you on his behalf, to acknowledge receipt of your letter which was a pleasant surprise. We have spoken to the other siblings of Larry and we are humbled and honored by your idea of writing about him. Indeed, it is a worthwhile project and we would be willing to help you with information and even take you to the place where he grew up. He has one other brother and three sisters living. We would be delighted to correspond with you.
>
> Looking forward to your reply.
>
> Sincerely
>
> Hughie and Tommye Byford

I was thrilled and energised. All that initial digging had been worth it. I had established contact with the Byford family, who seemed keen to help. The journey of discovery about Larry Stephen Byford, some 45 years after his death, could begin in earnest. Now, I could start to unravel the threads of his life, with the help of his family, childhood friends and some of the Vets with whom he had served. I wanted to find out more. Where he came from and how his early experiences impacted on his life. His early years and relationships with siblings and family members. His teenage years leading into adulthood. His character, passions and friendships. His brief time in Vietnam. Where he fought. How he died. I needed anything that would help me to find the true Larry Byford, rather than just a faceless, characterless name on a wall.

I knew that this would be a venture undertaken by a man with no direct connections with the war. A man who'd never been in the military, who had never written a single word before about Vietnam. A non-American, working from his home in England 3,000 miles away. Who just wanted to learn a bit more: about the war; about Larry; about his own father; about himself. This would be a personal journey to Larry's homeland in Texas and to his battlefield in Vietnam. A journey to find out who Larry was and what happened on that day of 23 June 1967 on the Rockpile. A journey also to meet his fellow comrades, gathering 45 years on in remembrance and reflection. And finally a return to The Wall, hopefully with new knowledge and new understanding.

I did not expect it to be a story about the exceptional and the extraordinary. There would be no famous heroes, no epic encounters. I was not intending to find any direct genetic link between the Texan Byfords and their Yorkshire namesakes. I knew that this was not going to attempt to be a ground-breaking, eyewitness or historical account of war. So much had been written and immortalised already about famous battles such as la Drang, Khe Sanh, Ong Thanh and Hue. And who was I to claim that authorship role anyway? This would never attempt to be a sprawling novel of rich narrative based on a Vet's own story, 30 years in the making. It definitely couldn't be one of those personal downloads about the horrors of my own war experience: an extended psychological healing session through the printed word. For that job, I had no experience, qualifications, rights or insights whatsoever. No, I was simply setting out to tell a story about an ordinary man who registered for the draft, did his duty and lost his life. The ordinariness was to be at the heart of the matter. This was about the everyman on The Wall. I aimed to complete the work in time for the 40th anniversary of the final American combat troops being pulled out of Vietnam, which happened to coincide with the 30th anniversary of the dedication of the Vietnam Veterans Memorial. There at The Wall, like the rest of them, Larry isn't singled out in any way for being special. He is just one of more than fifty-eight thousand names.

But to his siblings and friends he is THE name on The Wall. The exceptional, the extraordinary, the hero. I began to realise that the telling of Larry's story could be a vindication, indeed validation, for his own family of a young life so tragically lost. So this venture would be especially for them.

Finally, I was on my way . . . to Texas.

CHAPTER 4

IN THE BEGINNING

I walked through passport control at Dallas/Fort Worth airport, aware that I was embarking on a path with no certainty, no familiarity and no idea of what I might find. The immigration officer asked if I was visiting for business or pleasure. It was a good question. This wasn't a business venture. And it was certainly not a holiday. It occurred to me that my visit was a kind of pilgrimage: a private and special journey to a home and a grave. But I couldn't share that with him. I said I couldn't answer his question. I was just hoping to meet people and visit a special place. He looked confused and intrigued but let me through.

Before boarding a connecting flight to Shreveport, I had a couple of hours to wait. I sat in one of those nondescript coffee bars found in airport terminals across the world and kept my eyes on the departure board. At the same time I caught sight of a guy just to my right wearing army fatigues, slumped almost horizontally, surrounded by large kit bags. On his shoulder I spotted a patch that I'd recently become very familiar with – the insignia of the 1st Cavalry Division. I tried to open up a conversation but he seemed tired and weary, reluctant to engage. He looked tough and was acting very surly. After a few minutes' awkward silence, he asked why I was in Dallas. I told him about The Wall, the journey I was about to undertake and how I was about to meet Larry's siblings. He looked ahead for what seemed like minutes but was probably only seconds.

'That's beautiful, my friend. That's an extraordinary story,' he exclaimed as he shuffled himself into an upright position and started to open up one of his bags. He put his hand inside and rooted around for some time before pulling out a grey-and-black arm patch that he then handed to me. I looked with fascination at the famous design: the black horse head in the top right-hand corner and the black diagonal slash across the shield. I had seen similar ones with a backcloth of gold in photographs in recent weeks. I felt the Velcro on the back and turned it over. There, written in bold, black marker pen were the words: 'To Ben Miller. From Zak and Jelev.'

He told me he was an infantryman returning home from Iraq having just completed his last tour of duty. He was leaving the army that week and this was his final journey home.

'Hey, take that badge,' he said 'Go on, you have it. I want you to take it everywhere you go on your story. When you see the family. When you're in Vietnam. If you go back to The Wall. Keep it close. It's my honour to give it to you.'

I looked at the patch again. I then realised the same insignia was on the old Vet's cap – the Vet I had met at The Wall; the one who'd told me to do the rubbing.

I was speechless. What a memorable encounter, just minutes after touching down in Texas. I told him I'd take his patch everywhere on my 'pilgrimage'. I was determined to keep faith with that pledge. It would remind me of the First Team's bonding, past and present. I forgot to get his contact details. I presume he's called Ben Miller. I'd never see him again.

*

Texas, the backdrop to Larry's life: the land of cowboys, cattle ranches, sweeping desert landscapes and cactus plants; the land of powerful oil barons presiding over lucrative oilfields. Today, huge swathes of Texas remain dedicated to cattle. Indeed, 20 per cent of all beef cattle raised in the United States still come from this region. Similarly, much of the Texan landscape continues to be engulfed by the oil industry. A process that began on 10 January 1901 when a lucky strike from a discovery well at Spindletop produced a famous 100-foot high gusher of 'black gold'. By the 1930s, the surrounding area had become the biggest oilfield in the world. Today, the Gold Coast, on the bend of the Gulf of Mexico, remains one of the most concentrated stretches of refineries and petrochemical plants anywhere on earth, establishing Texas as the engine room of America's oil industry. Two of its metropolitan areas, Dallas/Fort Worth and Houston, are among the largest commercial and urban centres in the United States: sprawling conurbations that provide home and work for millions of Americans. Texas: a land of plenty, of production on a large scale, of dense populations and relentless progress.

But there's much more to the Lone Star State than this. Texas is big. The sheer enormity means it is truly a land of contrasts. Nowhere is that diversity better exemplified than the area in the north-east known as east Texas. There, it is a land typified by pinewoods, rolling green pastures, creeks and lakes, with poultry farming, watermelon growing, logging and agriculture. This is a softer Texas: less brash, more intimate. That distinctive Texan drawl is still there, the pick-up is still the vehicle of choice, but this rural landscape tucked up next to the Louisiana border feels like it belongs to a different country from that of Dallas, San Antonio or Galveston.

Texas may have a worldwide reputation for its strong streak of confidence and the swagger in its step. But, in contrast, east Texas has been called 'the buckle of the Bible belt'. Alongside traditional Catholics and Methodists live Baptists, fundamentalists and evangelicals – tight, conservative Christian communities – in every village and every town. This is the western edge of the Deep South. And it is there, east Texas, and specifically Shelby County, where Larry Byford was born and raised, and which helped shape his brief life.

*

The rickety Weaver-Gates house on Pecan Street in Center, built in 1910, is one of the oldest buildings still standing in the town. Today it's the Shelby County museum. As I opened the front door, nobody seemed to be around. Walking in, I was transported back to the time of the first settlers in the area, and to a Native American way of life. For more than 1,000 years, this land was the home of the Caddos, the first community to build settlements and to establish trade routes in the area. There on the wall in the first room was a large painting of east Texas's first farming community. The Caddos were shown naked apart from basic loincloths and were depicted fishing in the nearby Sabine river using primitive nets; carrying deer, hanging from poles, to be butchered for their meat and hides; celebrating the autumn harvest at the Fire Temple; building mounds to bury their dead. I looked in awe at the exquisite bowls displayed in the nearby glass cabinet. Made of coiled clay, the pottery was baked over open fires using cinnabar to impart a distinctive rich red colour.

Soon I was learning how, by the sixteenth century, Spanish explorers had crossed the Sabine river from the east and entered the area. They called the Caddos 'Tejas', meaning friends, and the place evolved into the name Texas. The Caddos were courted by both the Spanish and the French up to the eighteenth century, although, according to the museum, the Europeans found the Caddo custom of weeping and wailing to be rather disquieting.

By the beginning of the nineteenth century, settlers, primarily of English, Scottish and Irish descent, were coming in from the north and east, and this western expansion saw the Native American tribes being driven out. By 1859, the last Caddos had been removed from their ancestral lands and sent on to Indian territory in Oklahoma.

I moved on to the Civil War, in which Texas chose secession. Passions ran high in the east Texas area. Some local towns were suppliers and mustering points for the Confederate Army. Most lost a significant number of men. With the coming of the railroad in the 1870s, the 'Piney Woods' of east Texas, untouched for thousands of years, became the centre of a new lumber industry that was to explode over the next 50 years.

I immersed myself in the history of the place. I found it all fascinating. A Shelby County Historical Society volunteer came across to enquire if he could be of help. Teddy Hopkins, recently retired, clearly loved working in the museum and researching Shelby County's past: 'I like to fulfil people's dreams here and find that needle in the haystack,' he said. I told him about my mission and we both set to work.

Teddy began opening up maps, looking for clues. The first he passed to me didn't even identify the town of Center. 'Must be mid nineteenth century, certainly before the 1860s,' he declared. I spotted the Sabine river meandering through the area. The town of Nacogdoches was there. So, too, a Caledonia and a Buena Vista. Even nearby Shelbyville. But Center had not yet been born. It was just an empty space above the Attoyac river.

Teddy sat back in his chair, keen to impart his knowledge. He told me how Shelby was neutral ground at the start of the nineteenth century and settled by Anglo-Americans between 1824 and 1836. Center had become the county seat in 1866. I noticed a large antiquated map for Shelby County hanging on the wall behind him. There, at the bottom of the frame, I spotted a small wooden road sign facing west. Ingrained were the words 'Possum Trot'. I recognised that as the name used by Don Jensen when posting his message about Larry's death. I knew I had to go there.

Teddy opened a crumpled book with a collapsing spine, called *History of Shelby County, Texas*, and rifled through the pages. He also started pulling out drawers and looking through filing cabinets and shelves, searching for clues. Soon we were both delving into the pasts of the Stephens and Byford families.

*

In 1867, Joe Stephens, who was to become Larry Byford's maternal great-grandfather, travelled with his mother in an ox wagon from Georgia to east Texas to establish a new life. Joe was 11 years old and part Choctaw Indian. On reaching adulthood, he became a horse and mule trader in the area. He married Emma Eulala Fausett in 1888 and they settled in the Mt Pleasant/Jericho area, a remote, rustic farmland six miles south of Center, the small town that had just become Shelby County's new seat of government. Although Center was to become the main town in the area, with a courthouse and jail constructed on a freshly laid-out square, it was a relatively small community with just

3,000 residents. Joe and Emma Eulala had twelve children, of whom six survived. Their first, Lenton Asalph, arrived a year after the marriage. 'Lent', Larry's grandfather, lived in the area for more than eight decades. A small-framed man, he enjoyed company and had a keen sense of humour. He was known throughout the community by many names – Mr Stephens, 'The Colonel' and, most popularly, as 'Big Daddy'. Lent was known as a moral person who judged a man's character by his willingness to work. He would often emphasise to his family: 'Remember, a man's word is his bond. If he doesn't keep it, he isn't worth a damn.' In his early years he worked as a foreman on the building of Highway 96 from Center to Beaumont before farming watermelons, corn and peas.

Lent married the pretty, stylish Eunice Samford on Christmas Day 1909. They had two daughters, Jewel and Cecil. Eunice died aged thirty, when Cecil was eight years old, and Lent's mother Emma moved in to help care for the two daughters. As children, Jewel and Cecil would work hard at home, churning the milk, carrying slop to the hogs and collecting firewood from the surrounding woods to keep the kitchen stove burning. Schooling took place in a single makeshift classroom in a barn by the cemetery at Mt Pleasant.

In the same year that Cecil's grandfather Joe travelled from Georgia to Mt Pleasant, 22-year-old Henry Wall moved from Georgia to Alabama to begin married life with Nancy Bailey. When he found that there was no prospect of work there, he, too, decided to go to east Texas, first to the adjoining Panola County and then, in 1886, up to Shelby County to Jericho, the small farming community south of Center. By then they had an eight-year-old daughter, Emma. When she was twenty-four years of age, Emma married a local farmer, Hugh Franklin Byford, and they went on to have five children: Dandy, Narnie, Maude, Fate and Hazel. The second son, Fate, was born in 1911.

Twenty years later, on 23 January 1931, Fate Byford and Cecil Stephens were married in Mt Pleasant. Following their forefathers, they made their living as farmers. Fate's father, Hugh, had decided to split up his land in Shelby County, giving 66.9 acres to each of his five children. Fate and Hazel swapped their allocations, and it was on their new smallholding in the nearby tiny community of Short that Fate and Cecil were to work the land and raise their family. Over the next twenty years there, Cecil gave birth to nine children. One was Larry Stephen Byford.

I went to the files. The land at Short was first settled in 1870. The arriving farmers had wanted to call it Crossroads but as that name had already been taken they opted for the name of a prominent local lawyer, Daniel Short. In 1890, it had a population of 30. By 1930, it was still a small hamlet of fewer than a hundred, with a church, a sawmill, a few farms and a general store run by Sim Holt.

Teddy passed me a map showing land allocations for the area 80 years ago. We examined the boundary lines for various family plots, including those of the Baileys and the Stephenses. Then we noticed a small rectangle of some 24 acres marked out as belonging to Hugh Byford. Next to it was a 67-acre allocation identified as B. Pantalion. 'I think that's it, around there.'

So it is in Short, a small, scattered rural community, six miles south of Center, where Larry's story begins. And that's where I headed to next.

CHAPTER 5

TO THE WHITE HOUSE

Soon after arriving in the area, I called in on Hughie and Tommye at their home in Mansfield, Louisiana, 35 miles northeast of Center. I introduced myself, told them a little more about my project and showed them the rubbing I'd made at The Wall of Larry's name. It was a warm and emotional meeting. They said they were keen to accompany me to Hughie's and Larry's childhood home. The next morning we were on our way.

'These roads are so different to when we were kids. Then they were white sand. Too hot to walk on in bare feet in the summer. Too muddy, often, to pass in winter.' As we bumped along the farm track, just west of Highway 96, approaching Short, Hughie Byford was filled with excitement at the prospect of seeing his first home once again. 'We're getting real close now,' he bellowed.

After a while, the dusty track became squeezed between two steep red-clay banks that rose to ten feet tall on both sides and transformed our route into a partially enclosed, claustrophobic passageway. The banks spilled stones and small boulders onto the path, and overhanging trees cast deep shadows on the red soil. These tall, spindly pine trees clung in silent desperation to the precariously eroded bank edges. They hung on to the ruddy soil, their gnarled roots looking for all the world like witches' fingers. It reminded me of a scene from a scary children's fairytale.

'These are the banks young Larry used to run up and down all day,' Hughie enthused, as he pulled down the car window and looked closely at the red-clay walls, pitted with holes from the dirt dobbler nests. 'He'd pick mulberries here and stick out his purple tongue. Such a good kid. Grinning all the time. Big for his age. No skinny minny. Not a meddlesome boy. More do as I say.'

Hughie and Tommye Byford were the ideal travelling companions for my journey to Larry's childhood home. Now 74, Larry's brother Hughie looked casual and at ease with himself, wearing baggy blue jeans with blue braces over a red T-shirt, and sporting a yellow baseball cap. Rotund, shorter in height than I'd imagined, and full of life, he couldn't stop talking. His booming east Texan drawl was appealing but difficult for me to decipher.

'You'll soon see that Short is short of everything other than the church,' chuckled Tommye, sitting in the back of the car with her eldest daughter, Cindy.

We were heading down County Road 1005, sandwiched between Highway 96 and the 711 farm to country road, six miles south of Center. Short wasn't a village; it was more a scattering of farm holdings and homes. The old Byford family house would be difficult to find, they'd warned me, and access to it even today remains rudimentary. Back in the 1940s, the approach was on a rough two-rut dirt track that had since been upgraded to a narrow, single-lane asphalt road.

'143 Route 6 was our postal address then. You had to know where you were going and what to look for to find it. We had a telephone, J4J, I remember, shared among the four houses nearby and only one house could use it at a time,' Hughie recalled.

The nearby poultry farms were then, as now, at the heart of the local economy. Tens of thousands of chickens were slaughtered each week in the broiler houses scattered across the area. Hughie remembered that if the wind was blowing in the right direction, the smell from the birds would form a pungent cloud that would sit suspended over the land. Sandy soil was ideal ground for growing watermelons throughout the summer. Sixty years on, Center's annual watermelon festival in July, and its poultry festival in October, still remain the two most prominent community events of the year.

'I loved him. So kind-hearted. A genuine friend. A hero,' Tommye mused about the brother-in-law she came to visit regularly down this same track more than 50 years ago.

'So handsome, smiling, with those apple-plump cheeks,' Cindy reminisced. 'He'd bring trinkets and gifts. "Got you a little something," he'd say.'

'War is cruel. He was cheated out of something. He fell short of the things he could have enjoyed,' bellowed Hughie in his southern drawl, 'A man don't show his love open like he should, but I do about Larry. He was a good boy.'

I could feel both the affection and the pain, still so acute almost half a century after his death.

We chugged down the track until we came to the bottom of a gentle hill, seemingly miles from anywhere. Hughie took in a deep breath and tapped me on the shoulder. 'We're here, boy!' he shouted.

Larry's childhood home – the old 'white house' in Short, east Texas

And there it was. Larry's childhood home: the old 'white house'. Resembling a log cabin that had been tucked away in the depths of the country and long forgotten, with no other building in sight. It was a single-storey pinewood dwelling that had been painted white, with a gently sloping slate roof. A red-brick chimney on the front of the house, to the left of the porch, broke up the symmetry of the facade. The house, a 100 ft by 30, was simple, modest and compact.

The Byford family had lived together in this little home for many years. Inside was a small living area with a wood burner, which led directly through to a kitchen-diner. Three bedrooms and a bathroom lay to the right. All had bare wooden walls and floors. Then, Larry shared a room at the back with his brothers, painted in blue. Untended grass, peppered with weeds and wild flowers, grew in uneven patches all around the house. Beyond lay a rich mixture of broad leaf and conifer woodland, and in the distance lay pastureland.

I noticed that a small extension had been built on the back since those days but, basically, the house looked the same as the one in the photograph I was holding.

It was taken sometime around 1950 and showed Larry standing at the front of the house. I examined it carefully, comparing it with the scene before me. The distinctive chimney was unchanged but the small canopy above the front door was now held up by two red-metal pillars.

Although the grass was a little tamer now and had been cut back, the area was still very wild. I noticed that there were more trees, several of which were growing closer to the building than before. Conifers, cedars, sycamores and sweet gum encroached on the wooden house in a mosaic of shifting shadows so that it merged seamlessly into its surroundings.

Today's owner, Hirst Barbee, came over to check out the strangers looking so closely at his home. Wearing a cowboy hat, big buckled belt and blue jeans, he looked to me like the classic Texan. For years, he'd worked at the NASA space centre down in Houston but had come to Short to retire to his family roots and 'to get away completely from the noise and hassle of the rat race'. He'd certainly managed that.

Here was isolation. Tranquillity. A place at one with nature.

The Barbees and the Byfords had been long-time neighbours. Hughie and Hirst began exchanging news of latest family developments. I could sense that Hughie was nervous and unusually reticent. It felt poignant seeing him there, reluctant to move out of the front car seat. Looking across to the old family plot, he was now the outsider.

I persuaded him to come out and we began to wander around. Several squirrels scampered across the scrub and clambered up the tall pines. From high up in the branches, blackbirds, sparrows, robins, blue jays, wrens and doves created a cacophony of sound. 'This is where it all began,' he declared in a cracked voice.

*

Like so many people living through the Great Depression and the Dust Bowl, Fate and Cecil's early married life was challenging and they struggled to make a living. A modest sharecropper, Fate made little money from the 18 acres he'd been allocated for the cotton crop. Much of his farming focused on subsistence – keeping cows and chickens, growing corn and vegetables – to provide for his growing family.

Larry's parents – Fate and Cecil Byford

Fate was a strict disciplinarian who kept control over his children through an eagle-like stare. A serious man, he 'never joked or kidded'. His wife, Cecil, was a quiet, attractive woman with a beautiful face, featuring a high forehead, stunning wide dark eyes, an aquiline nose and square jaw, her dark skin and jet black hair hinting at her Choctaw Indian heritage. She remained remarkably trim for someone who had given birth to nine children.

Larry was born on 1 May 1945, delivered by Dr Spencer Warren at the nearby Hurst Sanatorium in Center. Named Larry Stephen – in recognition of his mother's maiden name – he was Fate and Cecil's seventh child. Harold was the eldest, aged twelve; David, nine; Hughie, seven; Nancy, six; and Patricia, just three. A first daughter, Barbara, had been born 18 months after Harold, but had died within a fortnight.

Family life at the white house was happy but tough. As sister Pat would later describe to me: 'We may have been poor but we were rich in so many ways. It was a simple, safe life rooted in family, friends and keeping the home together.' Nancy helped Momma with the cooking. Pat washed the dishes, cleaned the floors and made the beds. The boys roamed out and about in the fields and woodlands, hunting and fishing.

Momma Cecil prided herself on her cooking. Stews, cornbread, fresh vegetables and rich soups formed their staple diet. Pot roast laced with potato wedges, carrots, onions and butter beans, fried ham in bread, and especially chicken dumplings were particular favourites. Desserts included homemade cobblers, fruit pies and cakes. There were never any leftovers. There couldn't afford to be.

We ambled by the side of the house as I drank in Hughie's memories from more than 60 years ago. Cotton, corn and sugarcane fields were laid to the back, wild deciduous trees to the front, and a vegetable garden to the side. A well was sited by the back doorsteps but the water contained too much iron so a replacement was dug further away. Filling up buckets of water from the well was an essential part of everyday life. Hughie recalled how he'd help wash clothes with his momma down at the nearby creek. There was no mains gas provision but the house was connected to electricity. A butane gas tank ran the kitchen stove and provided hot water. However, the Byfords' space heater would be switched on only on special occasions. A chainsaw was in regular use, cutting up logs to feed the ever-hungry wood burner. Cecil prided herself on her own landscaping at the side of the house, planting crepe myrtles, althea bushes, elephant ears and lantana. It was simple, rustic living close to the earth.

Family life was very much guided by daylight. Up at 5.30 a.m., Larry would help bring in the firewood, turn the chickens out of their coops and collect the eggs, helping Momma as she milked the cow and prepared the vegetables. And all this before packing his bag and heading off for the early-morning school run. On his return in the afternoon, he'd try to hoe the vegetable patches or go into the fields to help handle the plough with his daddy. He'd have an hour to play in the woods before a good meal of homegrown produce at the family table. He was tucked up in bed before eight o'clock. Outside, night prowlers – raccoons, possums, armadillos, foxes and wolves – would be searching out their prey.

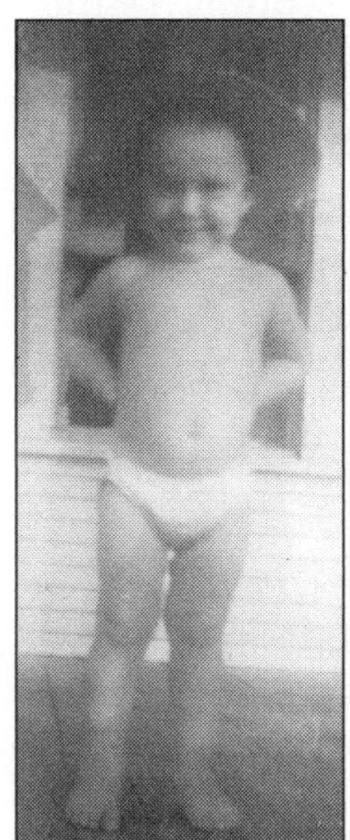

Young Larry

I looked through some of Hughie and Tommye's photographs of Larry as a young boy, given to me the day before, and imagined him running through the nearby bushes. Wearing a wide-brimmed hat, hands on hips, looking straight at me, he appeared to be chuckling at the fact that I was there on his patch. His smile was radiant and innocent. I shuffled the photographs and there he was again, a few years on. With dark-blond hair and large brown eyes, wearing a striped T-shirt and shorts, he smiled shyly at the camera. The next showed him to be the all-American kid – short back and sides, his hair turned brown but with the same bright eyes, and freckles covering a nose which was becoming more aquiline like that of his mother.

I noticed Hughie looking up high to the top of the trees, remembering how the hawks would swoop down suddenly by the side of the house to grab a chick wandering in search of seed. Seven years older than Larry, he'd been a boy of the woods here. Out and about hunting for squirrels, cats, raccoons and quail, shooting for deer and fishing for catfish and bass.

'I'd call him "Tag Along",' Hughie laughed. Wherever he would go, Larry would try to follow. Larry soon learned from Hughie how to ride bareback on the family horse, Sissy. He was devoted to the family dog, Dinky. 'He'd be grinning all the time; that boy was so lively.' With his buddy, Delbert Graves, he'd pretend to be Gene Autry, the Singing Cowboy, or Roy Rogers, and loved playing Cowboys and Indians in the local woods.

Harold was 12 years older than Larry, and the first to leave the nest when he joined the Air Force. David, who was more serious and conformist, with strong aspirations to be a teacher, took on the mantle of the eldest sibling at home. After receiving training, Harold went to serve in the Korean War. The Korean peninsula seemed light years away from the peaceful surroundings of Short, and far removed from their own experience. The family would pray together every evening for him to come home safely. It was then that Larry first heard members of his family use the phrases 'going away to fight communism' and 'doing his duty for his country'. Two expressions that would come to have such direct personal resonance a decade later.

Three years after Larry arrived, Cecil gave birth to another baby daughter, Carroll Darliene, but she died of a heart defect aged ten months. Debbie was born eight years after Larry. They became very close despite the age difference. Although he was treated by his elder brothers and sisters as the 'young boy' in the family, he became a father figure to Debbie. They shared the back bedroom for a time when they were kids. That made them close. He'd tease her remorselessly, they often fought like cats and dogs, but they loved each other deeply. Larry became hugely protective of her and she doted on him.

I was gazing at the house when Hughie pointed out that lightning had been a constant danger when living in an all-wooden home. Then he recalled how it once almost wiped out his young brother: 'We would milk the cow down there in the early morning before getting ready for school. The calf fed for a few minutes then they were separated until evening. The calf stayed in the lot and the cow went out to pasture. There was real bad cloud and lightning that day. As we were going down to the barn to separate the cow from the calf, Larry was running to undo the chain on the gate to let the cow out. With his hand holding the metal chain, a lightning flash struck him. Came right down from the tree. He fell to the ground all blowed up as the lightning hit the post. It sent Larry into the little gully and swelled his arm up. He didn't break a bone or nothing; he wasn't badly hurt, but he was real blue for a while. He was real lucky.'

I didn't want to leave the house. I wanted to stay all day in this bucolic idyll and dream more about Larry's childhood. But I could sense that Hughie wanted to move on. We headed into Center in search of further places that had shaped Larry's young life.

When Larry began at Center Elementary school, aged six, he'd catch the yellow school bus at 7.15 a.m. outside his home which then meandered through these same country roads, heading to the little town, picking up pupils along the way. On the back seat would be his friends, Delbert Graves and Tommy Murphy. Every week day, they'd drive past the creek where they fished regularly for minnows and perch. Past the steep red-clay banks where he'd challenge his siblings and friends to a race to the top, clinging precariously to the spindly tree roots as he scrambled up. Past Short's wooden Methodist church where he regularly attended Sunday service with his family. Now replaced by a more modern building with a steeple, the church was the centre of the hamlet: a magnet for a tight, mutually supportive community that would come together to pray and give thanks for their lot, and where everyone knew everyone. The place where, each October, people would bring a covered dish and gather along long rows of tables on Homecoming Day.

At 7.55 a.m., the bus would arrive at Center's main square, passing the John Rogers drug store, the Farmers State Bank, Sammy Dance's hardware store and the Rio cinema, before dropping off its young passengers just behind the quadrangle outside the school's main gate. And that's where we arrived next.

The original yellow sandstone school building was closed down several years ago and appeared desolate. I peered through the dirty windowpanes. The classrooms were locked up and dark; the sound of children's voices a distant memory. I turned my attention to the old playing area, which was full of weeds. Four rusty swings hung together, swaying and creaking in the light breeze. I sat on an old wooden bench and imagined Larry running around. He'd enjoyed his days here in the early '50s but he was no scholar. He was better at fixing things and being practical. Kind-hearted, fun, a joker, I'd been told, he learned to read and write here but he didn't relish the academic experience.

It was the same at Center High. In the alumni publications, there appears to be no mention of him anywhere. He was no great musician, nor did he have any sporting prowess and there was certainly no record of any prizes. Apparently, he was always smiling, popular and good-hearted. But it seemed that Larry was an unremarkable pupil. So it was no surprise to hear that he was keen to leave school as soon as possible to get a job, earn money and, in part, supplement the increasingly pressurised family income.

For, as the years went by, it had become harder for his daddy, Fate, to generate a sufficient return on his farming. The cotton sharecropping was too small and he wasn't allowed by the authorities to allocate more of his land for cotton growing. The cows and corn were not providing enough cash either. So tight did life become that Fate was forced to find manual jobs via the WPA (Working People of America) such as gang work, loading gravel into dumper trucks. It was irregular money and often it could be months before he found a fresh hire. There was just enough food on the table for the family each day but Fate eventually decided he had no option but to leave Short and head south to the petrochemical conurbations to find more regular income. He wasn't the only one deciding to do this. Many men were leaving east Texas at that time in search of jobs in the shipyards, in construction or at the refineries. He soon secured work as a pipe fitter in the Texas-US chemical plant in Port Neches and stayed there for 30 years.

By now, David had left home and was pursuing his dream of going to college. Hughie had moved south, like his father, and worked at Neches Concrete before getting a job as a fuel-tanker driver. The rest of the family headed out of Short in 1957 to join Fate in Port Neches. Although Fate's income was more stable, Cecil soon missed Short, her wider family and the familiar, traditional, rural way of life. Within a year, she returned to the family home with the children, while Fate continued to work down south during the week. He'd leave Short on Sunday afternoon and not return until late on Friday evening. That arrangement, however difficult and testing, was to last for the rest of their marriage.

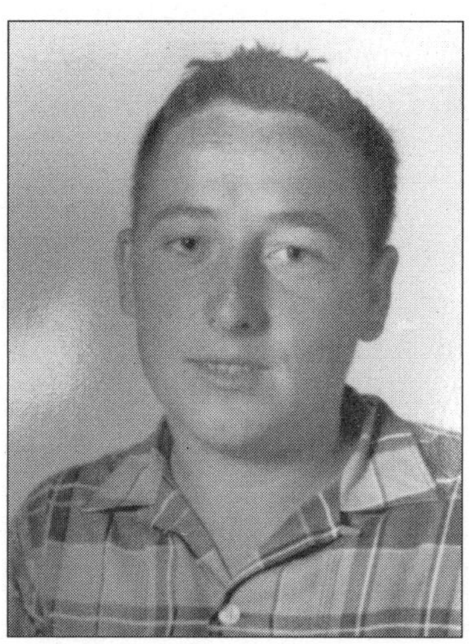

The Texan teenager

With his father away so much, Larry entered teenage life as the weekday man of the house. For Cecil, it could be a lonely existence and the luxury purchase of a black-and-white television helped take away a sense of isolation, especially in the evenings. She loved the soaps and became hooked on *Love of Life*, *In Search of Tomorrow* and *Guiding Light*, apparently believing all the storylines to be true.

Larry became something of an entrepreneur in the summer months, tending his own watermelon patch and heading off to Shreveport on Independence Day, where he could sell each fruit for 75 cents. The idea of earning his own money appealed greatly but any thought of working in the broiler houses nearby filled him with dread. Working in the poultry industry would mean spending every day with the thousands of 'dirty birds' as they squashed together tightly on their litter. There was no chance of that happening.

New teenage friends grouped together – Melva Lee Tomlin, Jerry Hughes, Shorty Andrews and Bill Rushing – as well as established pals like Tommy Murphy and Delbert Graves. More and more of his time was spent hanging around Sim Holt's community store in Short, playing endless games of dominoes, Monopoly and cards – 42 and gin rummy were big favourites – as well as horseshoes and dodge ball. He and his friends would muster a few coins together for cola and lemonade. Ice cream was a special treat. Just hanging around together. Not doing a great deal. Dommies and cards. Cracking jokes. Hanging loose. Just like teenage boys do. The store, directly opposite Short church, closed down many years ago and today the building no longer exists.

Larry left school in 1962, aged 17. By then he'd filled out. He was a strong kid with a mischievous streak that he'd exercise more frequently away from home. With little prospect of getting a good job in Center, he decided to follow in the footsteps of his father and brothers and try his luck elsewhere. He moved in temporarily with Hughie and Tommye at their new home in Seminole in west Texas and worked part-time on a land drilling rig. From there he wrote a letter to Debbie in November 1962 – one of the very few pieces of memorabilia relating to Larry still left in the family:

> How is everyone, doing fine I hope. I have been working a little. Did you get my money I sent you and mother. Well I hope you have by

> know [*sic*]. I may get to come in Christmas if every thing is fine. I have you a present for Christmas all ready picked out. It is real nice. Thoes [*sic*] grades were not good. I will give you ten dollars for every A you make in school from here on out. Hope to see you soon.
>
> Love Larry

However, his carefree attitude was to be knocked sideways by a devastating development in the family home. At the end of the summer of 1963, his beloved mother, Cecil, became unwell and was taken for tests to the John Sealy Hospital in Galveston, more than a hundred miles away. Larry returned to the family home and Hughie went to stay with him there temporarily. Debbie moved in with her Granddaddy Lent and his new wife Alene while her mother was absent. Fate continued working away during the week in Port Neches.

On her return home to Short, Cecil started to lose her sense of balance and her condition quickly deteriorated to the extent that Fate had to put rails on the back door steps to stop her from falling. From that point, the illness marched on inexorably, systematically stripping Cecil of each one of her faculties. Before long, she became unable to drive. Larry was granted a special permit to transport her around. Then she lost the ability to walk and would sit for hours on the back patio in her wheelchair looking at the trees and fields. Some months later she was bedridden and unable to talk coherently. The family understood Cecil's illness to be a degenerative brain disease but no one in the family ever understood the exact nature of its cause nor its prognosis. For the family and, of course, especially for Cecil herself, the rapid decline of her health was devastating.

Fate remained the breadwinner, working away from home. He employed a maid, Gladys, to live in with Cecil, Larry and Debbie from Monday to Friday and it was her job to cook for the family, do the household chores and help bathe and dress Cecil. It was a hard time for everyone but Cecil was certain of one thing: she was determined not to hold Larry back and wanted him to advance in life both in work and in play.

Leaving the two school sites in Center, we soon found ourselves on the 711 main road on the way out of town and parked in front of a nondescript, faceless warehouse that had clearly seen better days. Inside, a few paint cans lay stacked on wooden shelves. Old fluorescent lighting, covered in cobwebs, hung from exposed steel girders and an empty central bay of fading grey concrete made the place feel desolate. In the early 1960s, it had been a thriving GMC garage called Watlington's, and Larry had got a job there working in the spares department. He loved it. Around that time a whole new passion had started to shape his life: cars. Being surrounded by automobiles, engines and mechanics at Watlington's made Larry long to buy his own vehicle.

Within a few months, with the money he was earning, he was able to purchase his first car and was soon the proud owner of an old Plymouth Fury. Later, he bought a Chevrolet Chevelle. But his absolute pride and joy was to be an old red Corvette, which must have clocked up very serious mileage for him to have been able to afford it: a brand-new version then cost around $4,000 (approximately $31,000 in today's money).

At that time, the Corvette was the all-time classic American sports car. Larry loved it like a treasured girlfriend. The roman red colour, the sleek curves, the pert 'duck tail' rear deck, the four round tail lights and the chrome mesh screen were the essence of style. The two low seats and the red paintwork that contrasted with the white coves on the side panels gave it an eye-catching, sporty, carefree style. This was a car touched by glamour. Only 11,000 were made of that 61 edition and only 1,794 of them were in classic roman red. For Center, this was something really special, and Larry was the owner.

Larry loved driving his 'Vette' through the country roads and opening it up on the highways to Nacogdoches, San Augustine and even to Shreveport if he could afford the gas. A king of the road, he loved offering to take the local girls for a spin. He'd park up outside the Rio cinema in the square or take it to the local Crystal drive-in. His strong, muscular build and outgoing personality made him an attractive proposition. His brash confidence, jokey sense of humour and forwardness with the girls became the envy of his friends. So, too, was that little red Corvette.

His practical aptitude came to the fore, and in his spare time he and his friends would spend hours stripping down engines and tinkering under bonnets. This obsession soon evolved into a new hobby – drag racing – which saw him competing with friends and local drag rivals on any available local 'strip'.

The long wooden bridge crossing Flat Fork Creek on the way to Logansport and Highway 96 south of Center were particular favourites. Hughie had pointed out that same old bridge earlier in the morning when we drove in from Mansfield. The 96 south, out of the town, was arrow straight, so had obvious drag-racing appeal. As we drove along it, I imagined the scene: rival racers spinning and squealing their wheels to warm the tyres, trying to outstare each other as they edged towards the start line. Then, when the race started, shifting through the gears as quickly as possible to be the first to cross the finish line exactly a quarter of a mile away. Larry may not have had the fastest car around, but apparently he was one of the most courageous drivers, with a real daredevil attitude. He was difficult to beat and soon built a reputation as one of the best road runners across Shelby County, often completing his 'e.t.' (elapsed time) on the strip in under 25 seconds.

Some close friends of Larry shared their memories with me. Bill Rushing remembered: 'He loved excitement, he was real daring and wanted to do things that put you on edge. We were night owls sitting in those cars. Showing off. And he loved chasing the girls. He was kind and outgoing but if he was pushed over the edge he could show a temper and he took no prisoners.'

Melva Lee Tomlin remembered Larry being: 'Lots of fun, laughing all the time, just real carefree.'

Delbert Graves considered him: 'A leader of the local group in the Short area. He wasn't real aggressive but he could look after himself the best. And he'd look after you. He was real loyal.'

Another friend put it this way: 'He could get a bit wayward in his late teens – all boys at that age do and he didn't have his daddy around as much – but he was a real good guy, and with such a great sense of humour.'

Some time later, David, his elder brother, related to me an incident from that period: 'One time I went back home and one thing bothered me about Larry. The only thing that I know really bothered me about him. I went out to his car and gave him some money to go to the store to get something and there was a turn chain on the floorboard. I said, "Larry, that needs to be in the back. You needn't be riding with a chain under your feet." He said, "David, that's what I protect myself with."

'There was a method that, you know, those boys his age used. I questioned all that. You know what I'm talking about – that long – you can ruin somebody with it. I said, "Larry, have you ever used that?"

'"No, I haven't had to," he told me.

'But I believe that he was the type that, if you put him on the spot, he would do it.'

It was time to cross the Texas–Louisiana border and take the Byford party back home to Mansfield. The conversation, inevitably, remained centred on Larry.

'I have a sense of pride about what he did. He gave up his life to help somebody,' Tommye reflected, 'It was his time to go. I don't question God because he is always right.'

'It's one thing to defend yourself, but to advance to help somebody, and to do all he could to rescue him and he didn't even have to,' Cindy interjected. 'Now, that's a genuine sacrifice. That's as pure as it gets.'

We stopped by for a Cajun dinner at the home of their eldest son, Charlie. Big, warm, affable and open, I took to him immediately. He worked at a nearby open-cast mine. His bulky figure and gregarious nature belied a sensitive soul. He took me to his study before we sat down to eat. I saw a long row of guns stacked neatly on the wall and fishing tackle laid out ready to use. And there above his desk, prominently displayed, was a large, coloured etching, set onto glass within a smart teak wooden frame. I recognised it immediately: it was a sketch of Larry wearing his uniform, and was based on that very same photograph I'd first seen of him on the Internet when my journey of discovery had first begun.

Charlie took it down and looked at Larry proudly. On the desk was another photograph of Uncle Larry, aged fourteen, back at the white house, proudly holding in his arms the new addition to the Byford family: three-month-old Charlie.

'He's still my hero. I think about him every day. Every time I'm in this study. I think about his red and white Vette. He'd say,

"You want to go for a ride hey, Charlie?" And Mama would say, "You'd better not go too fast now, Larry!" So we'd set off real slow from the white house. Then over the hill, when Mama and Daddy couldn't see or hear us, he'd burn off and we'd make the big loop. Real fast. Then we'd come back over the hill real slow again. It was so thrilling.' He rubbed his eyes.

'He did his duty. He didn't have a choice. He was just a kid.'

He suddenly broke down uncontrollably. Once again, I was witnessing deep affection matched by agonising anguish. All those years later, the emotion on display was raw, even in someone who was so young at the time his own life had overlapped with Larry's.

We returned to Hughie and Tommye's home. It was late. I noticed four simple, coloured glass beakers laid out next to a group of photographs of Larry on the dining room table. Tommye began to speak: 'I remember the last Christmas he was here and he brought them as a Christmas gift. His final present to us. Later, I dug them out of the ashes when our house burnt down. They are so precious. I never use them. I just keep them up in the cabinet. When I look at them, they remind me of Larry. Always happy, happy-go-lucky.

'I remember one thing. I never told anybody about this. I don't like alcohol. I don't like drinking at all. He knew that about me. As he was about to leave for Vietnam, he had a drink with somebody, and when he saw me he held my face and put his breath on my face. To aggravate me. And I slapped him. I just hit him in a jokey way. But he liked to aggravate.'

She continued: 'Once, when Cindy was only 20 months old, Hughie backed over her in a 1959 Impala Chevy. What a nightmare! After that, whenever I heard a car start and Cindy and Charlie were out playing, I would run to the door to make sure they were out of the way. I was really antsy about that. Larry caught on to how nervous I was about my children. So if he saw them playing outside, he would crank his car and rev up the engine just to see me fly out the kitchen door. Then he would laugh at me. I felt like pinching him.'

As I bid my farewells, I could see her shuffling the photos on the table. Chuckling, adoring, reflective, sad.

CHAPTER 6

DOING YOUR DUTY

I was heading up a grass driveway towards the single-storey house just off Highway 85 in Joaquin, seven miles north-east of Center, when I first spotted her. She'd come out to greet me and was standing outside on the verandah, dressed in a purple shirt and white trousers, the wind rustling through her neat grey hair. As I got closer, I couldn't help but notice her stunning facial bone structure and graceful elegance. A woman of rare beauty and poise. Like her momma.

She smiled and waved serenely. I remained a little nervous. This was the woman who'd hung up on me when I'd rung to arrange the appointment, slamming the phone down abruptly, saying, 'I don't want to talk.' Tommye had assured me it had been a mistake and that she'd thought I was a cold caller selling insurance or double glazing. That's what she did with all those calls, she told me. However, I was still apprehensive. I got out of the car and before long I was shaking hands with Larry's elder sister, Nancy, who was six when he was born and twenty-eight when he died. Today she's 72.

She was insistent about the time I should arrive. Lunch was taken every day at twelve o'clock precisely. Coffee was at two-thirty. I could come in between.

Inside her home, I could sense the influence of her mother. Everything spotlessly clean. All spick and span. Everything in its right place. Her love of art was tangible; the many paintings and drawings on the walls gave the house a sense of individuality and creative flair. I shook hands with Herbert, her husband of more than 50 years. He was sitting in his own chair. And now Nancy was relaxing in hers. The scene reminded me of my mum and dad in Dalefield. Everything neat and proper. 'Orderly, just so,' I noted down.

She opened the conversation by showing me a photograph of Larry taken when he was a tiny boy. It was that same image of him standing on the porch at the white house aged maybe two years old, certainly no more. His hands were on his hips and he was pushing out his chest. The brim of his straw sun hat made his ears stick out. He gazed directly at the camera with a cheeky little smile. 'I just looked after him, kind of mothered him,' she smiled, staring into his eyes. 'Cute but a little rowdy. A fun person. Very special.' She spoke slowly, calmly, somewhat wistfully about her kid brother.

I told her I was keen, in particular, to talk about the draft and Larry's call-up. I'd understood he was with her when his actual call-up letter came. What had happened?

In the summer of 1966, when Larry was 21, he left Short for New Orleans, looking for better-paid work. For a while, he lived with Nancy and Herbert, an older man he particularly liked and respected. Herbert knew a lot of people in the local oil industry there and was able to secure Larry a job on the rigs, cleaning big paraffin drums. 'Working with the wireline bunch' was dirty, tough work but comparatively well paid. Larry was determined to earn as much money as he could and his life at that time revolved around finding the most lucrative work possible. Herbert recalled the time he spent with Larry when they were not working: 'We'd go fishing for perch and bream in some ponds when we'd come in for a day or two. Not say much. You're quiet when you fish.'

Larry's quest for work soon led him to move on to the city of Houma, where he lived in a motel seeking out the best manual jobs he could find.

At that time, the US was becoming increasingly entrenched in the Vietnam War, and it was clear more troops were needed. The US Administration had already instigated a process of conscription, utilising the Selective Services Act. Over an eight-and-a-half year period, almost two million young Americans, aged mainly between eighteen and twenty-three, found themselves called up for military service in Vietnam. Soon Larry Byford was to be one of them.

Under the Selective Services Act, men between 18 and 35 had to register for possible conscription. Those who passed their pre-induction physical, which tested eyes, ears and stamina, were considered eligible and designated 'One A' and fit to go. They were issued with a draft card and all waited anxiously to see if they would be called up. Larry kept his card in his wallet. The 4,000 local draft boards across the country collectively had to meet the overall national quota levels that were set but each board had significant discretion on selecting the men it put forward.

Nineteen sixty-six was a peak year for conscription. Letters were posted all across America, informing 380,000 card carriers that they were being drafted for 'universal military service'. The draft order was for two years' service, with the likelihood of spending a year in Vietnam. Eighty per cent of the draftees were from poor or working-class backgrounds, hence why it became known as 'the blue-collar war'.

In late August 1966, Larry's letter arrived at his motel in Houma, forwarded from his family home in Short. Some of his fellow Americans found ways to exempt themselves from the draft or to defer their training. Most cited a commitment to continue their studies by attending college. Some failed the medical or highlighted physical disabilities. Others even decided to emigrate to Canada. A few claimed they were needed in a caring role at home. Recalling this particular detail, Nancy sighed.

'He could have got a deferment,' she said quietly.

Larry's father, his brother David and Nancy all wanted him to avoid the draft by citing his mother's failing health and her need for round-the-clock care. David was prepared to find a local pastor or judge who would write a reference saying how he was needed at home. But in moving away, Larry knew that the argument about his indispensability had been weakened. More importantly, he declared that he didn't want to be seen to be 'any different to others' or a 'chicken' and that, as he had been called up, he should go and serve his country. He decided to act patriotically and do his duty.

Hughie thought that the decision was Larry's alone to make and that no one should stop him if he wanted to serve his country. 'When you are drafted, you ain't got no choice. You do as they say. That's what he was doing,' he'd told me. David felt especially afraid that he wouldn't come back and told him he thought it was 'all a waste of time'. Nancy remembered telling her husband Herbert: 'If Larry goes, I fear he won't come back. I don't understand why we are in that war. It isn't to defend our own country or to save it. It has no meaning. And even with the training he's going to have, it won't prepare him for war. Sure he can use a gun. Sure he goes hunting. But he doesn't have the experience. I don't want him there.'

But it was all to no avail. Larry was determined to go. He wanted to do his duty.

When he left south Louisiana to head home to Short and prepare for his departure to boot camp, he called in on Herbert and Nancy, who had cooked him his favourite shrimp supper. He'd brought a bottle of wine for the occasion. But Nancy refused to open it, saying: 'The time we are going to drink this bottle of wine, Larry, is when you come home safely and we can open it up in celebration.'

When he drove away, Nancy feared the worst. Indeed, the bottle stayed with them at their house and never would be opened.

As she spoke eloquently about that night, I recalled the photograph I'd seen the previous day, which showed Nancy clutching her baby brother, with David, Pat and cousin Judy by her side. They were all sitting on top of Dinky's kennel in the garden. The photo was taken in 1946 in the aftermath of the Second World War. It had been a time of peace, a time of hope, and all their futures were filled with possibilities. I looked at Nancy across the room and saw that same high forehead and deep-set eyes that were so distinctive when she was a young girl. Now, she was staring into the distance. Thinking about her lost brother. Looking desperately sad.

*

Larry's two-year draft meant first having to go off to boot camp with the likelihood of spending a full year in Vietnam. In October 1966, he was saying his temporary farewells to family and friends. Packed up with three days' of clothing, he went on his way on a chartered coach to begin the US Army's basic training programme. He was heading east over the Sabine river back into the state of Louisiana, travelling just a hundred miles away from Short, to the major infantry training centre at Fort Polk.

Having left Nancy's, I headed along Highway 84 westwards, through Tenaha and towards Timpson to my next port of call, just north of Nacogdoches. During that journey, a word kept coming into my mind. I couldn't get it out of my head. The word was 'DUTY'.

What does it mean? I realise that its basic concept is rooted in ethics. Various definitions describe it thus: 'duty revolves about a moral obligation . . . a moral or legal commitment to act . . . a sense of sacrifice owed to your country or homeland . . . committing yourself without considering your own self-interest'. But that is merely abstract thought devoid of emotion. What does 'doing your duty' really involve? For a start, it requires people to leave their families – parents, partners and children – follow orders to the letter and risk not coming back alive. That's a very tall order, a big ask for anyone. Our instinct for survival is deeply ingrained, so I was interested to try to understand why the vast majority of young men felt that they should honour the draft call in both World Wars and the Vietnam War, even when they knew they had a high chance of losing their lives. Was it to do with deeply instilled patriotism? My thoughts turned to the minority who refused to cooperate, risking derision and contempt from the wider community. Maybe those who refused to fight did not feel the same level of connection with their country as those who took up the draft? Maybe they were conscientious objectors who morally couldn't support the cause? Or was duty more about being a law-abiding citizen? Did the separation between those who served and those who didn't simply reflect a division in society between those who followed the rules and the crowd, and those who did not want to conform to the norm?

Opting out of the draft had clearly not occurred to my father.

In fact, he was so passionate about serving his country that he changed jobs to ensure that he could volunteer. But why? Was it that a sense of duty had been instilled in him from an early age? Or was it more to do with his personality? He certainly likes to conform, to fit in and not ruffle anyone's feathers. Maybe it had something to do with the fact that, at that time, the First World War was sufficiently fresh in everyone's memory for them to feel passionate about the outcome of the next conflict. Most importantly, Hitler posed a direct and immediate threat to the safety and security of Great Britain, so a sense of urgency and an intense desire to help defend his homeland was unsurprisingly strong.

There'd never been a draft call in Britain in my lifetime, so I'd never faced the same dilemma. But what would I have done had I been called up? Would I have gone too? 'Depends on the cause,' I thought to myself. Like my dad, I tend to conform. But, on the other hand, I would stand up strongly too for something in which I believed. On reflection, I concluded that if I felt I was defending the security of my own country, then I was confident that I would have gone to fight.

But what if I thought the cause was morally wrong or mistaken? What if the draft had been to fight in Iraq? Some faraway place, just like Vietnam, with seemingly little direct relevance to my home and family? Well, that would be difficult. Maybe I'd adopt Larry's mindset: just get on with it; don't be a chicken; don't break the law and face imprisonment; be a good citizen; do your duty. Or maybe I'd have said we shouldn't be there in the first place, fighting a war that had no moral justification, and refused to go on those grounds. And what if the call-up involved one of my two sons, Sam or Harry? I recognised that was a different ball game. I wasn't sure. I have always encouraged them to think for themselves; to make their own decisions based on their sense of morality, and to question, always question. The only thing I realised I was completely sure of was that I was extremely grateful my own family had never had to face the issue of conscription.

I dragged my thought processes back to Larry's situation. He'd had the chance to apply for exemption but had decided not to take it. I had to question whether I would have made the same decision, either for myself or for my sons. Of course, the Vietnam War occurred within recent memory of the First and Second World Wars, so the concept of responding to a draft call was still fresh in the memories of the whole of the western world. Perhaps the defeat of Hitler's regime had infused the US with confidence, and those who went to fight felt sure of success. The general consensus at the time was that it was best to be patriotic and that if you were called, you went. That chimed with me. It is so easy to be wise after the event. That's the privilege of history. But at the time . . .

*

The green canvas of the east Texan countryside whisked past me. My thoughts started to wander again and took me back to an event that had happened at home some years ago. I'd set my parents a simple task: to write on a card their favourite saying of all time. My mum had answered: 'Spread a little happiness.' My dad had written in big bold capitals using a black marker pen:

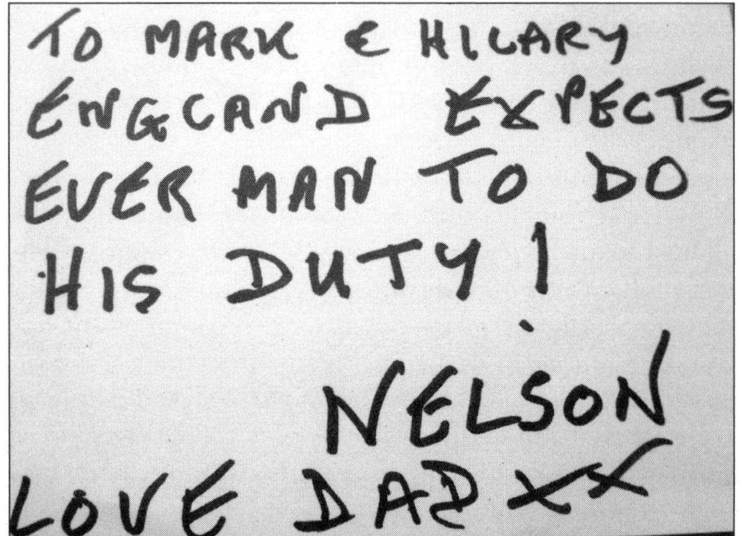

TO MARK & HILARY
ENGLAND EXPECTS
EVER MAN TO DO
HIS DUTY !
NELSON
LOVE DAD XX

I'd kept that card in my desk drawer alongside the rubbing of Larry's name. It had intrigued me. Like Larry's rubbing, it was a memento that I'd wanted to store away. I recalled that my dad had a portrait of Nelson hung prominently in his study at Dalefield. It was clear that the phrase meant a huge amount to him. But why? I knew the quote; every English schoolboy does. It's probably the greatest phrase in British naval history. I decided to look into its origins and purpose just to satisfy my curiosity.

The words originally formed a signal, ordered by Admiral Horatio Nelson, to be sent to his fleet from his flagship, HMS *Victory*, just before the Battle of Trafalgar was to commence on the morning of 21 October 1805. That was to be the most decisive naval engagement between England and France of the Napoleonic wars. Nelson knew something extra was required to inspire his men. It was a final clarion call before battle began. He'd wanted the message to read: 'England confides that every man will do his duty.' But his signals officer, Lieutenant John Pasco, realised that the word 'confides' would have to be spelt out letter by letter and there simply wasn't enough time. He suggested changing the phrase to 'expects', which was in the signal book. Nelson quickly agreed.

Immediately, 31 flags were raised up over 12 columns on the mast of *Victory*, using Popham's recognised Telegraphic Signal of Marine Vocabulary. Then the message: 'England expects every man will do his duty' was sent across the whole fleet, from ship to ship. However, that morning, some ships recorded the signal mistakenly as 'England expects every man to do his duty.' Both versions soon entered folklore. The historic victory at Trafalgar, and Nelson's heroic death there, meant it was to go down as one of the most inspiring call to arms ever to be declared, one of the greatest moments in British military history.

Today, the words take pride of place on the plinth at the bottom of Nelson's Column in Trafalgar Square in central London and are carved into the marble floor below his black sarcophagus in the crypt of St Paul's Cathedral. Shortly before setting out on my journey, I'd rung my dad to ask why Nelson's words meant so much to him.

'Is there anything better than that? You don't have to add to it,' he'd answered. 'In wartime, when you're up against it, put your mind to those words. There's no better rallying call.'

But what did duty mean for him? I was eager to hear the

response from a man I'd always seen as wisdom personified.

'To do your duty means to die for your country if needs be. It's as simple and straightforward as that. It means when you're in the heat of it all, you're prepared to die for your country and for the cause.'

That was the interesting wording for me – to die for your country AND for the cause. My thoughts had turned full circle and now I was faced again with the crux of the matter: was Vietnam the right cause? Was it worth it? To die for your country was one thing. But to die when the cause was in relation to a far-off land, connected to the USA by the seemingly tenuous link of fighting communism, was something else. When the cause was controversial, debatable, maybe mistaken or possibly even wrong, should that matter? Should that be seen as doing your duty or be more like blindly obeying an order? I felt like I had been wandering through a moral maze, had got lost along the way, then found myself right back at the start again.

*

Laid out neatly across the pine table in her kitchen, ready for my arrival, were the few treasured artefacts in Debbie's possession from her brother's brief period in the military: his bag label; a green neck cloth; his neatly folded green cotton US Army shirt with fading colour round the collar and cuffs, BYFORD still faintly readable above the right breast pocket; and his metal dog tag, stamped with his name:

BYFORD
LARRY S
US 54 760 752
O
BAPTIST

Most of Larry's personal belongings from his time at boot camp and in Vietnam have been lost. Some letters were burnt in a house fire at Hughie's; some were discarded by Fate when he moved out of the white house; others were removed years ago by relatives as they sorted old boxes and spring cleaned their homes; and the rest simply disappeared over time.

Just a handful of letters from him remain. Two are with Debbie, both sent from boot camp. One, from Vietnam, is with cousin Judy. Another is with David. Not a single photograph exists within the family from his time in Vietnam. No logbooks. No diaries. A small collection indeed.

Debbie handled the dog tag, feeling the letters and numbers engraved into the metal. She was 13 when Larry was killed. Today she's 58. She's married but never had children. She wore a brown sweatshirt and blue cotton trousers, her greying hair cut neatly in a short bob. She spoke with a gentler dialect than her brother Hughie. She was warm and friendly, and at the same time calm and collected. Even though she was the youngest sibling and the one closest to Larry, she remained composed throughout our conversation, even when recalling the most sensitive of times.

'He always looked after me. That's what big brothers do. He was always there for me,' she said affectionately.

She kept emphasising how she was keen to help but at the same time apologising that she found it difficult to remember any detail. 'I hope this project brings back a few memories for me but I'm most looking forward to hearing new things about Larry.' It was a comment that stuck with me. I might be able to tell her more during the course of my journey than she could tell me. It would spur me on.

She started to leaf through a book. I noticed the pages were full of photographs. 'This is Larry's book given to him when he passed out at boot camp. Look, here he is,' she exclaimed proudly. There, set among rows and rows of smiling recruits in uniform, was her brother. The same photograph I'd seen before, now used four decades later on the memorial sites. I'd discovered its origin. Fort Polk. December 1966.

'He didn't want to be different. He was called and that was his duty. He saw it that way. I knew he was going to have to go but he's coming back, right? I don't think it ever really crossed my mind that he wouldn't.'

She passed the book over to me and I began to look through it carefully. 'Who'd come home safely out of all these faces here?'

I wondered. I turned the pages slowly, and as I did so, I could feel myself being taken back to when Larry entered boot camp. It was the winter of 1966–67. The scene was Fort Polk.

I saw a photo of the huge sign that would have greeted Larry on the afternoon of 28 October 1966:

> Welcome Soldier to the United States Army. Stand Proud!

Next to the reception block another billboard announced:

> Fort Polk. United States Army Training Centre Infantry.
> Fight to Win. Engage and Destroy.

From 1962 to 1974, more soldiers were shipped from Fort Polk to Vietnam than from any other training base. It was known as 'the last stop before "Nam"'. Fort Polk was enormous: 198,000 acres of pine woods, creeks, swamps, mock battle zones, rifle ranges, parade grounds and row upon row of green and white barracks. It was another world. The nearest town was Leesville, eight miles away. Set in the forests of west Louisiana, the terrain was similar to that of east Texas. But although it would have felt familiar to Larry, this place was altogether different in terms of layout, atmosphere and purpose.

The recruits nicknamed it 'Fort Puke Lousyanna'. Although not always appreciated by those who were trained there, the base was steeped in the history and traditions of the US Army. Hailed as the birthplace of the infantry soldier, its status was legendary. Some of the greatest US generals – Eisenhower, Bradley and Patton – were stationed there. It had a strong reputation for discipline and steel. The place where boys became men; where civilians became soldiers. Where the smoky-bear-hatted drill sergeants instilled a special brand of fear and loathing. Fort Polk strove to be the best; it didn't believe in second place or in compromise. It trained men to be champions.

The nervous young recruits were as diverse as the United States itself. Larry a 21-year-old southern boy: white, rural, a religious patriot. Surrounding him, a wide-ranging group of white, black and Hispanic recruits, aged between 18 and 23: some urban and streetwise, others straightforward country folk; from the east coast, west coast, Midwest, Deep South; some proud to be there, others deeply sceptical or even resistant. A melting pot of draftees and volunteers. 'From cities to farms, from slums to mansions,' was how one recruit had described it.

Within an hour of his arrival, Larry was ordered to fill out his 201 records file. As he did so, he must have felt scared and lonely: everything he found familiar and comforting was starting to vanish. His background and identity were fading fast. There would be no room for individuality there. From now on he was to be known as Byford: US 54 760 752. The road ahead would be totally focused on building his physical fitness, developing his aptitude and attitude, and instilling in him a readiness to change from being an 'ordinary Joe' citizen to a tough, courageous killing machine in the most powerful army in the world.

I took the pre-printed standard-issue postcard from Debbie's book, which Larry sent that same first evening. Addressed to: *'Mother, Dad, Debbie and All'* it confirmed that he had arrived at Fort Polk and would be spending three to five days 'being processed' before being transferred to a unit for training:

> Please do not write me until I send you my permanent address. In case of emergency you can contact me through the local chapter of the American Red Cross.
>
> Love Larry Byford

Stark words. There was no allowance or room for personal messages, reassurances or endearments. The wording conveyed efficiency but lacked any emotion. The picture on the front wasn't exactly warm or assuring either: a photograph of recruits wearing gas masks, queuing up outside a long, single-storey shed, with the words alongside: *'Preparing for a trip into the gas chamber, trainees learn the correct use of the mask. A brief exposure to tear gas and chlorine gas without benefit of masks teaches them the importance of masks.'*

As that first night fell, he was sent with the other recruits to one of the two-storey white and green wooden barracks that spread across the southern area of the base. Built to house Second

World War recruits, the aerial photo in the book showed how the barracks were laid out in a grid pattern. Inside, metal bunk beds were two feet apart, in two rows either side of an open bay. At the end were basic shower facilities and the 'Head' – eight toilets laid out in a semi-circle with no doors.

Two drill sergeants accompanied Larry and the rest of his group everywhere throughout the first few weeks of training. Bellowing questions and orders at the top of their voices, their faces merely inches away, they were there not only to teach and guide but also to instil fear, respect and discipline. Their intimidating, tough behaviour was euphemistically described as 'personal mentoring'. For the next eight weeks, everything would be tightly controlled: when you got up; when you sat down; when you ate; when you slept. Up sharp by five-thirty. Lights out by nine-thirty.

The boys were formed into companies of around 200 and split into platoons of between 30 and 48 men. Larry was a member of Company B, 4th Battalion, 2nd Training Brigade, Fort Polk. Based with him in his platoon squad were two guys who were to become close friends over the following weeks: Charlie Boley from West Virginia and Bobby 'Bee Bee' Bevill from Tennessee. Charlie was also a country boy who liked hunting and fishing. He was four beds down the line from Larry, who'd been allocated one of the bottom bunks.

The first appointment at the camp was with the barber, where each recruit had his hair shaved off to stamp out individuality and instil uniformity. After numerous inoculations, they collected their uniforms.

Now he was ready to begin the Basic Combat Training programme. During this time, he and his fellow recruits would learn the proper way to address a superior; understand basic fighting techniques; undergo the rigorous programme of physical training to prepare their minds and bodies for combat. March, march, march. Fall into formation. Stay in step. Stand to attention. Hump the kit bag. Avoid the fat camp. Instil self-discipline. Basic principles were reinforced at every opportunity: 'Fight and destroy the enemy.' 'Win and never surrender.' 'Be champions.' 'Kill whenever and wherever necessary.'

Charlie Boley recalled later how Larry had arrived at boot

camp rather stocky and out of condition. But, after a month of that tough physical endurance programme, he lost around 15 pounds to become lean, trim and fighting fit.

'Get up, you assholes! Rise and shine!' The same routine seven days a week: wash, shave, dress and inspection. I became immersed in the photographs of their training programmes. Two hundred white-vested new recruits in regimented rows, running on the spot, lying on the ground, doing their 'daily dozen' class of early-morning push-ups and sit-ups before boarding the cattle trucks that drove them to different locations across the base to undergo the designated exercises of the day. Some of the recruits called the vehicles 'watermelon trucks', because on the uneven roads their green helmets bobbed up and down the side railings. That nickname would surely have made Larry think of home.

The Basic Combat programme lasted for eight weeks and was like living life in a pressure cooker. Intense, intimidating. Non-stop. Macho. Boisterous. At times, bullying. Larry could handle it. He could look after himself. He worked hard. Kept his head down. There was to be no blanket party or sandbagging for him.

Nearly all the daylight hours were focused on training. The recruits were up at dawn, back at five, with time to shower and change before having to polish their boots and organise their kit. Then there'd be dinner in the chow followed by an hour to relax between eight and nine. This provided a chance to play cards, write letters home and read before lights-out.

Letters provided the soldiers' only contact with the outside world. As such, they assumed a level of monumental importance. The letters that Larry sent from Fort Polk were still in their original envelopes, kept safely inside his passing-out book. I opened the envelopes eagerly but carefully, to see his handwriting for the very first time. It felt like a big moment. Each was written in blue ink. Slanting gently to the right, the writing was neat and legible, quite extrovert in style, with plenty of loops and flourishes. Sometimes he used capital letters for emphasis but punctuation and spelling were not his strong point.

On 10 November 1966, he'd written two letters addressed to his sisters, Debbie and Pat. He appeared to be feeling a bit lonely, missing home and wanting to receive more mail. The first letter was written to '*Mother, Dad and Debbie*' on Fort Polk-issued paper, the words written over a photograph of marching men on the move:

> How is everyone doing fine I hope. I am just fine. Debbie I want you to start writing me. Yesterday we got more shots. Today we got our M-14 rifles. They sure are nice. This evening we went and got another hair cut. We get one every week. I just haven't got any hair to cut. I bet you wouldn't even know me in my uniform. Every evening we all go over and see if we got any mail. So just write me even if you don't say anything. Tell Melvin Tomlin to be sure and write me. Call him and give him my address. How is my car doing. Why don't you Debbie clean it up for me. I may get me a week-end pass in two weeks so you may all have to come and get me. Well I have to go to bed, lights are out at 9.00 o'clock. We have a holiday tomorrow but can't leave the barracks. We have to work a half day on Saturday. Well be sure and write me. I have to go.
>
> Larry

In the second letter, sent to his sister Pat, her husband at the time Benny, and their children Jeff and Mel, Larry wrote:

> Yesterday we took a PT test and more shots in the arm. We get two every Wednesday. We get our M14 rifles assined to us today. We learned how to disassemble them and put them back together again. We are sospose to respect them like they are our own life. Thats the army Ha. A boy got his ass chewed out for calling it a gun. You have to call it a rifle or weapon. That's army again. I sure was glade to get a letter from you. We all run over every evening to see if we get mail.
>
> Make Debbie write me if its not three lines. You to. I want you to drive my car and keep an eye on it for me. I don't want any of my hard headed brothers to get a hold on it. Ha. We are having a lot of class work to. We are learning to march to. Say why don't you get Patsy Woods address for me and send it to me or call her and have her write to me. Know I want you to be sure and do that. Tell Debbie to write.
>
> Larry

Patsy Woods was a few years older than Larry. He'd admired her from afar ever since he had first met her. Patsy used to cut and style his mother's hair, and it is unclear whether she was aware of Larry's interest in her. Although it appears that she did not respond to Larry's puppy-dog-like infatuation, he was undeterred. It's apparent that keeping in touch with her, in his absence from Short, was important to him. Presumably so he could show his colleagues that he, too, was receiving mail from a girl.

I continued to look through the photographs that showed the recruits engaged in different activities around the camp and discovered his first off-day pass to Leesville, more commonly known to them as 'Sleazeville'. For most of the guys, that meant seeking out the bars, getting drunk and wooing the many available girls there, before returning to the camp before the strict midnight curfew.

A few hours later, it was back to the grindstone. A night-time infiltration course was particularly challenging, as Larry and his colleagues crawled under barbed wire, in the dark, with pits exploding all around. Hugging the ground closely, chins touching the soil, with live ammunition flying over their heads, flashlights going on and off at unpredictable times.

I opened up a third and final letter, written on 24 November 1966:

> Dear Mother and all. How is everyone doing fine I hope. I am just fine. This is Thursday night and we had the day off. And had turkey for dinner. I ate all I could hold. HA. Every day is the same to me in here although it is not to bad. We got past prividgles but no passes this weekend. May be next weekend if we look real sharp next week. We are going to get off for Christmas as far as I know. We had a real good time today and went to the picture show this evening and saw Shane. A western movie. Then we came back to the barracks. I am sending you a postcard Debbie and for your information Miss Woods has all ready written me. HA HA. I am taking out Bonds (government) and I am sending you a receipt for one. I have started. We got our pictures and I look bad. Will write soon. I am going to bed. Hope to hear from you soon.
>
> Love Larry

By December, Larry had received his Basic Training certificate and the special commemorative Fort Polk, Major General Reaves wrote in it:

> You have succeeded in making the difficult change from citizen to soldier. There will be many other challenges in your military career which will call for the same spirit of dedication and hard work demonstrated in your first eight weeks of service.

Before leaving, Larry exchanged photographs and addresses with his friend Charlie Boley. The photo of Charlie was still there left loosely inside the book. 'He was such a nice guy was Larry. He'd do anything for you. Such good memories of him,' Charlie later recalled. On the back of his photograph he'd left a message to:

> Larry:
>
> To a good friend of mine who'd raised hell with me in basic training.

That was the last time that he would ever see or hear from Larry.

After graduation, Larry returned home for the Christmas holiday to see his bedridden mother and the rest of his family. Ten days later, at the start of 1967, he was back at Fort Polk, this time to begin the Advanced Individual Training programme (AIT) that would enable him to qualify as an MOS 11B infantryman. He was now addressed as a soldier and would be treated as one. He had come out of Basic Training having learned how to salute, how to march, how to shoot a rifle, but he didn't really have a clue yet about real combat. AIT was about to change that.

He was now based on the north side of the camp in a place called Tigerland. The eight weeks ahead entailed ever more intense physical training exercises, achieving much greater proficiency in the use of his rifle, and tough, arduous combat sessions. The programme had been designed to make him as ready as possible for his forthcoming deployment. By the end, not only had Larry learned how to use his M14 rifle proficiently, he'd fired a 40mm M79 grenade launcher; a 3.5 in. bazooka rocket launcher; a 0.50 M2 machine gun; an M60 machine gun and a .45 calibre pistol. His training, shaped by all these experiences, would make him ready to 'fight like a tiger'.

On the first day back at Fort Polk, Larry met a new trainee also starting out on the AIT course. They were to become 'buddies'. Gene Ashcraft was a country boy from Arkansas.

'We just clicked immediately. As soon as we shook hands I knew we'd be real close friends. He was funny, so easy-going and friendly,' recalled Gene later. 'He didn't have ill manners and he didn't speak rough, not like me. He was easy talking, not short-tempered or angry like some of them. And we had similar country backgrounds. We'd both hunted and knew the woods, the creeks and the outdoor life, and we'd both worked real hard. That was our background. Some of the boys had come down from the big cities, and if they weren't street-wise, they found Tigerland real, real tough. Larry and I were country-wise. We'd been raised to work hard. We could both use a rifle. We knew how to survive. And we just clicked.'

Forced marches remained very much on the agenda. Yelling out cadences at the top of their voices as they ran along, they'd repeat each line of the drill sergeant's call:

Mama and Papa were laying in bed
Mama rolled over, this is what she said
Oh give me some, give me some, PT, PT
Good for you and good for me
Up in the morning to the rising sun
Gotta run all day 'til the running's done
Ho Chi Minh is a son of a bitch
Got the blue balls, crabs and seven year itch

Another regular cadence would turn out to be especially poignant:

I don't want no teenage queen
I just want my M14
If I die in a combat zone
Box me up and send me home

Pin my medals on to my chest
Tell my momma I did my best
Tell her when she goes down to sleep
Remember me but don't you weep.

The toughest part of the AIT course took place during the last week, when the recruits were sent to the infamous Tiger Village. The whole of the North Polk area reserved for the AIT infantry course was known as 'Tigerland'. But the main focus of Tigerland's notoriety was reserved for Tiger Village, a locked-off area of land that had been transformed into dense jungle-like vegetation to help the US Army prepare men specifically for Vietnam. A fortified Vietnamese village had been constructed at Peason Ridge, to acclimatise the infantrymen to the conditions they were about to face and teach them essential survival techniques.

I turned another page and saw a photo of a large sign: '*Tiger Village – Village Warfare with the Viet Cong.*' Alongside those words was a large illustration of a Vietnamese peasant holding his hands up in surrender in front of a hut as an American soldier took aim. On a board at the entrance to Tiger Village, to one side of the wooden gates that were heavily guarded, were the words '*Fight To Win*'. Once inside, the soldiers were in a completely different world.

Authentic-looking straw huts – hootches – were built within a heavily wooded area. A small tunnel complex was hidden below ground. The village was booby-trapped, with trip wires hidden in the undergrowth, and the area around it was littered with mines. This mock jungle area was completely covered by a thick canopy of dense foliage, which made visibility poor. There were other dangers too: snakes and scorpions were a regular sight.

Larry Byford enters Tigerland, Fort Polk, January 1967

More photos. There was Larry standing next to a large ridgepole tent surrounded by dense foliage. He looked much trimmer now, his puppy-fat cheeks lost through constant exercise.

Inside Tiger Village, the soldiers role played, acting as

Vietnamese peasants, undercover Vietcong who had infiltrated a village community, or American soldiers arriving on the scene as part of a daylight or night-time search-and-destroy mission. Effectively it was a week-long war game. Camping out using pup tents. Sometimes sleeping in foxholes, which they had to dig out. Waiting for that sudden ambush. Sleep deprivation was guaranteed, with an average of just one or two hours as the night patrols consumed their lives. In the escape-and-evade exercise, they were dropped into no-man's-land. The challenge was to get back to the safe point without getting captured. On the run. Like animals hiding from nearby predators. If seized, don't surrender. The treatment handed out would be brutal. Some cracked up under the sheer intensity and pressure of it all. But the exercise was all about staying alive in Vietnam. No training could guarantee that but Tigerland had the highest number of safe returns from the field of anywhere in the US military.

Larry passed the AIT training at the end of February 1967. Like nearly all his AIT infantry comrades, he was informed that his 'reward' for graduating would be to head to Vietnam within the month.

He had limited knowledge of Vietnam, the war or its political and military history. He took little interest in developments over there, and his colleagues at boot camp say he didn't engage much in talking about why the US was involved or debating what the right solution should be. He just accepted it. He was going there to do his duty. To fight communism. His country had called on him and, proudly, he'd obliged.

He knew Vietnam as a far-off land somewhere near China that had dense, forbidding jungles. He'd heard about the leader in the North called Ho Chi Minh, who was trying to unify the North and South as a communist state. He and his supporters were brutal and aggressive, so he'd been told, and if they were not stopped, the domino theory would kick in and communism would spread across the region, followed by the world. He'd also heard about that incident, two and a half years ago, when the Vietnamese fired at US warships stationed off the coast in the Gulf of Tonkin. How it had sparked the deployment of US combat troops to 'Nam. He'd heard how in February 1965 they'd attacked a US airbase in South

Vietnam at night when American soldiers were sleeping. Seven were killed and a hundred more wounded. That was why the US began bombing campaigns in North Vietnam and why thousands of American ground troops had been sent to the South. The mission, he'd been told, was to stop the North Vietnamese Army entering the South, and to kill Viet Cong communist guerrillas operating within the country. The goal was to secure a non-communist, democratic South Vietnam and to halt the spread of communism. That's why he had been called up and why he'd just been sent to Tigerland. To keep the South free. To fight communism. That's as much as he knew. And that's as much as he cared to know.

After his passing-out parade, when he was presented with his special Tigerland Certificate, Larry bade farewell to his colleagues and wished them luck. He exchanged addresses with his closest buddy, Gene Ashcraft, and they agreed to write to each other regularly while in Vietnam. They also agreed that if one of them was killed, the other would try to keep in touch with their family.

'We told each other to watch it and to try to make sure we saw each other at the end of the damn mess that was Vietnam. But we both knew one of us was possibly not going to come back. The odds told you that,' Gene would tell me later. 'I remember we embraced each other and Larry wished me luck and also my wife. She was seven months pregnant at the time.'

It would be the last time that Gene Ashcraft would see Larry.

Larry and Gene Ashcraft say farewell, Fort Polk, February 1967

In the final photo taken of Larry, on that very morning in February 1967, he was wearing his combat jacket and standing next to Gene in front of the white weatherboarded barracks. Gene was smiling optimistically, with his right arm over Larry's right shoulder. Larry looked more pensive. His head was shaved and he looked solid but more streamlined than before, his jacket a little baggy over his taut body. This was the family's last image of him alive. Within minutes, Gene had caught a chartered bus heading north while Larry had boarded one going west.

After enduring Tigerland, he'd expected his time back home to be a short period of rest and relaxation with a chance to have a bit of fun. But the week before leaving Fort Polk, one of Larry's best friends from his home area, William Larry Andrews, known as 'Shorty', was killed in Vietnam.

On 16 February 1967, Shorty, together with the rest of his platoon, was ambushed while on a reconnaissance patrol in the Plei Trap valley in Kontum province. Surrounded on three sides by enemy forces, and under heavy machine-gun fire, the platoon had fought for their lives. Shorty, along with 22 other American soldiers, was killed. Like Larry, he was just 21. They had been at school together. They'd played dominoes together at Sim Holt's store. They'd hunted in the woods. They were best buddies.

What should have been a vacation period of recuperation and anticipation became a time of shock and deep sadness for Larry and his friends. Going back to Short had re-emphasised the dangers he was about to face, the fragility of life and the brutality of war.

Shorty's funeral was at Mt Pleasant cemetery, two miles from his home. Delbert Graves remembered Larry going across to Shorty's parents and saying, 'I'm going to Vietnam and I'm going to get even with them.'

Three of Larry's closest friends there that day had avoided the draft. Delbert had failed the medical three times, as he was too overweight. Melva Lee Tomlin had a heart murmur. And Tommy Murphy had just got married and had a child, so his draft order had been deferred. While Larry was determined to go, Shorty's death made a big impact on him. Debbie's best friend Jo-Ann Barbee remembered being in Larry's house just before he left for Vietnam and seeing him sitting at the end of his mother's bed and expressing real worries to her that he might not come back. His cousin Judy Samford had a bad feeling about it all, a kind of sixth sense that there was something 'real dark' about his upcoming deployment.

The usual group of buddies gathered together at Sim Holt's store to play their final games of dominoes and cards, to have a few beers and bid their farewells to Larry. They all shook his hand and then, unusually for them, each of them embraced him.

On Saturday, 8 April, Larry bid an emotional farewell to his family. His father, mother and Debbie were all at the white house to say goodbye. So, too, was his eldest brother Harold and his wife Marie, who had travelled up from their home in Port Neches. Larry's beloved little sister, 13-year-old Debbie, was crying and distraught, dreading the moment when he actually walked away. His best friend Melva Lee Tomlin came to pick him up, and Debbie's last memory of Larry is seeing him leaving the house, dressed in civilian clothes, waving as Melva Lee's car drove down the dirt road heading for Dallas airport.

'The last time I saw Larry he was walking out by the runway,' Melva Lee would later recall. 'Then he was climbing up the steps with all the other guys onto the specially chartered aeroplane and looking back to check if he could see me. He couldn't. "See you when you get back, buddy," I said to myself.'

Larry was on his way to Vietnam. An assignment set to last three hundred and sixty-five days as part of his two-year draft obligation. He didn't know if it was going to be a return ticket.

I closed his Fort Polk book. I realised I'd gone into another world for quite a while. With a startled look at the clock, I realised how late it was. I wanted to go on talking with Debbie. There was so much more to cover. How she'd heard the news. The funeral. The medals. Life for her after Larry. But I sensed I needed to come back at another time. I made my farewells. Next time we'd meet together with her sister Pat, who had recently suffered a stroke and, understandably, wanted to be with Debbie when she met me.

It had been quite a day.

CHAPTER 7

RED ROSES IN A GREEN AND PLEASANT LAND

Of all the visits I was to make, I was certain that the place where Larry was buried would be the most poignant. I'd seen the photograph of the gravestone on my laptop but I knew I had to go there. I had allocated an afternoon for the visit, as I wanted to gather my thoughts, take stock and review all the information I'd collected over the previous few months since beginning my research. To do this at the graveside of the person in whose life I had become so intertwined seemed right and proper. It would, I felt, connect me more deeply with Larry's story.

It was a beautiful crisp morning. I drove slowly through the verdant countryside, which was sprinkled lightly with farms and small dwellings. The graveyard was a couple of miles from Larry's home, in Mt Pleasant, the hamlet where his great-grandfather, Joe Stephens, had first settled more than a century ago. Eventually, I found it at the top of a gentle hill, next to the Mt Pleasant Church of Christ – originally the site of the old school that Larry's mother had attended.

The cemetery was rectangular and situated to the north of the church. The fenced-off boundary was around 200 yards by 100; the ground a clearing of parched grassland, bare in patches and set on level land. Seven hundred gravestones were scattered across the wide enclosure: some upright; others laid out horizontally; a few with ornate columns. Some of the graves were festooned with flowers. Most lay bare. Many other graves were apparent but unmarked. There was still plenty of free space. This was the place where generation after generation locally had buried their dead. I turned the latch, opened the gate and went in.

There wasn't a cloud in the sky. The tall, leafless trees in the distance, completely static on this windless day, formed a natural boundary around the cemetery's northern perimeter. To the west were open fields. Peacock Lake lay in a dip to the east and was clearly visible from where I was standing. This tranquil stretch of water was where Larry had learned to swim. It was silent and peaceful now, but 60 years ago, it would have been packed in the summer with youngsters cooling off and having fun. Larry used to jump in the water even on Christmas Day as part of the annual festive ritual. Remembering this place as playing a significant part in Larry's childhood prompted his cousin Judy to recall a powerful memory of him as a child.

'Larry was the real caring type,' she'd later tell me. 'I remember when the dam on that nearby lake broke and all the water was gushing out. It was Larry who ran out with his basket to save the catfish and take them to safety in the nearby creek.'

I paused when I heard this. I couldn't help but see the parallels between young Larry trying to move the dying fish to safety and the young adult trying to save the Major.

Most of the graves were clustered around family plots. Near the eastern rim, a small rectangular grey marble stone engraved with the name BYFORD marked out the family's designated area. Below it, set out in an evenly spaced line, were six modest marble slabs, lying flush with the ground:

BARBARA UNICE BYFORD MARCH 10 1934 MARCH 14 1934
CARROLL DARLIENE BYFORD JAN 24 1949 NOV 9 1949
LARRY STEPHEN BYFORD MAY 1 1945 JUNE 23 1967
CECIL BYFORD MARCH 19 1911 JAN 13 1968
FATE BYFORD APR 28 1911 NOV 12 1987
HAROLD GENE BYFORD AUG 3 1932 DEC 26 2002

Larry's gravestone, Mt Pleasant cemetery, Shelby County, east Texas

A wild flower, each in bloom, grew at the head of each one. And in the middle, between Carroll and Cecil, was Larry. His stone was square and slightly bigger than the others. Upon it sat a raised rectangular bronze plaque a little off-centre, towards the top edge. Above his name was a cross but otherwise the plaque was unadorned:

LARRY STEPHEN BYFORD
TEXAS
PFC CO C 5CAV 1CAV DIV
VIETNAM PH
MAY 1 1945 JUNE 23 1967

At the bottom of the granite stone a small, shallow square hole had been cut into the marble. It was empty and clearly damaged. Originally this had been the place for a plastic casing that had been designed to display his two war medals. Hughie had told me that they'd disappeared from the grave many years ago and were later retrieved. But Debbie had a different story. The frost had cracked the casing and, fearing that the medals would be damaged, the family had given them to her to look after. I knew then that I had to return to her home to see them for myself. That would be important. But not yet.

The empty square hole gave the grave a forlorn look. I imagined how, when in place, the medals would have added character, imbuing it with a sense of distinction. I wished they were there now.

Above his plaque was a small blue vase with a display of fresh flowers in red, white and blue – the colours of the American flag. The careful arrangement felt very appropriate. I'd brought six red roses with me as a symbol of my own respect. Taking them carefully from my bag, I knelt on the ground and pushed them into the soil just above the plaque. Red roses, the symbol of England, now planted in another green and pleasant land. The flower heads nodded gently, creating shadows that danced across the lettering.

Rising to my feet, I realised I was completely alone. All was quiet. Then, without warning, a large flock of blackbirds flew overhead, beating the air and breaking the silence. I looked again at the plaque and checked my watch. I wanted to make sure that I stood for at least two minutes. I recalled the scene at The Wall. I had experienced this feeling before: sadness tinged with anger and bewilderment. There was an element of confusion too. Here I was, 3,000 miles from home. Alone. In Texas. At a grave. Looking down on Larry. I was a stranger to him and yet here I was.

Looking at the plaque again, I homed in on the word 'Texas'. Clearly, his family were proud of him being a Lone Star boy. I was reminded of my dad, who has always been inordinately proud of his Yorkshire roots. I remembered a photograph I'd seen the day before of Larry as a teenager perched on top of a Texan state boundary stone carved in the shape of the state. He looked confident and proud, with a certain swagger. Crew cut. Checked shirt. Blue jeans. Muscular. Tough. Manly. He looked a Texan all right.

My eyes focused on the letters PH. The Purple Heart. I reflected again on his time in Vietnam. He'd been out there just two months. And he had come back home to here. Dead and buried, aged just 22. He was a hero to his family, I knew that. Up here he seemed forgotten to everyone but them. Almost anonymous. And that made me even more determined to tell his story.

I sat on the ground, looking at the grave, and let my mind wander to the time that Larry was in Vietnam. The spring of 1967. I was eight years of age and living in the Yorkshire mill town of Huddersfield. I was obsessed with football, watching every home game of Huddersfield Town with my dad and my brother. I could still name the team: Oldfield, Parkin, Cattlin . . . I attended St Patrick's primary school and was in Mrs Molloy's class: Fleming, Hepworth, Zito, Byford . . . I could visualise those desks laid out in the old Victorian classroom. I'd just made the school football team. How proud I'd felt to wear the green-and-white hooped shirt with the number 11 on the collar. The memories and emotions came flooding back.

Vietnam. It was a name I was only vaguely aware of back then. I recalled my parents watching the TV news and remembered that my boyish interest was piqued when I saw helicopters on the screen. I probably knew that there was some kind of war involving Americans in a far-off land but it hardly registered. I wasn't interested. Nor were any of my friends. Why should we be? Britain wasn't involved. Life for me then wasn't about war and carnage but about football and fun.

I'd realised at the outset that I needed to do a lot of homework to fill the huge gaps in my knowledge. I'd read as much as I could in recent months about that period, devouring every relevant fact, comment and recollection relating to Larry that I could find. I had researched Vietnam, the politics behind the conflict, the fighting, as well as the social context. The study had become my war room; maps, charts, yellow stickers decorated the walls so that the paintwork was completely covered. By the time of my visit to Center, I had made contact with a number of Vets who'd been with Larry in Vietnam. Some had been willing to talk. Others said they couldn't remember him. Some said they were still too traumatised to recall those days again.

What had I been able to discover? What had happened during those two months in Vietnam from mid April to mid June? Where was Larry posted? What did he do? What exactly occurred on that fateful day – 23 June 1967? I moved up close to the grave and traced the lettering on his plaque with my forefinger. I closed my eyes and began to assemble my thoughts and sift through the acres of information I had collated. Facts, figures, snippets of information swirled around my head in an untrammelled stream of consciousness. Before long, I found myself slipping back in time to the spring of 1967. Immersing myself in the events which took place at that time. Following Larry and his journey.

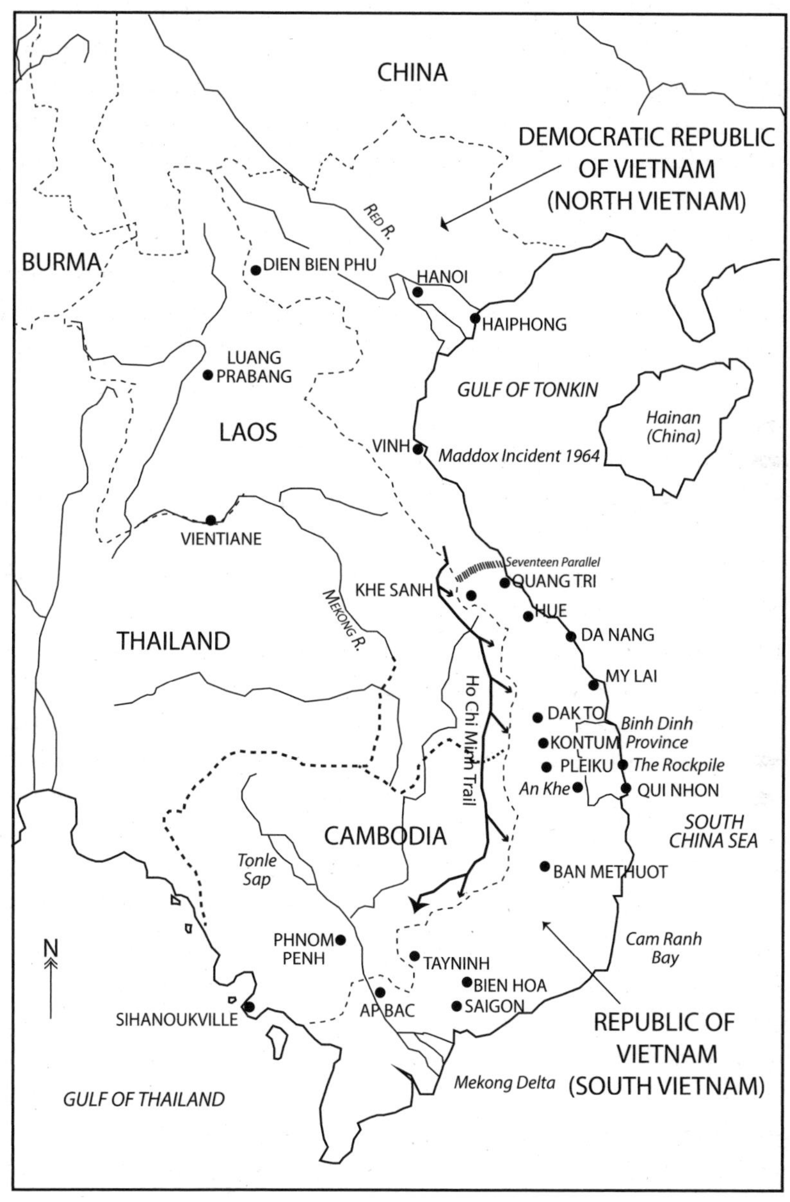

South-East Asia, 1967

CHAPTER 8

ON HIS WAY

By early 1967, Lyndon B. Johnson, the President of the United States, was feeling increasingly frustrated about the course of the Vietnam War. He desperately wanted his 'Great Society' social-reform programme at home to be the symbol of an ambitious, successful term of office: his legacy to the nation. He'd focused his Great Society agenda on improving education, health, poverty and civil rights in the United States and he wanted it to mark him out as a president who cared deeply for his people, actively dispersing civil unrest and racism while improving living and working conditions. However, as each month went by, he found that his attention, as well as that of the American people, was being diverted ever more to the war in Vietnam. The economic cost, by now $2 billion per month, was increasing exponentially. The talk was of budget deficits to finance the war. Johnson was even being forced to consider seeking the introduction of a special surcharge on American taxpayers to help pay for it.

But the cost to the nation was not just financial. By 1967, thousands of US soldiers had been killed and, with steadily increasing fervour, the American people were questioning the wisdom of sending innocent young men to die in a far-off foreign land and in a war they didn't fully understand. Johnson was acutely aware that public support was starting to drain away at an alarming rate. In 1965, 80 per cent of the population had been in favour of the war. By the middle of 1967 that had dropped to less than 50 per cent. The following year would be the presidential election. Johnson knew that clear progress was essential and that time was of the essence.

Despite an upbeat military assessment from his Joint Chiefs of Staff that the situation in Vietnam had improved and that 1967 would prove to be the decisive year, Johnson was starting to have serious misgivings about its outcome. In his State of the Union address, delivered to Congress on 10 January that year, he stood firm in his resolve to 'stay as long as aggression commands us to battle'. However, he revealed more than a hint of concern at the slow rate of progress as he warned the American people it was unlikely to be over in the near future:

> I wish I could report to you that the conflict is over. This I cannot do. We face more cost, more loss and more agony. For the end is not yet. And I cannot promise you that it will come this year or come next year.

The harsh reality was that America was failing to secure the strategic victory that it desperately sought. The President felt constrained both politically and diplomatically. He feared that significantly escalating the bombing of the North could lead to a much wider war, directly involving the Soviet Union or China. Also, rapidly expanding the level of American ground troops would generate more opposition at home and around the globe. But he knew that if he showed any willingness to compromise with North Vietnam or support for a gradual US military withdrawal, it could spell defeat, destroy his presidency and America's anti-communist leadership across the world. So he continued to pursue a middle ground, promoting a policy of gradualism, slowly increasing the scale of the American military effort in the hope that the North Vietnamese would hit breaking point and be forced to back down on their goal of unification.

'I'm going up old Ho Chi Minh's leg an inch at a time,' the President once proclaimed. But that compromised position meant that neither victory nor peace could be secured speedily. The hawks in Congress who wanted a major escalation in American firepower remained dissatisfied. Yet so, too, were the doves who felt the war could not be won quickly and wanted negotiations to be pursued more actively on a potential political settlement. The American people were deeply divided too. By the spring of 1967, 45 per cent of the population wanted to increase the military presence whereas 41 per cent favoured withdrawal. The President was in a dilemma.

Johnson wanted a political settlement but only on the right terms, and he was wary and sceptical about Ho Chi Minh's motives. Any secret peace initiative up to then had got nowhere. So, the President remained determined to drive out the North Vietnamese Army from the South and to take out the Viet Cong guerrillas hidden across the country. He hoped that strategy, alongside the intense bombing of the North, would pressurise Ho into submission and to accept the South's long-term future as a democratic, independent nation. But unless Ho backed down, there could be no settlement. No compromise. No ending of the war.

On 11 February 1967, a month after President Johnson's State of the Union address, Ho emphasised his refusal to compromise in a response letter to the President:

> The US government has unleashed the war of aggression in Vietnam. It must cease this aggression. That is the only way to the restoration of peace. The US government must stop definitively and unconditionally its bombing raids and all the other acts of war against the Democratic Republic of Vietnam, withdraw from South Vietnam all US and satellite troops and let the Vietnamese people settle themselves their own affairs.
>
> The Vietnamese people will never submit to force. They will never accept talks under the threat of bombs. Our cause is absolutely just. It is to be hoped that the US government will act in accordance with reason.

Ho Chi Minh was resigning himself to a long, bitter war that he believed the North could endure more effectively than the Americans. He'd drummed up an extraordinary revolutionary zeal and passion in his people, rooted in the region's history. The people, he'd told them, had constantly struggled against foreign invaders who'd ripped apart their independence. They'd endured a thousand years of Chinese occupation until the tenth century. They'd been humiliated and humbled by French colonialism in the previous and present centuries. Now the Americans were the latest in a long line of 'unwelcome visitors'. They had to be driven out. 'Nothing is more precious than independence and freedom,' he'd proclaimed.

Independence and freedom – those same words were emphasised by both Johnson and Ho Chi Minh, but, for each of them, they had polar opposite meanings. Johnson described North Vietnam's infiltration into the South as 'an invasion'. Ho hailed it as a 'liberation'. Like the two countries they led, they were miles apart. Effectively, by early 1967, the Vietnam War had turned into a stalemate.

Ho believed that stalemate favoured the North Vietnamese strategy of a protracted war. The tactics of his military command team, led by General Vo Nguyen Giap, were to remain nimble and flexible; to draw out the Americans; stretch them thin; make contact but then withdraw quickly. Ho thought the conflict could last for at least ten years. It would be a test of endurance. He believed the American people had no stomach for a long war and, therefore, Johnson would be forced to break first. As General Giap later reflected: 'We knew we were not strong enough to drive out half a million American troops but that was not our aim. Our intention was to break the will of the American government to continue the war.'

Both China and the Soviet Union, leaders of the communist world, backed the North Vietnamese. The Chinese wanted Ho to persist hard with the military struggle to the very end, at whatever the cost. Ho was attracted to the Chinese leader Mao Zedong's tactical proclamation: 'The enemy advances, we retreat; the enemy camps, we harass; the enemy tires, we attack; the enemy retreats, we pursue.'

Although Mao was determined that the conflict must not lead to a wider US–Chinese war, he was eager to support the North Vietnamese directly with huge quantities of food and military hardware, and, through it, promote China's leadership of the communist cause.

The Soviet Union was more in favour of a diplomatic solution, President Brezhnev declaring that he 'didn't want to sink in the swamps of Vietnam'. Yet, although Moscow was also careful to avoid becoming directly involved in a major war in South-East Asia, the deep rivalry between the USSR and China meant that the Soviets also wanted to be seen to be the North's key backer. Therefore, they too pledged all necessary support to North Vietnam.

Like President Johnson in Washington, the North Vietnamese leadership in Hanoi faced a serious dilemma in that spring of 1967 about which military tactics to deploy in the coming year. The hardline Party General Secretary, Le Duan, favoured stepping up the offensive and planning for an all-out decisive strike. General Giap supported continuing to play the long game. Ho Chi Minh, very much his own man and no puppet of either China or the Soviet Union, decided to pursue both options. By then, Ho's health was failing and he spent most of his time living quietly, tending the gardens next to his stilted house in the grounds of the presidential palace in Hanoi.

Ho Chi Minh recognised that although the North had suffered a series of defeats in individual battles in South Vietnam during the previous year, there was no sign that the US was capable of inflicting a knockout blow, despite its extraordinary military might and resources. In that context, he believed American public opinion would turn against Johnson such that he'd have to back down. So the immediate agenda remained to hang in, expect a prolonged war but plan for a surprise offensive to be launched sometime in the coming months. Ho ordered that no official talks should be conducted unless the US blinked first and unconditionally ceased its bombing of the North. Ho had come to the same conclusion as President Johnson: 1967, the year of the goat, would be critical in the 'American War'. The turning point.

By the early summer of 1967, Johnson's inner cabinet and advisors were increasingly divided. A private communication sent by Defence Secretary, Robert McNamara, originally a hawk strongly behind the Vietnam mission, showed that even he had serious misgivings about the American bombing tactics. As the man with responsibility within the administration for the armed forces, he wrote to Johnson:

> The picture of the world's greatest super power killing or seriously injuring a thousand non-combatants a week while trying to pound

> a tiny, backward nation into submission on an issue whose merits are hotly disputed is not a pretty one.

The words may have been written in confidence but they were extraordinary, clearly intended to re-direct the President's moral compass.

At the same time, thousands of anti-war protesters were convening more and more marches across America, protesting at what they believed was an unjust and worthless foreign venture and pleading for the troops to be brought home. The world heavyweight boxing champion, Muhammad Ali, was about to announce that he would refuse the draft. Thousands of other young Americans were doing the same. President Johnson urgently needed to demonstrate clear progress and achieve tangible success. And he needed to do it fast.

General William Westmoreland briefs President Johnson and his advisors in the Cabinet Room, White House, April 1967
(Courtesy of LBJ Library. Photo by Frank Wolfe)

While Larry was flying out to Vietnam in April 1967, General William Westmoreland, the US military commander in Vietnam, flew back to Washington that same month to give a briefing on the state of the war. The tension in the capital was palpable. The

General was seeking another significant uplift in the number of ground troops in the South to speed up the path to victory. In an attempt to reassure the politicians and gain their support, he made a public appearance before Congress in which he claimed, optimistically, that there was steady and encouraging success, the enemy was on the run, and that a further increase in the number of troops was needed to finish off the war. However, inside the White House, briefing the President and his senior team in private, Westmoreland admitted that the military situation was much more complex and worrying. Far from being on the verge of victory, American troops were struggling to make significant headway.

The strategy to search out and destroy the North Vietnamese Army and Viet Cong guerrillas wasn't working quickly enough. Even when it appeared that the Americans had secured a small victory, the NVA and VC would regroup, replenish and resume the fight. Indeed, American troops often found themselves having to return to areas they thought they'd already secured.

It was clear that bombing the North had made no difference to the enemy's willingness and capability to fight. The North Vietnamese Army was still able to transport men and supplies across the border. The vast majority of rural villages in the South remained in Viet Cong control. For much of the time the enemy was elusive. There were also growing tensions between the South Vietnamese and American armies. The US Command doubted the local soldiers' resolve and commitment. Most of the people of the South believed its government to be corrupt and wanted a fairer redistribution of wealth. Their support for the war, and for the Americans, was, at best, patchy.

General Westmoreland concluded that the situation meant a US victory was unlikely to be secured for several years and the war was set to continue indefinitely. With 500,000 American troops, they could only hold their current position. With 600,000, the war could last another three years; 700,000 and, hopefully, it could be over in two.

In the hope of securing a speedier victory and yet also trying to appease his critics, President Johnson compromised again. He reluctantly agreed to increase the intensity of the American bombing of North Vietnam but sanctioned only a small increase of 45,000 ground troops for the South, taking the overall number to just under 500,000. At the end of 1965, there had been 185,000 US troops in South Vietnam. By the end of 1967, the number had risen to 485,000.

The hope was that the increase would enable the 'crossover' point to be reached, whereby more of the enemy were killed than were replaced. That was already supposed to have happened some time ago. KIA ratios became the key performance indicator of success in a war with no conventional front line or attempt to take territory. Johnson may have described it in the past as 'a bitch of a war' involving 'a damned little pissant country' but he knew progress was vital. 'When will the war end?' was the unavoidable question he faced wherever he went. He needed an answer.

More than 100,000 bombing runs would be carried out in 1967 alone as part of Operation Rolling Thunder – dropping over 200,000 tons of explosives, destroying 80 per cent of the North's power plants and 55 per cent of its major bridges. But, anxious to avoid a public backlash at home or a wider escalation of the war that would directly involve the Soviet Union or China, Johnson refused to sanction a catastrophic knockout blow. The North, having scattered its industrial base across the country, remained dug in, counting on the passion of its people to withstand any punishment meted out by the US, however intense.

There was still no light at the end of the tunnel. The President remained under siege.

Mark Atwood Lawrence, Associate Professor of History at the University of Texas in Austin, is one of America's leading contemporary academic historians on the conflict and published a highly acclaimed book in 2008 entitled *The Vietnam War*. I rang to ask him about the state of the war in 1967.

'1967 is the year when the US commitment was going full bore and if that approach was going to work, there had to be striking results. The year "Rolling Thunder" was really going all out. The year when the American troop commitment approached its maximum level. The biggest search-and-destroy missions were being undertaken, like Cedar Falls, Junction City. So it strikes me that it was the year at which, if the US strategy was working, it would demonstrably achieve significant results,' he began.

'But, instead, it became the year to get a fix on the acute frustrations they were feeling; the underlying reasons why it wasn't working despite the intense pressure to show results; the looming election campaign and Johnson's upbeat public-relations strategy falsely claiming they were making significant progress.'

He went on: 'We're also now learning more and more these days about the communist side of the war – what was going on within the other side in 1967. There, it was also a time of uncertainty about the course of the war. In Hanoi, the hawks who had driven the agenda were getting pushback from the pro-negotiation supporters. It was a year of political purges. And then came the decision to plan the Tet Offensive, in part in order to re-dedicate the North to the war.'

I asked him which of China or the Soviet Union was giving more support to the North at that time.

'1967 is also a moment of profound change in North Vietnam's reliance on its major supporters. Before then, its number-one supporter was China, but in 1967 there was a re-orientation and the Soviets started to take the lead. That had a lot to do with the Cultural Revolution in China and the decline of China's ability to exert power outside its own borders.

'Giving the go-ahead for the Tet Offensive was also a way for Le Duan and others to say to the Soviets: hey, look, we're not totally reliant on you and your pro-negotiation stance, even though we'll take your military equipment.'

*

Larry Byford was part of a new wave of troops arriving in South Vietnam in April 1967. But, as he left on that flight from Dallas, he had no idea in which part of the army he would be serving, or to which part of Vietnam he'd be sent. He touched down first on the west coast of America at an Overseas Replacement Station, where he was processed before embarking on a 16-hour flight to South Vietnam, eventually landing at the US base at Cam Ranh Bay. The huge transit depot handled the thousands of new arrivals who were being assigned to serve in the northern regions of South Vietnam in the I Corps and II Corps military zones.

Larry arrived in Vietnam on 18 April for the start of his designated 365-day tour of duty. The countdown to his DEROS (date eligible to return home from overseas) had begun. He was now an FNG: a 'fucking new guy'. One of 400,000 American troops in Vietnam. One of 80,000 combat troops. A grunt with a one in twenty chance of being killed.

The first thing that hit the new arrivals as they got off the plane at Cam Ranh Bay was the intense, damp wall of heat. Temperatures in central Vietnam were already soaring towards 100° Fahrenheit but it was more the high level of tropical humidity which produced an atmosphere that could be suffocatingly close and tight. The air was heavy and breathing was difficult. It felt like inhaling hot cotton wool.

Don Demchak, aged 20, from Clairton, Pennsylvania, was a fellow draftee who arrived in the country at a similar time: 'It was almost 24 hours on an air-conditioned plane and then you walked down the ramp and all of a sudden the heat just hit you and you almost passed out. It was then that I thought, "I don't know what I'm getting myself into here."'

Don Jensen, a draftee from Iowa, had arrived in May: 'You just got off that plane and – woosh – you started sweating profusely immediately. The plane door opened and the heat hit you like a ton of bricks.'

Larry spent five days at Cam Ranh, where he was informed that he was to be deployed in the 1st Cavalry Division (Airmobile). This was the first ever airmobile division, considered to be one of the elite units of the US Army. The 'First Team', packed with courage, loyalty and combat spirit. It had already killed more than three thousand North Vietnamese soldiers and annihilated two of the three regiments of a North Vietnamese Army division. But why had Larry been chosen to serve in such a prestigious division? Was it a random decision or had he achieved top-class reports from his Fort Polk training? The answer seems to be that it was simply a matter of chance. Replacements were constantly needed to strengthen the divisions and to take the places of those who'd just died, been injured or had served their year out. The system was like a conveyor belt, with soldiers slotted in to fill the gaps as they arose.

Larry's MOS (Military Occupation Speciality) was designated as 11B10. Eleven for infantry. B for light weapons. Ten for his Private First Class grading. A light infantryman, about to be sent out to the Second Battalion of the Fifth Cavalry. A skytrooper ready for daily air assaults. His location was to be in 'II CTZ' – the Second Corp tactical zone – based in the middle of South Vietnam in the eastern coastal plains of Binh Dinh province. He'd be joining Charlie Company, C 2/5, as soon as possible.

He was transported from Cam Ranh Bay by a C130 Hercules plane to Camp Radcliff on the eastern side of the Central Highlands, a mile outside the town of An Khe. Camp Radcliff was the 1st Cavalry's main headquarters in Vietnam. The busiest helicopter landing strip in the world, it was populated by swarms of Bell UH-1 Iroquois helicopters, known as Hueys, buzzing around the rows of helipads like wasps hovering around their nests. There, he spent a week attending the First Team Academy, also known to many newly arriving grunts as the 'Cherry School' or 'Re-Mount'.

The mandatory course was designed as a seven-day acclimatisation programme. Classes were held on the 1st Cav's history and values, guerrilla warfare, rappelling and combat-assault tactics. The division was the pioneer in airmobile deployments, moving troops fast by helicopter over different terrains in search of the enemy. There were also tutorials on the importance of malaria control. Fifty cases were being reported each month in that battalion alone and the men were ordered to take preventative tablets as instructed. Although at boot camp Larry had had extensive training with the M14 rifle, now he was taught how to use the recently introduced M16.

A copy of the *Standing Orders of Roger' Rangers* was handed to each skytrooper. The card reminded them of the instructions given out by Major Robert Rogers to his own cavalrymen way back in the 1740s. The guidance included the following words:

Don't forget nothing
Keep your Musket clean as a whistle
Don't ever take a chance when you don't have to
When on the march, march in single file and enough apart so one shot can't go through two men.

Major Rogers' sound advice would remain just as relevant in Vietnam, more than two centuries later.

Major General John Tolson had just taken over the reins of command of the 1st Cavalry Division but Larry would never get to meet him. Based at LZ Two Bits, Tolson was an army legend: an airmobile pioneer who'd participated in the very first ever tactical air movement of ground forces by the US Army back in 1939. It was now his overall responsibility, as part of the ongoing Operation Pershing attrition strategy, to ensure that all North Vietnamese Army elements in Binh Dinh were destroyed. Also, he was tasked with eliminating the Viet Cong guerrilla units that were hiding in the hills, operating undercover in villages protected by the local people, or ensconced in caves on the coast by the South China Sea. In essence, his job was to catch the enemy in the act at night and destroy his work in the day, thereby preventing 'Charlie' from being effective in any way. Larry Byford was about to become a small cog in Tolson's mighty First Team machine. One among twenty thousand men. After a week at Camp Radcliff, Larry entered the C-123 cargo plane and took off for the 30-minute flight to LZ English, the base of the Second Battalion. He was about to be dispatched to the coastal plains of Binh Dinh, to link up with his new company colleagues in the field. They were based in an area south of Bong Son in the Phu My district – part of a lush agricultural region rich in rice cultivation. One of the most densely populated areas of South Vietnam ever since the days of the French occupation.

'They don't tell you anything about the culture,' Don Jensen remembered. 'You were like sheep being led. You didn't know anything about the country or the people when you got to the Company.'

Captain Don Markham, the head of Charlie Company, was the highest military commander with whom Larry was to have contact. Markham was a thirty-year-old officer who'd graduated from the US Military Academy at West Point nine years earlier and had been in charge of C Company since January. Born and raised in Virginia, he would serve two tours in Vietnam and would be awarded two Bronze Stars with valour for bravery. Markham ran a tight, solid company. He had a reputation for fairness and for taking care of his men. He was 'the tops', one grunt remembered. Jensen described him as: 'A very good commander; he had the stance of a leader. There was no doubt who was in charge. He never sent anyone out on foolhardy missions.'

It would be Larry's forthcoming platoon leader, Lieutenant Clarence Kehoe, who'd be the leader who would matter most to him. One of the Vets recalled that Young Kehoe had a 'John Wayne style, gung-ho, but he wasn't foolish but smart'. Kehoe would direct what his platoon did on the ground, and the men realised that he could mean the difference between life and death.

However strong Larry's personality, I imagined that he would have been terrified as he and his fellow FNGs flew off to join their Charlie Company colleagues that day. He was entering an alien land to fight an alien people and must have questioned whether he would survive. His training had lasted just twenty weeks: eight weeks Basic; eleven weeks at AIT, then that last week at An Khe. Sister Nancy was right: it wasn't a lot.

Leaving the relative comforts of base camp and going into the war zone was bad enough. But by early May temperatures regularly reached more than 95° Fahrenheit in the daytime, and the humidity was constantly high. Conditions were exhausting, energy sapping. Would he be strong enough? The next day would be his 22nd birthday. Many of the recruits around him were even younger – some just 18. Loyal, dutiful, obedient – and frightened.

When the plane landed at the base of the Second Battalion, he transferred to a Huey chopper. The dull thunder of the rotor blades started up and before long Larry and his fellow FNGs were flying over a land of many colours: mountains, forests, plains, swamps and paddy fields, all in different shades of green, which contrasted with the pale-yellow sands of the coastal beaches and the brilliant azure blue of the South China Sea. From the air, the scene was one of exceptional beauty and tranquillity. None of the soldiers knew what really lay beneath them in the serene-looking landscape – of the dangers that lurked in the shadows.

Eventually, the helicopter landed in a clearing on the Bong Son plains. Larry unclipped himself from the safety wire, moved to the side door, stood on the skids and jumped.

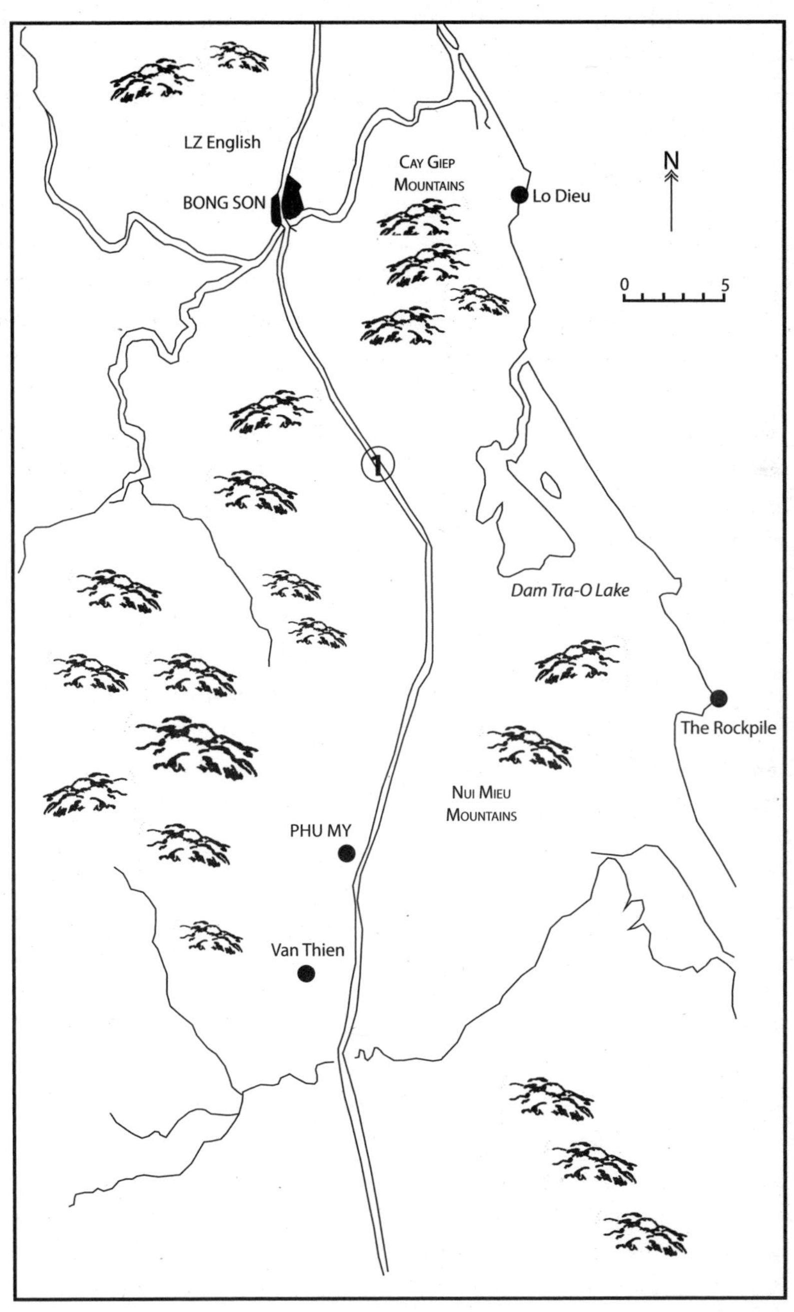

Bong Son Area of Binh Dinh, South Vietnam, 1967

CHAPTER 9

POSSUM TROT ARRIVES

Rousing myself from my reverie, I reached for my bag and took out a folder in which I had stored a library of information. Sitting next to the gravestone, I flicked methodically through the contents, reacquainting myself with the details I'd gleaned from emails, telephone chats and transcriptions of conversations with Vets who'd served with Larry. I tried to imagine him arriving at the Company camp early that evening. What sort of a reception would he have been given?

My notes reminded me that in March 1967, just a few weeks before his arrival, nine men from the Company had been killed in a ferocious battle at Phu Ninh. In all, 22 US soldiers had been lost and 26 were seriously wounded. Eighty-one North Vietnamese had died. It was the costliest battle suffered by Charlie Company during the entire war. That was the day when, in Markham's words, they'd 'disturbed a hornet's nest' of soldiers from the North Vietnamese Army's 18th Regiment. The Vietnamese had tried to separate, outnumber and overwhelm the Americans. Brutality and carnage had ensued and there were terrible, unforgettable scenes. Both sides had smelled the stench of death and witnessed, as well as perpetrated, the sheer horror of human butchery.

Markham and his men had been deeply scarred by the experience. Markham later described the scene as a 'great trench of bloody hell'. SP4 Grenadier Denny Henzi from the First Squad of the Third Platoon also recalled how many of his colleagues left the battlefield numb with the 'thousand-yard death stare' and were still in some kind of shell shock weeks later. Many would carry the nightmares of Phu Ninh with them for the rest of their lives.

John Wnek, from Chicago, was 19 years old and with the Fourth Platoon that day. He told me: 'Afterwards, the mood was very, very, very depressed. It was sad. The KIAs were all lying out there. Some had ponchos over them, some not. We'd policed up the bodies. I was overwhelmed by the grief. Oh my God, it was just terrible. It was a consciousness of doom. You were in another world after that.'

Then, only a fortnight before Larry's arrival, two men in the Company were killed by landmines and two others seriously wounded. Similarly, D Company lost two men in mid April.

On arrival, Larry was assigned by Markham to the First Squad in the Third Platoon and was sent across to meet up with the platoon leader, Lieutenant Kehoe. The Third was one of three rifle platoons in the Company. It had between thirty-five and forty-eight men, and the First Squad was a team of between eight and twelve.

The new recruit, wearing fresh fatigues, would have been closely scrutinised by the battle-scarred squad. FNGs were generally held at arm's length by those who had been in the field for some time. According to Tom Blancett, a 20-year-old draftee from St Louis, Missouri: 'The FNGs were shunned at first. They had no experience. You were nervous to be with them. They didn't know how to spot a booby trap.'

'FNGs were treated stand-offish,' Don Jensen told me. 'Here's a new guy. We know he don't know a damned thing. He'll do something stupid, get someone shot. Stay away. Keep him at arm's length.'

Tom Rutten, a nineteen-year-old draftee out of junior college in north-west Iowa, had been a member of the First Squad of the First Platoon for six months when Larry arrived. He remembered: 'FNGs were interlopers, bullet magnets, inexperienced. You'd leave them on their own in the first two months. They were shunned when they first arrived.'

Don Demchak also recalled those early days: 'So many of the

newbies would get wounded within the first month, so you tried to get educated real quick. You soon learned how you depended on each other. But you didn't get any orientation on how to survive the elements, the booby traps, the punji stakes waiting for you. You were thrown into the frying pan not knowing what you were about to be cooked with.'

'I was intimidated by the guys,' remembered John Wnek. 'You still had your nice skin, your colour in your face. But they were all dirty with well-worn fatigues. They looked like they'd been in a fight. They were cliquey at first. They began to probe me. They were suspicious. You got the impression you weren't seen as responsible or reliable enough. But within a month or two that would go. Soon every day would become a hump and a fly.'

Despite the initial wary nature of the platoon, Larry's new colleagues asked him his name. He replied that he wanted to be known as 'Possum Trot'. No one can explain fully why he chose that name. He had never been called it before, either at home by his friends or at boot camp.

Possum Trot was a small hamlet back home in east Texas about 15 miles east of Short. Nestled in the thick woodland of the Sabine Forest, near the village of Huxley, it was a poor black community of around 60. For those in Possum Trot at that time who were fortunate enough to find jobs, nearly all worked in the local logging industry. Nobody knows if Larry had ever even visited the place. Was there a specific connection there? Apparently, all he'd said in the past was that he thought the name Possum Trot had a real funny sound to it. He told his platoon colleagues that he liked the name. So, for the next six weeks, he became known as Possum Trot, or simply Possum.

Clinton Endres was a 19-year-old fellow Texan who'd been working as an apprentice electrician alongside his grandfather before his own call-up. He remembered Larry coming on board: 'We were both in the same rifle squad. The First Squad. I became squad leader and Possum Trot became a very dependable member of our squad. As a character, he was just a good boy from over in east Texas. Taller than me and bulkier. He didn't look well groomed. None of us did. He was heavier than me, huskier.

'We loved to sit around in the evenings when we could tell

each other stories about our lives back home. He would talk about his hunting and fishing and his cars and stuff. He was the kind of guy who was always ready to volunteer and do what needed to be done. He had it together.

'He was an open guy, not shy, never unpleasant or cocky. A real likeable, pleasant guy. I remember him telling me he'd worked in a GMC dealership in Center in the parts department. He had a country Texas accent, not the tangy west type. A deep voice. He'd talk about the piney woods.

'I remember when he said to call him Possum Trot he said it was a place that was real near to where he was from. So that's what we called him. It was kind of a catchy name. We all called him Possum.

'I was 19 when I got drafted back home in Muenster in Texas. I remember in Vietnam I always got sent my home-town newspaper. It was a weekly newspaper and my parents would send me it, and Possum Trot would always want to read it when I got finished. He got a big kick out of it, joking and laughing because it was a kind of cheesy newspaper but it was ours. He would always say, "I love this place Muenster and when I get out of the service I'm going to come and work in the GMC dealership in the town." He was quite a guy.'

I opened up the 1st Cavalry's Operational Report for that quarter, May to July 1967, which noted that the Division: '*conducted search and destroy and village cordon and search operations, together with pacification programs in the area,*' and that at that time, '*morale throughout the division remained excellent.*'

The report stated that the First Team faced: '*low-level enemy activity directed primarily at attempting to draw the support of the local populace back to the side of the enemy*'.

A more detailed log report of the unit activities for the Second Battalion of the Fifth Cavalry, now archived at the Texas Tech University, recorded that:

> April ended on a low note with negative action or finding in Bong Son. As May took over, the mission for the battalion was to catch the enemy in the act at night and destroy his work in the day. The enemy was trying to regain the foothold

> they had lost during the battles of March and evidence of this revival was found over wide areas in the valley and in the lowland lake site.
>
> Although the crust of an enemy infrastructure had been permeated, and the interior infested with the cancer of disorganization, they were trying for a comeback. The enemy, like the wilderness itself, will leap back with a vengeance unless constantly controlled.

The log also noted that a concentrated effort on the part of the enemy to regroup and resupply was in progress and the battalion was there to stop it:

> Intelligence reports continued to indicate the possibility of a notable build-up in the beach area – a point on the map that had not received close scrutiny in several weeks. These reports carried a low credibility rating, but were not beyond the realm of possibility as was discovered later.

Ken Burington joined Charlie Company in the field as an infantryman in mid June. Many years later, he chronicled the day-to-day operations of the Company over that summer period for the Tall Comanche website:

> C Company's usual daily operations during May 1967 consisted of surrounding and searching villages in the Crescent, the flatlands in the vicinity of Dam Tra O Lake. This was a rich agricultural area of rice paddies, with the large freshwater lake and the nearby sea providing substantial additional resources. New infiltrators entered the area both from the western mountains and by the sea. The Viet Cong attempted to blend into the legitimate populace of the many hamlets while the NVA troops generally seemed to stay in the two mountain groups, the Cay Giep to the north of the Crescent and the Nui Mieu to the south.
>
> The cordon and search missions could be slow. The practice was to surround a hamlet early in the morning and then physically search the ground and the houses while

> South Vietnamese police or the ARVN [Army of the Republic of Vietnam, i.e. the South Vietnamese Army] questioned the inhabitants with particular attention being paid to military-aged males. Often nothing significant was found but every so often a violent fire-fight would flare up. The usual method of approach was by helicopter. The unpredictable appearance of cavalry troops at scattered villages contributed to area security and helped keep the enemy off balance and unable to establish political control over the local population.

On the day that Larry arrived, the Company's camp was based inland from the coast, near to the Dam Tra O freshwater lake. In recent months, Charlie Company had seen action in all kinds of territory: from mountains, forests and deep jungle to leech-infested swamps and brush scrubland. Now they were in Bong Son, they faced a mixture of rugged mountains, gentle hills, narrow river valleys, coastal plains and deep, sandy, remote beaches. The Cay Giep mountains to the north of the camp were steep, heavily vegetated and challenging to negotiate. The Nui Mieu mountains to the south were solid rock with a thin covering of red clay that made it difficult to dig foxholes for night shelter and safety. Both these higher grounds were good hiding places for the enemy. So, too, were the rice-growing areas in the coastal plain – 'the flatlands' – which were a stronghold of the Viet Cong. There, the VC mingled in small groups in the local villages and hamlets, wearing ordinary clothes and accessing food supplies of rice, chicken, fish and vegetables. They'd often live below ground in the day in specially built tunnels and holes that were almost impossible to detect. Then they'd come out at night and try to ambush the Americans.

Tom Rutten recalled his early experiences: 'You were scared to death in the first month. So frightened. Then you came to the realisation you were fucked and you came to grips with it. No use thinking about it. Don't take chances but you were resigned to the fact you're screwed.'

For Clinton Endres, life in Vietnam was totally opposite to the gentle lifestyle he had enjoyed back home in sleepy Muenster, Texas: 'We'd start the day with a mission nearly every day. Sometimes we were walking on the hillsides. Sometimes on a mountain top. Sometimes in the valleys. Sometimes we were searching out villages. It was hot, very hot, at that time. Of course, later in the monsoon season it would be real wet but then in May it was becoming really hot. We'd spend the morning on an air assault somewhere, flying to where we were supposed to be. If we didn't have any contacts then the day went pretty well. By mid to late afternoon we'd start to look for a place to set up for the night. Then we'd build a perimeter, dig out foxholes and make a place to stay. The Hueys would come out and bring fresh supplies that we needed, especially fresh water each day, C rations and the mail. We stayed out in the field from April onwards and it felt like it was for eight months. We didn't see a lot of action a lot of the days in April and May but then suddenly it would all be happening. I remember we were once in this isolated valley; I don't remember what our mission was or what we were doing exactly. Nobody was saying anything and nothing was going on. Then one of the men said to me, "You know, we are in the asshole of the world."'

After hearing that account from Clinton Endres, I knew I wanted to form an even clearer picture of life on the front line, to try to understand what Larry and his platoon went through. I wanted to tease out specific details of practicalities, conditions and routine, as well as how the men felt both physically and emotionally during that time. Establishing contact with members of Larry's Company had been invaluable. Each member was able to add to the steadily increasing layers of information, providing me with a more textured understanding of the men's experiences in the field.

Mike Martin, at the time an 18 year old from New York State, was known as 'Upstate': 'We didn't go back to an LZ [landing zone] and stay there each night. No, we spent every night in the field. We had to dig a new foxhole every night in a new area. Then we'd set up a perimeter for security and lay out the trip flares and claymore mines. Then everybody would stay in themselves. They would sit quietly and write home. I heard that some of the other companies would go out once in a while, do their mission, and then go back and be at the LZ for three to four days. Well, we sure didn't have that at all. C Company was out in the field for weeks, maybe months, throughout that summer.'

John Wnek remembered his typical routine in succinct style:

'Wake up early. Shit, shower and shave. Get all your things ready, then you'd hear the birds [helicopters] were on their way.'

Don Jensen recalled a little more detail: 'We were up before daylight. The most dangerous times to get hit were first light and last light. They'd wake everyone up. Get your sleeping bag rounded up. Take your pack to the cable slings. The first choppers would then pick up your packs and sleeping gear.'

The troops were ordered to saddle up. Then, as the Hueys arrived at Papa Zulu (the pick-up zone,) they hovered, their propellers slashing at the heavy heat haze, producing a rhythmic, deafening, thrumming sound. The men would run fast, heads down and turned to one side, battling against the strong, angry blasts of hot air. They'd duck under the rotor blades and jump inside. 'Pull pitch!' would be the check call, indicating that the helicopter had started to rise and was leaving the pick-up zone. Each chopper carried between six and eight men. The whole manoeuvre would take seconds.

Hueys fly in formation, Binh Dinh, South Vietnam, 1967 (Photo courtesy of Don Jensen)

Often the skytroopers flew in formation, resembling a cluster of mosquitoes on a mission to deliver their lethal poison. The choppers hugged the contours of the land, skimming just above the treeline or the hilltops. They'd hover, tilt and pitch from side to side, making the flights exhilarating and gut wrenching.

Led by Cobra gunships armed with rockets, automatic grenade launchers and mini guns, the helicopters would be on the look out all the time for evidence of the enemy. At the same time, they acted as a lure, enticing Charlie to come out and reveal himself. As they approached a proposed drop point, the door gunner would shout out whether the landing zone looked hot or safe. Don Demchak again: 'When you came in to land in the Hueys, you might hear a "rat a tat tat", which meant it was a hot LZ. Three would jump out of one side, three out the other, leaving the pilots and gunners in the chopper. Then we'd shoot out to the perimeter.

'If you knew it was a hot LZ, you'd start sweating even though you were a thousand feet up. It was cool up there but that cool feeling soon went,' Tom Blancett remembered.

'When you saw red smoke, you thought, "Oh my God, please get me out of this,"' John Wnek recollected. 'You knew it would be chaos and noisy. You'd look down below and think how beautiful it all was, fishing boats bobbing around in the bays, such peace, but in reality it was a killing field.'

Tom Rutten provided this vivid account: 'Saddled up to go on a combat assault you didn't know if it was hot or not and you were scared, you felt real vulnerable. You couldn't talk; it was such a staccato of vibration running full bore, very noisy. You could shout but you were just looking at each other, waiting. The chopper tips were breaking the sound barrier; they were like gunfire, especially when they changed the pitch of the blade and it hovered. It was so loud. Artillery would prep it first, shoot the hell out of the area, then the gunships would go in before our slick-ships [helicopters].

'We'd try to fly in simultaneously, two by two, at a time. If the LZ was hot, you'd have to jump out from above the ground, often with your pack on your back plus three rounds of basic, smokes, grenades, chow. Up to 80 lb. Boom.

'You'd hit the ground and three seconds later the slicks were on their way. The chopper was a target, so it went away in seconds. Gone. You'd get away from the noise of the chopper so you could hear any incoming rounds. You'd head for a treeline as cover as fast as possible. The ARA [aerial rocket artillery] ship would circle round the area with rockets while you took cover.'

The squad would begin the search immediately, on the alert for trap wires, mines, punji stakes, spiked balls and hidden pits, listening for any sign of noise from the enemy.

Often a security patrol would mean cordoning off a hamlet or village late in the evening. Then, at first light, together with the South Vietnamese police, known as 'the white mice', they'd move in to search the hooches, wells, compost dumps and concealed bunkers. These actions were called CAGs – Combined Action Group operations. Once completed, they'd be on the move again to the next search, the next patrol, the next encounter. 'In and Out' tactics. In by helicopter. Secure the area. Out by helicopter.

When out on patrol, the trooper in the lead – the 'point man' – was in the most exposed and dangerous position, and at the greatest risk of being shot at by an unseen enemy. That duty was rotated because it was so gruelling.

'I walked point on my very first day across some paddy fields,' remembered Don Jensen. 'The Sergeant said, "Shoot them fuckers." One fell down.'

'It was extraordinarily important you did it right,' Ken Burington told me. 'It was extraordinarily dangerous. You were the first person out: the eyes and ears of 120 men behind you. You felt very apprehensive.'

Some would volunteer to do point but it was so hazardous that most would accept the duty and hope and pray that they would survive. Each man walked ten paces ahead of the next. They never knew what was waiting for them around the corner. They had to be constantly alert – watching, listening, pausing for any sign or smell of Charlie. The soldiers' mission was to sniff out the enemy and kill him. They were always on the move: flying, walking, humping, searching, hiding and flying again. All the time thinking about one thing: survival. They could never feel safe. That sense of anticipation, not knowing who was out there or how he would strike, could inflict as much psychological toll as being in battle. The pressure, the fear of the unknown, was intense. Days of monotony would be followed by someone suddenly stepping on a mine, being shot at directly or caught in crossfire.

'Sheer terror, stepping in shit,' as Tom Blancett described it.

Effectively, the men were on constant standby – reaction troops ready to be sent to any place where intelligence or instinct thought the enemy could be. The grunts knew that they were being used as bait to tease out Charlie.

Mike Martin, who was in the Third Squad of the Third Platoon, told me: 'I was with Larry every day he was there. Remember that often we did four to five, sometimes even six or seven, combat assaults a day. Whatever information Intelligence would send us, then we'd go. Looking for the VC or where the North Vietnamese Army were. Always trying to make contact with them, getting into a fire-fight. We never knew where we were going. When we took off in those choppers, we were going into the unknown.'

Faced with an enemy that was everywhere and nowhere; all around yet hidden; silent but ready to pounce, put an extraordinary pressure on each soldier. Walking across the terrain in the sauna-like suffocating heat was made all the more arduous by often having to carry 50-lb packs on their backs while also wearing heavy ammunition. Flak jackets were left behind in the warehouses. They were too heavy to wear. Most of the men also discarded their undershirts and pants, which trapped moisture and caused bad rashes – so-called 'crotch rot'. As the intense humidity was stifling, the men had to be especially careful with their water. Two canteens carried by each of them had to last all day, so sips were taken judiciously. In addition, there was the overwhelming exhaustion. Tired from the heat, tired from irregular sleep patterns, tired from being constantly terrified.

'We kind of had to be real quiet in the evening. Do things very low noise, because you never knew who'd be coming at you or how many were around you,' recalled Mike Martin. 'They were all around us at night. They were just watching for us to get up in the morning and leave. So we had very little sleep. The Hueys would often bring in our gear at night on slings. You'd grab your pack then dig your foxhole ready for the night.'

The night sky above them was like nothing many of them had seen back home. Clear and free from light pollution. Packed with bright, sparkling constellations of stars. A night-watch duty required two hours on, two hours off. In reality, the soldier on duty would be so tired he'd feel half-alert at best.

'We'd be sent out to the listening posts; we called them Deltas. Usually about three men in each direction about a hundred metres beyond our perimeter. Those Deltas served as an advanced warning for the Company in case Charlie was coming,' Clinton Endres recalled. 'I remember one night Smitty [Dewey Smith], Possom Trot and myself were out on Delta. We found a spot where we had some cover and could see what was coming, if anything. We didn't dig in. We just did it on the ground and kept watch. We took turns to be on guard. While Smitty and I were sleeping, Possum Trot was on guard. All of a sudden he woke us up and said he could hear something. "I hear a noise, I hear a noise," he whispered. Here he was with a grenade in one hand and the pin in the other. We listened and looked for a while but heard or saw nothing. We told him to either throw the grenade or put the pin back in. And we went back to sleep. When he woke me up for my turn to guard, I asked him what he did with the grenade. Possum said, "I put the pin back in." What a feat, eh? In the dark.'

Every skytrooper, whether a grunt or a lieutenant, was acutely aware that between life and death hung a very thin thread.

'We all kind of looked and acted the same. We were all young kids. We were all skinny. We all had short hair. But no one got real close. We were told not to,' explained Mike Martin. 'We knew we'd be losing guys at a sudden moment. That's why nobody wanted to get close to anybody. They drove it into our heads. Don't get close to each other. Don't make friends. Don't get involved. Don't get into family things with the others because you're going to hurt yourself. You may lose him in the next fire-fight.'

In addition to helping me understand the conditions and emotions on the battlefields, the Vets had given me an insight into their feelings towards their enemy. I knew that the North Vietnamese Army were well trained and well organised. But I was unaware and surprised at the high level of regard in which many US soldiers held them.

'The NVA were very dedicated in what they believed in. They knew face to face they could never win but they could endure,' John Wnek told me. 'They were tenacious. We were thinking we've just got a one-year commitment, let's get out as fast as possible, but for them it was their life. A much greater commitment. I hope that doesn't sound unpatriotic but it was just the reality.'

'They were tough opposition. They weren't amateurs. Some of them had been fighting since 1952. They'd fought the Japanese, the Thais, the French. A lot of people for a long time,' Ken Burington reflected. 'I think it was rooted in their political motivation. We fought thousands of miles away for a diffuse purpose, to stop the spread of communism. It was a valid purpose but it wasn't the same as evicting someone from your region. They had a direct involvement and it showed in their commitment.'

'We respected them,' Jay Phillips recalled. 'They were wily. When you shot them, they still ran away. How could they do that? They were really hard to get down. And we were never sure who was the enemy.'

The VC guerrillas were particularly elusive. The ones wearing traditional black pyjamas were easier to identify, but so often they'd look like the rest of the local farm workers. Not surprising because often that's who they were. Recruited locally to be part of the insurgency, they were highly motivated, hardened to the elements and the outdoor life. Many of the VC were constantly on the move in order to evade detection, operating in small, tight, well-organised cells, seldom in one place for more than a couple of days. When the Americans moved around in daylight, they'd be in the hamlets, blending in with the rest of the local community, or hiding in their complex network of tunnels, underground fortifications, safe houses and caves.

Then, at night, they'd surprise the Americans with short, sharp bursts of attack, and then flee. They adopted a 'one slow, four quick' strategy: slow, careful preparation followed by a quick advance, a quick assault, a quick clearance of the area and a quick withdrawal. In ambushes and fire-fights, they'd get up so close that if the US called in air and artillery strikes, they risked endangering their own men.

'They were sub-human sons of bitches,' is how Don Jensen graphically described them. 'I'd have killed all the bastards if I could. But they were very, very clever. They wouldn't attack unless they had an advantage. We'd sooner stand toe to toe. Half a dozen would suddenly ambush, then disappear.'

Charlie Company's search-and-destroy missions were not all land based. Just over a week into his time with the Third Platoon, Larry took part in an amphibious assault. Members of the Company climbed into Navy swift boats late in the evening of 9 May off the Bong Son beach. Landing vessels from the 1098th Boat Company 1st Logistics Command, based in Quy Nhon, then proceeded north up the coast in darkness for about ten miles. Intelligence indicated that the nearby village of Lo Dieu was a secret depot used by the North Vietnamese Army to infiltrate men and materiel into South Vietnam. The US Army map for that period shows Lo Dieu to be nestled on the coastline below the rugged Cay Giep mountains, south-east of Bong Son. It was cut off from the mainland by the Nui Hoc Mit mountain to the north and the Dong Dai and Bo Hop mountains to the south, squeezed in between them as an isolated shore and beach. That's what made it ideal for the NVA to use as a disembarking point. It was difficult to approach overland, hence the need for an amphibious landing.

Larry and his colleagues huddled together in the two landing craft battered by raging surf. At 3 a.m., in silence, they landed on the shore, one boat to the north of the village, the other to the south. Mistakenly, the north cordon had been placed some distance outside the village and this left a potential escape route for the NVA. Larry and Don Jensen were part of the north team. As they moved inland, Jensen remembered he was told to take a position by a bush while the rest of his team moved on. He could hear gunfire to the south of the village and could see red and white tracers passing over and around him.

When light appeared, five North Vietnamese soldiers were found dead, killed by intermittent fire and naval artillery. Twelve other NVA soldiers were captured on that mission. They were sent to LZ Uplift to be interrogated by the 191st Military Intelligence team.

After the search was over, hot coffee and doughnuts were flown out as C Company was stood down for the rest of the day. The men were given permission to swim in the South China Sea and relax on the beautiful, isolated beach. The Company made camp near the village and left the area the following morning.

Although Larry sent a number of letters to his family and friends while he was in Vietnam, only two remain in existence. One, dated 14 May, three days after that amphibious assault operation, was sent to his cousin Judy and her then husband Jackie and daughter Bo. I held a photocopy and read the words slowly:

> Dear Judy and Jackie and Bo.
> Well just a few lines to say hello and to let you know I am fine. Well Vietnam is something else. What would you like to know about it. It is a real pretty place. I feel sorry for the people. I have been out in the field living the jungle way for two weeks.
>
> Well this afternoon I killed my first VC or Viet Cong. Don't let this get back to Jewel [Judy's mother] or Cecil as they may not let me come back to the big Center. Ha. We were on a patrol this afternoon when this happened. Nobody was hurt. Our Company hasn't had anyone hurt since March 11th. Well that's enough for that business.
>
> I am going to get me a camera and I'll send you the film and I'll take some of this beautiful country. We are in the Bong Son area. The mountains are real pretty. Yesterday we were on a high one and the South China Sea was on one side. We went swimming once in it since we have been in this area. I have a pretty good tan. It sure gets hot over here. We eat bananas and drink coconut milk all the time. The bananas are about half the size of the ones in the US. Well write again and I will as soon as I get time.
>
> Tell Bo to be sweet. Ha.
>
> Larry

Two days later, tragedy hit the Company when SP4 Freddie Robinson from Orangeburg, South Carolina, was killed by an enemy booby trap while out on a night patrol. He was 20 years old. A second soldier, SP4 Larry Evans, was wounded in the same explosion. It was a harsh reminder that death or serious injury came not only from direct fire-fights but also through the mines and traps all around them.

Sometime during that month of May, no one knows exactly when, Larry attached an item to his helmet that gave him a distinctive and somewhat sinister look for the rest of his brief time in Vietnam. As Don Jensen had posted on that Vietnam Veteran's Memorial Fund website back in 2005: 'That lock of hair on your helmet was your statement.'

Don explained to me why he'd written that phrase: 'Sometime in Vietnam he picked up, probably from a village house, a long lock of hair. It looked like a cut-off ponytail. He had it tied onto his helmet. I have no idea where he came up with it. I think he found it in a house during a search. He didn't cut it off but just found it. The native kids and women must have thought he had scalped someone. They were very afraid of him. We all had fun with his scalp.'

None of his colleagues can remember where or how he came to get hold of the ponytail or why he attached it to his helmet. Some don't remember it at all. Was it a peculiar fashion statement? Was it a warning of aggression to the enemy? Was it a symbol of victory following a search-and-destroy mission? Was it human hair? No one will ever know. The story behind that lock of hair would remain a mystery. And Larry was to take it to his grave.

CHAPTER 10

TO BE A HERO

I shifted my position, trying to get more comfortable on the hard cemetery ground. Glancing towards the plaque on Larry's grave, I was reminded that he had been awarded a Purple Heart and immediately my thoughts turned to the word 'hero' that kept cropping up time and time again on my journey.

I remembered the occasions when I had heard the word used. Recently, I'd been at the funeral of a work colleague. His daughter had stood by the coffin, courageously addressing the weeping congregation and ending with the words: 'To me, my dad was my hero.' It sent a shiver down my spine at the time; it felt like such a powerful word to use.

My dad had referred to Gerow as a hero; Ho Chi Minh was known as 'The Great Hero' by his people, and political figures such as Winston Churchill, Nelson Mandela and Martin Luther King are often referred to as such. The word is also bandied about in relation to sporting or musical celebrities. 'He's my hero,' is a common cry of fans of Alex Rodriguez, David Beckham or Justin Bieber. But surely using the word in that context devalues it? Heroes need to do a lot more than score the home run, the last-minute goal, or sing in front of thousands of screaming adolescents.

Flicking through the contents of my folder, I came across quite a few references to Larry being a hero. His sister had posted her message on a website: 'You are a hero to me and all your family and friends.' Tommye had hailed her brother in law as 'my hero', as we approached the old white house on the way to Short. Her son, Charlie, had used it later that same day. It is clear that the words 'Larry' and 'hero' are interchangeable in the minds of his relatives. I wondered: should he be seen by the wider world as a hero? Certainly, the notion of heroism seems to be inextricably entangled with war and, of course, he died in combat. But should dying in the course of duty automatically make someone a hero?

My thoughts turned to British soldiers who'd recently lost their lives in Afghanistan. The sight of a funeral cortège surrounded by grieving relatives, friends and the general public, processing solemnly through the streets of the Wiltshire town of Wootton Bassett had become heartbreakingly familiar. Significantly, each soldier returning home to Britain was automatically given a 'hero's welcome', despite the hugely varying circumstances of their deaths. It may be that one died performing a heroic act of bravery and another lost his life in an unfortunate accident. Yet they were always given equal weight.

If being killed in action is enough to incur heroic status, does that mean that each and every one of the more than 58,000 names that appear on the Vietnam Wall are also heroes? Or is it more complicated than that? Is there a minimum criterion? Are there varying degrees of heroism? If so, where does Larry fit on the scale? Did he do something that marked him out as a true hero, rather than as someone who had just been unlucky enough to lose his life? The Tall Comanche website stated that Larry had died 'Trying to save the Major'. Perhaps that was the clue. Had he lost his life trying to save someone else? If so, did that constitute heroism in its purest form?

Whilst back in England, I had noted down the definition of the word 'hero' and filed it in my folder. I sifted through the pages quickly until I rediscovered it: 'Illustrious warrior; one greatly regarded for achievements or qualities.' That was all. Disappointingly brief. Surely there was more to it than that? Wasn't it all about showing great courage and bravery in the face of acute danger and adversity? Wasn't it about self-sacrifice, in its truest sense, for the greater good? The word must be used sparingly, in my view, to recognise extraordinary acts of bravery, courage and moral strength. For those rare moments of supreme self-sacrifice. When somebody does something so brave and well beyond the call of duty.

Looking towards the trees in the distance at Mt Pleasant, I started to think once again about Larry's time in Vietnam and to consider it in the context of heroism. To do that, I needed to remind myself of the exact sequence of events that eventually culminated in his death, so I started to turn the pages of the folder once more.

My mind cast back to June 1967. I was fast approaching that fateful day.

*

The Second Battalion's official log for June 1967, written at that time by Sgt Ronald Punch, recorded the following:

> May slipped into June without incident as the companies continued their missions as before. In an effort to make use of the airmobility concept, several air assaults were made daily to cover a greater area to catch the VC by surprise. It was a common practice for the enemy to observe a company as it moved into a location and then work in another location in relative safety. The battalion was aware of this practice and plans were made to move a single company as many as four times a day to confuse and harass the enemy.

Historically, the first US cavalrymen served as dragoons riding into battle on horses. More than a century later, the 1st Cavalry Division was carrying on that tradition in Vietnam, except the horses had been replaced by helicopters. After the Second World War, during which the US Army had found itself often paralysed by mud and difficult terrain, American military leaders had realised that the flexibility of mechanised armies needed to improve dramatically. Accordingly, the concept of an 'Air Cavalry' – a new air-assault division – was drawn up in the early 1960s.

By the summer of 1965, a test unit of the 11th Air Assault Division had become the 1st Cavalry Division, led by Major General Harry Kinnard: the original pioneer of the 'air mobility' concept. He declared that the soldier was to be freed forever from 'the tyranny of the terrain'.

The new 1st Cavalry Division was established, activated and sent out to Vietnam within a 90-day period in 1965. Over the next 18 months, the sight of Huey helicopters coming in to land in hostile or remote environments, with skytroopers jumping from the skids, clutching their M16 rifles, was to become one of the most iconic images of the Vietnam War.

Ken Burington's summary of the month of June, written for the Tall Comanche site, made reference to how the airmobile concept helped shape Charlie Company's search-and-destroy activities:

> The efforts by the Communists to bolster local forces and re-establish a military presence in the Crescent, the coastal area of Binh Dinh province, continued with troops attempting to infiltrate both on foot and by boat, working their way south along the coast. The Cay Giep mountains, heavily wooded, and the Nui Mieu mountains, with its caves and rock formations, were located north and south of the Dam Tra O Lake adjacent to the South China Sea, and provided excellent terrain for concealment of the Communist base. But food supplies had to come from the villages below and this meant coming out into the open.
>
> In the beginning of the month, operations conducted with the South Vietnamese National Police in the northern Cay Giep uncovered weapons caches and the 2/5 Cav, working with ARVN troops and the Korean 1st ROK Regiment, searched the Nui Mieu. The constant presence of the Allied troops had the effect of forcing some of the Communist forces out into the lowlands where they were easier to find.
>
> The Companies of 2/5 Cav sometimes made air assaults several times a day to investigate evidence of enemy activity and to assist each other. During the second week of June numerous discoveries of weapons, new and hastily-built bunkers, ammunition and food caches, pointed to an increasing Communist presence.
>
> During the middle of the month C Company established

> its night positions along the beach and moved to cordon and search nearby fishing and rice growing villages on foot each morning before first light. Those who were there during this period remember the excellent swimming on that beautiful stretch of water we called Miami Beach and the wind-blown sand getting into every weapon and every meal.

The thirteenth of June 1967 was my ninth birthday. I still recall the actual day pretty well. Friends from my class at St Patrick's primary school in Huddersfield came round to our house for a party tea and a game of football. We ate jam sandwiches, jelly and ice cream, and drank dandelion and burdock. All the invitees were boys. You didn't have girls come to your party at that age. I remember that one boy, Marcus Bialkowski, bought me a Ladybird book about Richard the Lionheart, the great crusader of the Middle Ages heading off to war in far-off lands. Remarkably, I still have that book. It told 'the adventurous story of King Richard, the Lion-hearted, and of the Crusades which he led to recover the Holy City of Jerusalem from the infidels'. It made me think. On the very same day that Marcus had presented me with that book, Larry Byford was taking part in a new type of 'crusade' 6,000 miles away, in which the United States was trying to secure democracy, capitalism and what it called 'freedom' in a far-off land called South Vietnam.

While I was blowing out the nine candles on my chocolate cake, Larry was searching one of the coastal villages just east of the Dam Tra O Lake with his unit. On that day, Charlie Company captured and detained three Viet Cong members who'd infiltrated the area by boat. The VC mission was to bolster local forces for an upcoming offensive in the Nui Mieu mountains. More evidence was growing of an enemy build-up with an emerging pattern of increased activity along the beach at the base of the mountains.

Larry's final letter, 13 June 1967

During that same evening, Larry wrote what would be the final letter to his family. It was addressed to his eldest brother Harold and his wife Marie at their home in Port Neches. The date, 13 June, in the top right-hand corner, was clearly visible. As I scanned it, every word felt especially poignant:

> Well it is nice and quiet and the sun is getting hot and the birds are singing. That doesn't sound like Vietnam does it. Sunday evening we made a combat assault into the area where we are know and it was quiet and we got to the spot where we are going to set up our FOB, our place where we are going to camp. Some of the boys were hunting poles around the FOB to build hootch with and four of our boys stepped on a butterfly mine. It didn't kill any of them but it hurt one pretty bad. See those boys weren't looking for booby traps they were just wanting to get their hootch poles

first. I consider myself before a hootch pole. If you know what I mean.

Oh yes you said something about the M-16 rifle. I don't know what they say in the papers about the M16 but I wouldn't take anything for this one I got. That rifle will not jam if you clean it the first thing every morning before you go out on patrol. That little rifle will shoot about 700-800 rounds a minute. It's the best in Vietnam for this type of war.

We went up in the mountains yesterday and we found where a company of NVA had been about two weeks ago. The NVA are North Vietnamese Army. They are trained like us.

I got your package the third of June. I mailed a letter that evening and got your package after I mailed your letter, and have probably all ready told you but just forgot. HA.

We are getting to stay at the FOB today. That's the second time since I have been out here. We have the best platoon. The Third Herd. That's what they call us. HA. Yesterday evening about fifteen of us received our C.I.B. Badge from the Brigade Commander. The C.I.B. Is Combat Infantry Badge. It is the best badge in the army you can receive. You have to be under hostile fire from the enemy to get it. I am not going to tell mother about it because she will think I am to be a hero. All I want is to be a civilian again in the good old States. HA.

Darn this army. In another month or so I should be making Speck 4 as E-4. I have already put in for it. I think so anyway. Our Platoon Sargent just walked up. He is a good fellow. No sweat about work as long as he is out here. HA.

Well I have to go. Write when you get the chance. I'll do the same.

Larry.

His final written words.

The month of June progressed and the heat became ever more intense; daytime temperatures hit well over 100°. At the same time, encounters with the enemy were hotting up and the following days saw a significant escalation in violence. The Company was using scout dogs to scent out the enemy and detect their arms caches and tunnel systems. But the dogs found it as difficult to cope with the stifling conditions as the soldiers. Clinton Endres recalled: 'On one occasion, a dog and his trainer were sent out to the bush to help us. The dog was a German shepherd – a good-looking dog. He was supposed to sniff out the enemy and lead us to him. It was a real hot day. We were in an area that had a lot of small brush, say about two- to three-feet high. The dog was leading us down these trails. The trails reminded me of the cow paths on my grandpa's farm. The cows would make a path down to the pond to get a drink of water.

'Well, the dog was having a real tough time. He could not get enough air between those bushes. He was fixing to have a heat stroke. His trainer decided that we needed to medevac his dog, so we did. The medevac chopper came in and the dog and his trainer climbed aboard. As they were lifting off to go to a secure place for some cool refreshment and a time to recover from a hot day in the bush, my thoughts were, "I wish I was a dog!"'

On 15 June, the Company moved from its NDP (night defensive position) on the beach and crossed the wide expanse of sand dunes, moving along the paddy dykes, towards the village of An Hoa. As they approached, they received a few rounds of fire. There were no casualties, as the village was cordoned off. They returned to the beach for the night camp and the following day returned again to the same area east of the Dam Tra O lake to search the village of An Quang. Again, the men received hostile fire.

Clinton Endres remembered a memorable incident involving Larry which happened during that week: 'One very hot afternoon, "A" Company made contact with the enemy and we were called in to help out. The Hueys picked us up and dropped us off right in the middle of things. We landed in a clearing that was surrounded by hedgerows. There was quite a battle going on, with Huey gun strips and tanks blasting away. There was an opening in the hedgerow where a tank had gone through, so that's where we went.

'There was an enemy bunker just on the other side of the hedgerow and they pretty much had us pinned down. We had to hide behind rice-paddy dykes. It was then that we noticed that Possum Trot was having some trouble. He was raising hell, jumping around, up and down, cussing and fussing. He was lying in an ant bed and the ants were biting the hell out of him. When he couldn't take the ants any more, he would raise up above the dyke. And then Charlie would open up on him with his AK-47 rifles. Back down to the ants he would go. Up and down.

'This went on for a while until someone started to laugh. I knew it wasn't funny but we all started to laugh. We laughed out loud and I guess it seemed strange, especially to Charlie. He probably thought we were crazy. Through all the laughter, one of our men was able to work his way up close enough to the bunker to toss a grenade in. Well, that put an end to Charlie.

'It was almost dark by now. We called in a medevac for our wounded. Only one man from our Company was wounded. We set up our perimeter for the night and then a chopper came in with supplies, and this time there was a hot meal. Fried chicken, mashed potatoes and gravy with all the trimmings.'

On 17 June, an incident occurred which graphically illustrates the chaos and confusion that can so often happen in war. Charlie Company was gathered at its night-time defence position on the Bong Son beach when suddenly it came under fire. The problem was that the gunfire was coming from their own side. An American helicopter with a Night Hunter team on board was testing out night-vision equipment. The crew were not familiar with the beach A/O (area of operations) and opened fire on the Company, thinking it was an NVA force coming out at night. It made two passes, firing M60s at the camp. One man was wounded in the so-called friendly fire. The Company was not amused.

On the morning of Monday, 19 June, the Company began the search operation of a small village on the shore of the Dam Tra O Lake near Chanh Truc. All was quiet. At the same time, B Company ran into a large NVA presence further south in a hamlet located along the 505 Highway at the base of the Nui Mieu mountains.

A Company made an air assault over the mountains to act as a backup force. By mid afternoon, C Company was brought in to assist B Company and tanks from the 1/69th Armor as they pushed into the hamlet. D Company was also present, called in to help block escape routes to the south. In effect, the full Second Battalion was in action.

As the Americans met the NVA presence, ferocious fighting began with air strikes from above and artillery fire launched all around. American units swept through the village trying to secure the battlefield. The NVA was situated on high ground and attacked the lead element of B Company, situated below, as it moved in to the area. The Company became positioned too close to the enemy for further artillery cover to be used. The battle lasted for several hours. Thirty-two NVA soldiers were killed, eight American soldiers died and seventeen were wounded. Some lost limbs. Fortunately there were no losses suffered by Charlie Company. The battle was registered as a 4:1 kill ratio.

For Ken Burington, a 20-year-old-volunteer from Glen Burnie in Maryland, this was his first taste of action. He'd been in the field less than 48 hours: 'I was horribly new. They told me we were going to make a combat assault. As we were coming in as part of a six-helicopter insertion, it was exciting and threatening at the same time. I was frightened but not in a paralysing, unable to function sense. Call it extreme apprehension.

'We'd hit a couple of villages in the morning and were shot at. It was the first time I'd been fired on. Then we went in by helicopter to enter the battle. I thought, "I'm not going to survive a year here. It's too much, too fast." I remember it was a long day, not enough water, and trying to get a man out of a bunker.'

Still there was no let-up. The action shifted west to the other side of Highway One near Phu My, by the mountains that formed the boundary to the coastal plain.

On Wednesday, 21 June, an NVA prisoner captured in recent days led A Company to his unit's location in an area of 'occupied fortifications' near the hamlet of Van Thien, south west of the Phu My valley. There, the Company made contact with part of the 7th Battalion of the 18th regiment of the NVA's 3rd Division, who were sited on high ground by the Nui Mieu mountains. The contact was 'immediate and intense'.

B Company was sent in to assist. The NVA battalion was trying to re-establish a foothold in what was their prime recruiting ground. Those efforts were seriously curtailed by the ensuing battle but, as the Operational Report recorded, the NVA had 'an almost immeasurable will to be victorious'.

C Company was picked up from its location to help out and flew to the Van Thien area. As they approached, they set up a blocking position to the south and linked up on the ground with elements of the 40th ARVN regiment and tanks from the 1/69th Armor. Larry and his First-squad colleagues poured out of their helicopters. They could hear the barrage of noise: a deafening, deadly cacophony of grenades exploding, heavy guns firing and the sharp staccato drone of Kalashnikov and M16 rifles.

By the end of the day, Alpha and Bravo Companies had led the wipeout of the enemy company that had acted as an advanced party for the NVA's 18th Regiment.

The casualty figures for the battle vary according to different sources but it's thought that 101 Vietnamese soldiers were killed. The Americans lost 11 men overall. Eighteen others were seriously wounded and loaded on to medevac choppers to be taken to field hospitals. C Company captured seven rifles, two machine guns and some enemy ammunition. At the end, Markham pulled his Company into full formation. Larry and his colleagues were airlifted out of the Van Thien battle zone, most of them exhausted and shocked, others pumped up with adrenalin, but all of them relieved. They were ordered to remain in the area with the mission to prevent any further NVA build-up in the immediate vicinity.

The next day, Thursday, 22 June, fresh intelligence information revealed an enemy presence on a rock outcrop a few miles east of their camp between the coastal villages of My An and Tan Phung. The Company headed off in a swarm of helicopters to investigate, their propellers pounding the air loudly and rhythmically as they swooped towards the coastline. Before long, a solid black mass came into view. Breaking up the expanse of yellow and blue, it looked imposing, dramatic, its height and crenellated surface somehow unwelcoming. The Hueys approached from the north, allowing the soldiers a spectacular view from the side door: white-tipped waves crashing into the crevices and boulders of the mile-long barren rock, creating spray that arched high into the air.

They had reached their destination. Ahead of them lay 'the Rockpile'.

CHAPTER 11

THE FINAL DAY

The Rockpile viewed from the Nui Mieu mountains, 1967
(Photo courtesy of Ken Burington)

The Rockpile was a long, thin, isolated outcrop of black basalt on the Binh Dinh coast. This massive chunk of rock was a mile long, half a mile wide and 200 feet tall at its highest point. Along its entire length lay huge boulders and rocks, many of them leaning together, creating inlets and caves in the spaces between. Breaking up miles of fluid coastline, the dark stony mass looked threatening, brooding, almost sinister, creating a barrier between sand and sea. Its hard rocky surface was devoid of lush vegetation. Next to it was a wide stretch of golden sand that spread inland, eventually making way for irrigation channels and a network of paddy fields that led to the foot of the Nui Mieu mountains. There were no roads nearby and just a few rough tracks that meandered up to the summit.

The NVA had been infiltrating the coastline regularly in that area for some time, using small boats to drop off food, ammunition and men. It was trying to build up its strength in preparation for a potential surprise offensive in the region. Furthermore, retreating NVA soldiers from the recent battles were thought to have fled to the isolation of the caves. US air surveillance had recorded a number of enemy sightings, particularly at night, across the Rockpile and the nearby beach, and monitoring had also indicated radio noise coming from the outcrop. Several caches of rice and equipment had been seized nearby and one report suggested that several NVA were hidden in the caves. The Americans knew that it was vital for them to stem such a build-up of Vietnamese troops. That's why Charlie Company was deployed to the area.

According to Larry's final letter, the main thing on his mind at that time was his desire to be made an SP4 – a spec four machine gunner or a grenadier. It would mean advancement within his group and a pay rise of up to $50, which would raise his wages to $190 per month. In the meantime, he just needed to keep his head down, do the job in hand and make sure he got back home in one piece. With 66 days now completed of his tour, he had 299 days to go. He was '299 short'. For Larry, the deployment to the Rockpile was just another mission. He had no real knowledge of where he was and no real interest either. He just did what he was told. Ken Burington recalled: 'We had no idea where we were other than in very general terms. We were in a bubble. No maps. No bearings. We knew no more than 50 yards ahead, really. As riflemen, we had no access to detailed maps, either of the region or the specific area where we were.'

Once Charlie Company had landed on that Thursday, Captain Markham split up his platoons so that one group was placed on the top of the Rockpile, one by the side to the north, and one on the beach. The first sweep of the area proved negative. However, confident that enemy soldiers were secreted there, later sweeps eventually pinpointed a group hiding inside a cave halfway up the hill, looking out onto the sea. For more than 20 hours, the grunts surrounded the cave, waiting for Charlie to reveal himself and to come out of hiding. C Company spent the night on the Rockpile, as it became clear that the enemy was determined to stay put. The fact that radio noise was emanating from the rocks indicated that an officer of some sort could be present. As it was more important for intelligence-gathering purposes to capture an officer rather than to kill him outright, the decision was made to fly in a Psychological Operations officer from headquarters to try to tease him out.

The Psy-Ops officer arrived by helicopter the following day, Friday, 23 June. He was 33-year-old Edwin 'Woody' Martin, a major who had served in the US Army for a decade. A distinguished graduate of the US Military Academy at West Point, Martin had been in Vietnam for nine months. Assigned to the Headquarters and Headquarters Company (HHC) of the 1st Cavalry Division, he was a high-flyer. A single man, Major Martin was known among his own colleagues for his intelligence, his warmth and his wide smile.

Don Jensen, Clinton Endres, Richard Bratton, Jay Phillips and Mike Martin were all members of the Charlie Company operation on the Rockpile that Friday. In their own words, each had explained to me, either by email or by phone, how the events of that day unfolded. I'd put all the notes of their recollections in my folder to read again by Larry's graveside. Somehow that felt the appropriate thing to do. I wanted to absorb, slowly and carefully, what each of them had remembered. At the end of each description, I looked across to Larry's grave and to those red roses swaying in the light breeze. I was completely alone.

Like any eyewitness account taken from a range of sources, some of the details each remembered differed slightly. That's partly due to perspective: each witness was in a different location at the time of Larry's death, so was exposed to a slight variation of experience. Also, certain details tended to resonate differently with particular individuals, and memories varied in degrees of sharpness. However, the essence of the accounts remained essentially the same, although each soldier added information that helped me build up the overall picture. Sitting there at Mt Pleasant cemetery, I began to read each one again. I wanted to take in as much detail as I could and from as many sources as possible.

First, I began studying Don Jensen's account: 'I remember the day like it was yesterday. We got on helicopters at the LZ and air assaulted near the beach and then started patrolling south along the beach. We came upon a hill that became known to us as the Rockpile. There was a huge pile of rocks, maybe 200 feet high and a quarter of a mile long. The rocks were as big as houses. We stopped for a break, and I and some others walked among the big boulders. Someone went near a cave under the rocks. You could smell the gooks. They smelled like a combination of pee and rotten fish. So it was decided to surround the area. The call went in. A Psy-Ops officer, a Major, was flown in while the Company set up a perimeter. The Major went to the entrance of the cave. With a bullhorn, he tried to talk them out. They shot him. Larry was near and he went to the Major's aid. He tried to drag him out of the way but he was also shot. The guys got Larry out of the range of the gooks. A medevac chopper was called as Larry was wounded in action and the Major was killed. The chopper lowered a sling for Larry. By now the Major was dead and was near the cave and in range of the gooks' gunners. Larry was being raised up by the cable. He was being hoisted up. He was wounded but alive. The gooks fired up at the chopper, hitting a crewman. The chopper dived away, breaking the cable. They opened fire, as far as we know hitting Larry, and shot the cable in two. Larry fell back to the ground and among the rocks near the Major. They tried to get to Larry but the gooks fired and kept them away. Anyone trying to approach was fired upon. But by this time Larry was dead.

'We then had shootouts and grenade battles with the gooks. They would pop out and shoot and hide. They [the Company] brought in searchlights and shot parachute flares at night and kept the area lit at all times. Eventually a gook was captured nearby and they tied a rope on him and had him tie ropes to the Major and Larry. They were dragged out of the cave so we could get them out of there.

'We were there several days putting explosives in the caves. We were relieved as another company came in. They were putting explosives in holes. A large shaped charge was lowered to the mouth of the cave and set off. The Company left the area. An air strike was dropped on the Rockpile.

'May Larry rest in peace. He will always be a brother.'

I'd spoken to Clinton Endres on the telephone about that day just the week before I'd arrived in Texas. By the side of my transcription, I had written the words 'lucid' and 'vivid'.

'As I remember, C Company had a mission to go and check out the Rockpile. We hiked across the beach. The beach was like a desert. Lots of sand dunes and not at all easy to walk through. The Rockpile was a hill consisting of boulders, rocks, caves and rough terrain. We couldn't set up a perimeter like we were used to doing.

'Our squad, which Possum Trot was a member of, took up a position behind a big boulder for the first night. We were positioned kind of up the hill away from the cave opening. As the next day went on, there wasn't a lot happening. Our squad changed positions. I don't remember why. Our platoon leader came over and asked for a couple of volunteers from our squad to go over and help another squad who were short handed. Possum Trot decided to go ahead and volunteer right away. That's the last time I saw him – when he left. The last time I talked with him was when he went with the platoon leader down the hill and then round the side of the hill.

'Most of the day we were just sitting there kind of holding our positions. One of the guys did go down near the cave and looked around to see what he could find down there. He did find some weapons and things in there.

'Possum Trot was providing cover for the Major, who was trying to talk the enemy into coming out of the cave and giving themselves up. They did not give up. That is when Possum Trot was killed.

'I don't know what time of day he was actually killed or when that all happened, to tell you the truth. Late in the day the platoon leader came back to our position and said that one of our guys had been killed and that it was Possum Trot/Larry Byford.

'I was told about the Major trying to persuade them to come out. I wasn't there. I was about a hundred metres away when he was doing all this. I didn't meet him. I didn't see him.

'I understand they had a programme called Chieu Hoi or something, like an "open-arms" programme. If you give yourself up, then we'll receive you with open arms. I think that's what the Major was trying to do.

'I didn't really know what Larry was doing in his new position. We could hear there was sporadic shooting throughout the day but I didn't see the actual event.

'When the platoon leader came back up, that's when the medevac chopper came out. It couldn't land because of the rough terrain. So they dropped a line to his body. They were going to hoist Possum Trot's body up to the chopper. So the chopper was hovering there. As his body was being raised up to the chopper door, Charlie opened fire. He was about halfway up I guess, between the chopper and the ground. The enemy opened up with gunfire again. That's when the line was released, when they released his body and it fell to the ground. The chopper flew off.

'We, our squad, were watching all this from our position, which was up the hill. I just saw it. I saw when they let him go. I didn't see him hit the ground. But I saw him when he fell. I remember that for sure. We could see him there. The best I then remember was some of the guys carried him down the hill, then on down to the base of the hill where the beach met the water. Down there was a bigger area where the choppers could land.

'We spent three days on the Rockpile before we were relieved and went on another mission. Another company came in. We went on to something else. I don't know what they did after that.'

Richard Bratton, a 20-year-old draftee from Fulton, Missouri, was 11 months in to his tour of duty on this particular day. He'd attached a number of photographs with his initial email response and I examined them closely.

The first picture was taken from a helicopter side door as the slick approached the landing zone. The waves of the South China Sea, clearly seen below, were crashing into part of the Rockpile's exposed headland. Another photo showed 12 Hueys in the air, flying in formation, presumably approaching the drop-off point. There wasn't a cloud in the sky. In one of those choppers, I thought, somewhere would be Possum Trot. I wondered which one. The third was a grainy, almost indecipherable photograph showing a chopper on the ground with five soldiers taking cover, one of them in the lead with his arm raised forward, appearing to be giving instructions to the rest. The fourth appeared to have been taken at the foot of the Rockpile and showed fifty men, all standing to attention in four lines, presumably coming together to take their orders. Or maybe it was snapped at the end of the operation. I wasn't sure. Large boulders and rocky outcrops were clearly visible in the background and there were a few trees dotted around the foot of the slope. The final photograph showed four soldiers sitting down on a dusty pathway apparently somewhere on the slope of the Rockpile. None were identifiable. All were wearing fatigues, big boots and the familiar green steel-pot helmets. One was holding a mortar gun. Another was clutching his M16 close to his chest. All had their backpacks still strapped over their shoulders. They were taking cover next to a track, each man sitting about five yards from the next. All were looking up the slope, seemingly waiting for the next move, the next order.

Richard told me that there were lots of new FNGs in the Company and not many men with much experience: 'We'd lost many of the experienced guys in the March battle; so, many of the Company were either KIA or WIA. If I remember correctly, the only person that had been in the field for over four months at that time was me and two guys in the First Platoon. Everyone else basically was new. So it was bad for the FNGs.'

I began to read the words I'd noted from his oral recollection: 'I was a Forward Observer in all three platoons but I was not in the Third when Larry was killed. I was attached to the Third in April and May. But then the Second got a new platoon leader at the end of May, so I was put in the Second to keep him alive. I was wounded three times in Vietnam and received two Purple Hearts.

'It was hot, hot, hot – 110°. You were carrying five hundred rounds of ammo and two days of rations. I remember weaving up the side with the huge boulders. You couldn't carry enough water to get to the top. The new guys were having trouble with the snipers.

'Don't take this wrong, but it was just a small fight, a skirmish. We were just trying to get the NVA out of the caves during the day. They'd come out at night and snipe on us. I remember Larry. He wore a long lock of hair like a cut-off ponytail on his helmet. The Major walked up to one of the hole openings and the NVA had a machine gun set up. You could not get within 150 feet of it. He was shot and laid out in the open for quite a while. He was stone dead. There's not much you can do when it's open ground and there's a machine gun covering it.

'I was 200 feet from the cave entrance behind a boulder. They called for volunteers to go out and get him. The old guys stayed pretty tight, they stayed put. There was lots of fire from our guys trying to cover Larry but the plan didn't work. There was lots of new people and not too much experience. Larry was hit trying to save the body of the Major in front of the cave entrance. I remember hearing the shots and the body laying on the ground.

'When Larry was shot, a chopper tried to land to get him but that was shot up and I think the co-pilot or a crewman may have been hit. The next day we recovered the bodies. Then the caves were napalmed. It was just another day in Vietnam. You just thanked God you were still alive.'

Jay Phillips joined the Third Platoon alongside Larry, arriving at the end of May. An 18-year-old volunteer from California, he remembered Possum Trot as a popular colleague, well liked by all: 'On our first sweep over the rocky ridge, which took place a day before he was killed, we didn't find any sign of the enemy. That night, radio triangulation using offshore navy ships detected radio transmissions from the same area that we had passed through, so we were ordered to go back over the same area the next day.

'When we did so, we did happen to spot some human faeces

on top of a large boulder and that caused us to investigate the area in the immediate vicinity. That, in turn, led us to discover a cave that was really just a large passageway beneath some very large boulders. The outer cave was easily accessed once we found it. There were several NVA packs laying within.

'From the large cave mouth, there was a very narrow passage down between two boulders that appeared to lead further into the cave. At the time, I was an FNG and was also one of the smaller guys in the Company, weighing in at 133 pounds when I joined the army. I was also gung-ho and so volunteered to try to move deeper into the cave.

'Taking a .45 calibre pistol and a flashlight, I moved sideways for about twenty feet down below two boulders that were at least ten to fifteen feet high, until I was able to drop down into a very small second room that contained several machine guns and mortars.

'At that point, to manoeuvre around a four-foot boulder and a very rocky area, I needed to use at least one hand to be able to get around in the very tight and low space. So I put down the .45 and just used the flashlight.

'When I managed to get around the rock, I shone my light into a large underground room with a ceiling made of solid rock and only about three feet high. And that's when I saw the NVA soldier directly in front of me and perhaps 20 feet away from his AK-47. Since I couldn't really shoot him with the flashlight, I quickly moved back around the rock, retrieved my pistol and moved back up between the boulders to the entrance. Yes, I was terrified and, no, I never did try the tunnel-rat thing again as long as I was in Vietnam.

'Subsequently, after Larry was killed, we put CS tear gas down into the caves and a single NVA soldier came out to surrender. He was one of the largest enemy soldiers I ever saw and there was a rumour that he might have been Chinese, although I did not hear that confirmed. After his capture, he was sent back into the cave to retrieve the weapons I'd seen and he did so.

'I understand that after we left the Rockpile area, a B-52 strike was directed against the area, although that may have just been scuttlebutt, as it would have been a lot of explosive to use against just one possible radio site. Also, I'm not sure it would have had much effect against those huge rocks.'

Jay Phillips had volunteered to enter the cave and survived; Larry had volunteered to rescue the Major and had died. Chance. Fate. Bad luck. God's will. Call it what you will. War is like that. Cruel. Indiscriminate. A lottery.

'Upstate' Mike Martin, in a phone conversation with me a fortnight before, offered the most detailed account: 'We were doing patrols away from the ocean when we received a transmission. Helicopters would be coming in, so we had to secure a landing zone for them. They picked us up. While we were inside, we heard they were receiving radio transmissions off that Rockpile. They airlifted us up to about a mile north. They dropped us and we set up formation. It was very, very hot. Between 110 and 118.

'We started patrolling down to the rocky area along the coast. When we went over it the first time, we found nothing. We got down onto the other side and then got another radio transmission saying they were still receiving radio noise, so we went back up over the rocks again. We found nothing. We got about a mile up the other side and they said the same thing. But again we found nothing. We went back over the rocks again. We did this four times. Then, the fifth time we set up our perimeter for the night. We set our flares out, dug our foxholes and set up our listening posts for the night.

'Our helicopters were just coming in to bring us some gear. All of a sudden they turned and then went away. They had swings on the bottom of the Hueys but they suddenly decided to turn and pulled away. So we started back over the top of the rocks again. When we got to the very top, we could see we had guys down on the coast and guys in the middle of the rocky area. I was on the very top with my fire-team leader.

'As we came over the ledge, we saw a North Vietnamese running out of one of the holes below us. We shot him. Then we received fire from them. They started firing at us, so we brought the guys in. We set up a perimeter all around the whole pile and we started looking for where they were at. It was getting dark, so they called for artillery that would give us illumination all night long. We figured they were going to try and get out of the cave areas, get to the ocean and get away from us. So we had illuminations coming in all night from the 105 howitzers. Then the navy had four or five patrol boats go up and down the coast. They'd got into our radio transmission and asked if they could support us too. So they were shooting flares from the ocean as they patrolled up and down. We were there all night long. You'd see three or four of them when the flares lit up. We would get one or two of them on the beach and we'd whack them.

'Then, the next morning they were bringing in this Major Martin and military intelligence together with four North Vietnamese who he had turned into interpreters for him. They weren't prisoners. They'd surrendered. And he was running this Chieu Hoi programme. Well, that's what we were told. He used them to try to talk the North Vietnamese and VC into giving themselves up. What they were doing was like a re-supply point. They were bringing North Vietnamese down at night by boats. They were then going into caves, picking up ammunition, and then going into different units in the area.

'So, the Major and his men moved in to where the main rock formation was, down in an area that was cleared and where there was a big cave. It was right in the middle of the Rockpile, looking out to sea, maybe 75 feet up – about halfway up. The Rockpile wasn't big but it was all hard rock. There was more than one entrance to the cave. When they walked into that area, the four Vietnamese stayed back. He was walking by himself. With a bullhorn. He was talking Vietnamese. I didn't understand what he was saying. He seemed to be talking fluent Vietnamese. He was trying to talk them out. Get them to work for us. Saying, "We'll pay. We'll give you this. We'll do that." Stuff like that.

He'd actually started talking to them when he was down on the trail, explaining to them that all he wanted to do was to come up and talk to them. To see what he could do to get them to come out and stuff like that. Near the cave entrance, he dropped his gear. He had no weapons. He had nothing. Then they whacked him. It looked like a machine gun because of the way the flames were coming out.

'I was watching the Major laying there but from that position

I couldn't get a shot. If I had been towards the lower side, I would have been able to get a shot with my grenade launcher but from where I was they were underneath the cave, under the rocks in a hole. With a grenade launcher, if I'd shot down there, I'd have done more damage to the Major.

'Larry had been down on the beach to the right of them. There was like a trail that came up through the Rockpile that went towards the cave. When they shot the Major, that was when Larry went to try and get him out of there. I could see him coming up the trail towards the Major to try to drag him out. It was about 15 minutes after the Major had been shot and as soon as he went up they shot him too. He seemed to be killed instantly. When they hit Larry, he never moved after that. Then they had a medevac chopper come in overhead. The guy was coming down a cable to try to get the Major. As he was coming down, the North Vietnamese came out and shot at him. So they pulled him back into the chopper. They were then shooting at the helicopter and they hit it two or three times. So the helicopter immediately got out of the area.

'We'd then receive fire ourselves once in a while if they could get a good shot at somebody. But other than that all we did was to keep the place secure all the way round for a whole day and night. We used flares to keep them in the holes. We illuminated the area all night long.

'They then brought in the 1st of the 7th to relieve us and get us off the hill. So when they brought in the new unit, they relieved us in our post. We went down, were airlifted out and brought back to a field about a mile away to set up our perimeter. We didn't have anything. We didn't have any more ammunition, so they had to resupply us. And they brought us a hot meal.

'Then, we were later told, they brought the engineers in the next day who piped napalm into the holes and then they ignited it and set it off. The napalm might not burn you, because it might not even get to you. But it sucks all the oxygen out of the air and you die from not having oxygen. You suffocate to death.

'We started doing our normal patrols again like we did every day. For me personally, that was one of the battles that we were involved in over there. It was just something that never went away. And I was involved in a lot of fire-fights. We'd made a couple of recent combat assaults prior to this whole incident happening in different areas.

'I remember I had torn the crutch out of my jungle fatigues. We didn't wear our underwear because of the heat. So my balls and my penis were basically out in the open. They had ordered me a new pair of fatigue pants to be sent out on those choppers that turned around and flew away. That's also why it has lasted in my mind so clearly for all these years. I never got my pants.'

Larry's colleagues carried his body on a makeshift stretcher from the scene of his death to the beach area. There he was put into a rubber body bag and laid on the beach until a medevac helicopter arrived. He was loaded into the hold and flown to the grave registration area, where the details on his metal dog-tag were written down. As usual, the first letter of the surname and the last four letters of his serial number were noted as his medevac registration and the body bag was labelled accordingly: B0752. Larry had become another casualty figure. Another American soldier killed in action in Vietnam. Another grunt taken away in the field of duty. In the cold, brutal slang of the battlefield, he was 'greased'; 'a stiff'; 'hamburgered'; 'a sardine can'. One of 9,353 Americans to lose their lives in Vietnam in 1967.

But B0752 wasn't simply a number. This was Larry Byford. The country boy from Short. The loving son of Fate and Cecil. The adored sibling of three brothers and three sisters. Uncle Larry, the man who was always laughing. The 'caring, promising young man with the smiling face and the jovial personality'. Taken away at 22. Possum Trot, the grunt with the lock of hair attached to his helmet. The brother in arms who'd courageously tried to rescue the Major.

There's a maxim among grunts: 'Never volunteer. Just do what you have to do.' Well, Larry volunteered. He did what he thought was right. The consequence being that, within hours, he was on his way back to the United States. But he was not to travel in a 'Freedom Bird', taking those who had served for a year in Vietnam back home. There was to be no cheering as the plane took off, no excitement at the prospect of returning to see loved ones again. No, Larry's body travelled back in a commercial airliner. In a metal casket. Inside the hold. In darkness. Heading to Texas. Dead.

Reading those accounts again, I was struck by the futility, the wretchedness, the grief and the brutality of it all. So young. Twenty-two years of age. It had been such a pivotal age in my own life: one of great joy, excitement and advancement. The year I'd married the girl I was completely head over heels in love with. I'd met Hilary Bleiker at Leeds University two years before. On our wedding day, she was still 21 and I'd just turned 22: exactly the same age as Larry.

Major Edwin Woods Martin buried at USMA, West Point
(Photo of gravestone courtesy of Joe DeLorenzo)

Who was Major Martin that Larry had gone to rescue? I'd discovered that Edwin Woods Martin was a West Point graduate officer from the class of 1956 and was buried at the West Point cemetery in Section VI, site 301. His gravestone confirmed he was from Arizona. He'd graduated from high school in Carson City, Nevada. He'd served in Germany after West Point. He'd graduated from the University of Pennsylvania with a Masters

Dawn at the Vietnam Veterans Memorial, Washington DC.

Panel 22E, The Wall

Lawry Byford holds the rubbing of Larry's name.

Lawry Byford stands in front of the Normanton War Memorial.

Lawry Byford, aged 19, drafted to war, 1944.

Larry Byford, aged 21, drafted to war, 1966.

Larry Byford's childhood home, Short, east Texas.

Larry's gravestone, Mt Pleasant cemetery, Shelby County, east Texas.

1st Cavalry Division: 'The First Team'.

Company C 2nd/5th 1st Cavalry Division in action, Binh Dinh, South Vietnam 1967. (Photo courtesy of Don Demchak)

Company C prepares for battle, Bong Son, Binh Dinh, 1967 (Photo courtesy of Don Jensen)

Company C examine the dead at Lo Dieu beach, May 1967. (Photo courtesy of Dewey Smith)

Brother David with the final letter.

Brother Hughie with the funeral flag.

Sister Nancy with the favourite photograph.

Sister Pat with the report of Larry's death.

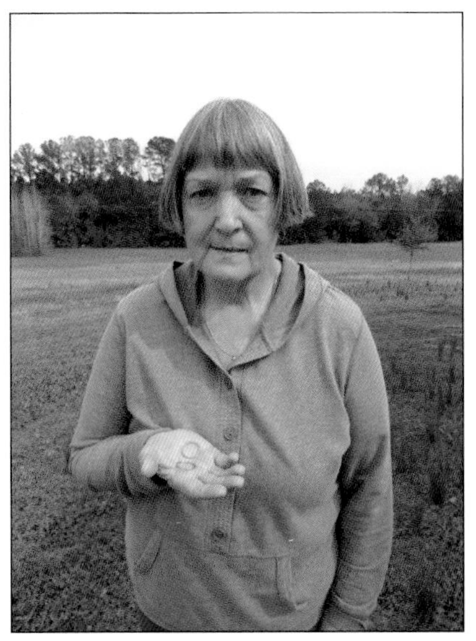

Sister Debbie with the earrings – the final gift.

Larry's Bronze Star and Purple Heart, both awarded posthumously.

Larry's dog-tag.

Larry's Military Merit Medal and Gallantry Cross with Palm awarded posthumously by the government of the Republic of Vietnam.

Dam Tra-O Lake and the Cay Giep mountains, Binh Dinh, Vietnam, 2012.

A rice worker tends her crop in the former battlefield at Van Thien, Vietnam, 2012.

The Rockpile, Binh Dinh, Vietnam, 2012.

Reunion of men from Company C who served alongside Larry in Vietnam in May–June 1967.

Don Jensen's photographs of Larry's body on a stretcher and in the helicopter hold, the Rockpile, Saturday, 24 June 1967. (Photos courtesy of Don Jensen)

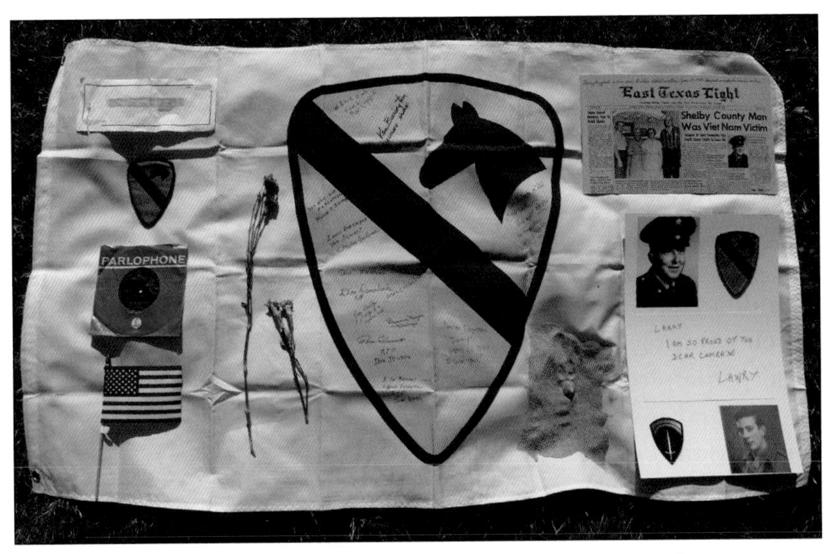

Mementos and tributes for Larry S Byford at The Wall.

Veterans Day at The Wall, 2012.

degree in English. He'd died aged 33. A photograph on one website showed him to have matinee-idol looks, with dark, deep-set eyes, an oval face and a high forehead. But I wanted to know more about his personality. I tracked down his obituary at the US Military Academy Library, published in the fall of 1967. It opened with the following words:

> Soldiers are frequently called upon to die in defense of their country, but few of them exemplify in their sacrifice the principles on which their lives were founded.
>
> Major Edwin W. Martin was such a man. He died, as he lived, demonstrating his unshakeable faith in the inherent goodness of Man.
>
> Woody Martin was the 1st Cavalry Division's psychological warfare officer working in its pacification program across the region. His mission was to induce enemy soldiers to surrender. That day, Woody, with his interpreter, was moving from cave to cave broadcasting surrender appeals when he came upon a small group hiding in a natural cave. In an attempt to avoid what he felt would be useless bloodshed, Woody offered generous terms of surrender. When they failed to respond, he instructed his interpreter to announce that as a gesture of goodwill he would enter the cave without his weapon and equipment. He entered the cave and was shot at point-blank range. Woody believed in his mission and had met considerable success in his numerous face-to-face confrontations with the enemy in which he induced many to lay down their arms peaceably. Just prior to his fatal encounter, Woody had volunteered for an extension to his Vietnam tour.

Lieutenant Colonel Jack Capps was his immediate superior at West Point:

> I cannot recall an officer so enthusiastically sought after by his students nor one who rewarded them so fully with the genuine idealism that Woody could convey so well.

A letter from his Commanding Officer in the 1st Cavalry Division, Captain Joseph Hultquist, written shortly after Major Martin's death, stated:

> His enthusiasm and dedication to duty served to distinguish him as an outstanding leader, held in the highest regard by his men. His soldierly bearing and conduct made him uniquely suited for his pioneering work in the new field of civil affairs.

Major William Haas wrote:

> He was almost too good for the world he lived in. I have seen him ridiculed for his actions, which were those of a man who believed and trusted his fellow men. I have seen the deep hurt when people failed his trust. Then, at other times, I have seen his sincere delight and satisfaction when people responded positively to the faith and trust he placed in them. Woody not only practiced the Christian virtues but believed in them wholeheartedly.'

A fellow student from his days at the University of Pennsylvania was Robert Berry:

> He was living proof that in this world it is possible to be all good. I have never known anyone who stood so firmly for all that was good. He was one of the most devout Christians I have ever met. He never wavered in his faith and it seemed to give him a great inner peace. He never doubted the meaning of life. Nor did he ever question the war in which he was involved.

Earlier that February, Robert had received a letter from Woody Martin, who revealed within it his strong belief in the war and his determination to succeed:

> We must fight this war. No one who has been here could advise otherwise. We must, as in the Marianne Moore poem:

'Fight the blind man who thinks he sees. We must know the cost and be sobered by the responsibilities it imposes.'

The tributes were bountiful, fit for an exemplary officer. But, sadly, within them there was no record whatsoever of Larry's exploits in trying to rescue his body. Of course not, why would there be? Indeed, Larry's death merited not a single mention anywhere in the 1st Cavalry Division's quarterly operations report for that period. Not even a line. The only specific reference to 23 June was about a battalion task force being sent to Dak To later that day. The only clue to Larry's involvement was hidden away anonymously in the quarterly statistics. Operation Pershing's latest numbers:

Enemy KIA: 764 VC and 522 NVA. 1st Cav Div KIA: 140.

It was the same with the Second Battalion's log. No mention whatsoever. Just another death. Nothing noteworthy.

Clinton Endres remembered the aftermath: 'We were all real quiet. Just quiet. I knew we'd lost somebody but I just hoped it wasn't Possum Trot. But it was. My good friend, gone.'

Lieutenant Jim Stanford took over as the leader of the Third Platoon the week after Larry was killed at the Rockpile: 'Unfortunately, I did not know Larry but I can tell you it was a traumatic time for every man in the Platoon. They were still personally feeling the effects of those several heavy days they were engaged with the enemy. And they were very upset at the loss of Possum Trot. He was a true hero in the finest sense of the word.'

CHAPTER 12

THE SADDEST DAY OF ALL

I felt woolly-headed, as if I were coming out of a dream. I must have been sitting there, sifting through my folder, thinking and looking at the grave for at least two hours. I'd read through notes, checked out photographs and let my mind wander down Possum Trot's timeline: his arrival at Camp Radcliff; the events in Bong Son; the savagery at Van Thien and the tragedy at the Rockpile. I felt stunned by the memories of my discoveries and drained by the emotions they had evoked. Now I wanted to move further along: to learn more about the time when his body returned home and to find out how the local community had gathered at this very spot.

Over the next two days, I was constantly on the move, visiting all five siblings and meeting the four pallbearers still alive. It would be a chance to understand what sister Nancy described as 'the saddest day of all'.

*

The soundtrack to American life at that time in mid June 1967 was 'Groovin' by the Young Rascals, with its laidback opening line, 'Groovin' on a Sunday afternoon'. The sentiments in the song, which was number one in the singles charts that week, were echoed by the scenes around Center that day. 25 June was a lovely, sunny, peaceful Sunday afternoon. The temperature was in the upper 90s with a light breeze. Nature was at her ripening, fecund stage in the fields, woods and rivers. Watermelons sounded hollow when tapped and the curly green tendrils were turning yellow. That meant melon harvesting was underway throughout the east Texan countryside. Bailey and Peacock lakes were full of children swimming, cooling down and having fun. The Shelby County Sportsman's Club Fishing Rodeo was nearing its end, its competitors striving to catch the heaviest bass and perch.

Fate Byford was sitting on the porch of the old white house in Short that Sunday afternoon, enjoying a rest day from his pipe-fitting job down south. It was a time to relax and enjoy the tranquillity of his surroundings. As he listened to the radio bulletin at one o'clock, Fate heard the main news report, which announced that President Johnson and the Soviet Prime Minister, Mr Kosygin, were set to resume their summit talks in New Jersey. Half an hour later, he heard another news story but from a different source that would be so shocking, so devastating that it would tear him apart and deeply affect every member of the Byford family for the rest of their lives.

Two officials from the Barksdale Air Force base just outside Shreveport had been dispatched to the home of Fate and Cecil that morning and were driving up the rutted clay track, approaching their home. They were bringing a telegram informing the Byfords of Larry's death.

Debbie remembers the very moment: 'We were at the old white house. I can recall some men arriving in uniform. I can remember them saying, "Mr Byford, I am so very, very sorry. Your son has been killed."'

As one of the officials handed Fate the telegram, he informed him that Larry had been investigating a cave on Friday when he was hit by small-arms fire.

Debbie recalled: 'When I heard it, it was like I heard it but like I didn't. It just wasn't registering with me or soaking in. "They're not talking about my brother," I thought. Then I remembered Daddy getting upset. Then the Murphys came round to be with Momma and Daddy. They were real close friends and neighbours. Mr Murphy then went to make the phone calls.'

Today, David Byford is 76, living in a comfortable home in Baytown, on the eastern edge of Houston. Married to Mary June for more than 50 years, he has been an academic for much of his life, specialising in business management. Although now retired, he still has an involvement in business estate. As I approached his home, I knew he was sceptical and concerned about my project. Who was this Englishman who'd contacted his family out of the blue? Why was he so interested in his brother Larry? Where was all this leading?

He was smartly dressed in a sharply pressed blue checked shirt and crisp blue denims. His silver-coloured, well-groomed hair gave him an air of authority and distinction. Surrounded by his wife and two sons, David Wayne and Mark, he listened to me explain what had happened at The Wall and how I'd taken the rubbing of Larry's name to my father. He took the very rubbing from me, held it in his hands and, at that point, broke down and wept profusely. The sensible, responsible, self-contained brother could not contain his emotion.

'Go on, Mark, keep going. It's a good thing. I want David to let it all come out after so many years,' proclaimed Mary June. I felt uncomfortable knowing that two grown-up sons were witnessing their adored father cry in front of a stranger he'd met less than a half an hour before.

David fetched an envelope, telling me that he wanted to share something with me. He recalled that on the very day Larry died, Friday, 23 June, he was at home reading his brother's latest letter from Vietnam, which had been sent on by his eldest sibling, Harold. The letter had been written on 13 June and it opened with those words:

> Well it's nice and quiet and the sun is getting hot and the birds are singing. That doesn't sound like Vietnam does it.

After reading it, David, by then a university lecturer, went straight to his study in his house in Highlands, Texas, and constructed a reply. He passed me that letter, which he'd typed out, dated 23 June 1967. I read it in silence.

> Dear Larry,
> Well how are you fairing over there in Viet Nam? I have been reading your letters and I hope you don't mind it too much. I just have one

thing to say about that place – you be real careful about everything that you do. Don't take chance one. I sure will be glad if they ever decide to do something about that place.

We were home two weekends ago and mother is doing as well as can be expected. She has a hospital bed and I took her a real good one and a half ton air conditioner unit and she really does like it. Granddaddy is doing fair but is gradually going down. I really wish there was something I could do for him, but I don't know what it would be. If you have a chance to write to him you should and tell him that you are not in any danger, even though you are, for I'm sure he worries a lot.

The boys are doing fine. Mary June is too. They have been at the farm in Livingston putting up things for the deep freeze. They put up corn, tomatoes, peas, butter beans, and home made soup. We would be fixed up for the winter if Fate would come through with a baby beef. Ha! That he will never do though. He thinks more of those baby calves than he does me. Ha!

Harold and Marie were over this past weekend and boy were we surprised. I sure was glad that they came over. They gave us your last letter and your address. I couldn't find anyone with it.

Larry write and tell us what you would like to have as we are going to send you a package of things – whatever you desire most. I am already looking for pre-sweetened coolaid. Marie said that that was one of the things they sent you. They have leased our land (daddy and mother's) and all the land around it. I called Houston this afternoon about it and they said they were probably going to drill on it in the near future. I sure hope that they do and also I have a feeling that they will find oil or gas there. I hope that they do as we need some supplement income very badly. I believe that they will find a gusher there somewhere. I will keep you informed about it and if they find oil while you are over there, I will call you. Ha! You will probably be able to hear it from Short!

I am running out of news and would like to type more, but I don't know anything else exciting to tell you. Write to us – send us a list of what you need – and we will send it. Tell me all the details of the place where you are and what you are doing.

Love Dave

The letter was posted on the morning of Saturday, 24 June. It was returned to David some weeks later, bearing the chilling words 'Returned to writer' with a stamp on the envelope: 'Verified deceased. Returned to sender.'

At that point, David remembered receiving the call from Sangie Murphy informing him that Larry had been killed: 'I completely collapsed and cried.'

Immediately, he drove up from his home in the Houston area in order to be with his parents and to help organise the funeral. Accompanying him was his wife Mary June: 'We drove up to Short in silence. We left our two baby boys at my mother's house in Livingston. Then we went right up to the house in Short. It was terrible. We stayed at the house until the body came back. We just cooked and helped feed everybody. We smiled a few times. We cried a lot of times. It was so, so sad.'

David remembered arriving at the house: 'We just looked at each other. Then I said to Daddy, "I told him I could get him out but he wouldn't do it." I can't figure him being old. In one sense that's the beauty of him dying young,' David commented. 'He was the dedicated type. He'd work hard for anybody so long as he was treated fairly. He'd work his tail off for you. He was dependable. So self-sufficient. He'd have been a great father and grandfather. I'm so, so sorry that he missed that. I've got three grandkids and they are my life now. He was someone who wanted to serve his country. He was pro-country. You'd have never caught him burning the flag. He did his duty and he did it well. I owe him for that.'

When Larry's sister Nancy and her husband Herbert took the call, Nancy remembered it being very sad, but 'in a way I wasn't surprised'.

Brother Hughie recalled that his call came from Uncle Gene Samford, Cecil's brother-in-law: 'I didn't think it was true but I knew I had to accept it. It completely wiped me out.'

His eldest daughter Cindy remembered the moment: 'We were helping Momma in the house. Our phone was mounted on the wall in the long hallway. I remember Daddy taking the phone call. He shouted "Aagh!" and he leaned back against the wall and he was sliding down and he fell over. He hit the vacuum cleaner and there was blood everywhere. He cried and cried and cried. Daddy never cried, so I thought the world was ending. I was so traumatised myself seeing Daddy's reaction.'

Hughie's younger daughter Kim also recalled that precise moment as though it were yesterday: 'I remember we had a big glass sliding door and a black leather sofa, and I just happened to be standing in between the hallway and the sofa when the call happened. Daddy just dropped to the floor. The blood was coming out of his head. I was just freaking out. I thought he'd died. Momma ran outside. She was throwing up. I remember she told my brother Charlie to call an ambulance, call the doctor, call somebody.'

'I can remember Hughie was semi-conscious on the floor and shouting, "Larry's been killed."' Tommye whispered. 'I got nauseated and ran to the sliding doors and started to heave. I was just so sick in my stomach. It was the shock of it all.'

Cindy remembered what happened next: 'Momma was trying to grasp it. She then started organising, going into her "running mode". She got a checklist together. Who to call. What needed to be said. She just handles things like that so well. Daddy kept on crying a lot. He was then real quiet. Silent. He was in deep mourning. No little girl likes to see her daddy cry, do they? He had to have counselling. He went to see our local preacher.'

'We went straight to Short. Everyone was in shock,' Tommye responded. 'Cecil was in bed. She was so deeply shocked. Her baby boy. I think she lost the will to live with the news. I probably would too if the same thing had happened to me. And their daddy was so shattered too.'

Debbie remembered being with her father at the time: 'Daddy remained straight. But then it was the only time I ever saw my daddy cry. We were sitting on the back porch talking about Larry. It wasn't right after we heard the news but a bit later. That's the only time I ever saw the man cry. I then remember them all talking about the body being transported and being on its way.'

'My parents were just devastated,' Nancy reflected. 'For my father, this was his youngest son and he was gone.'

Middle sister Pat was married with two young children and lived nearby in Center at the time: 'It was such a great loss. One thing I can remember when we got the news, some of us kids didn't want Daddy to tell our mother what had happened because she was in such bad shape. I was one of them who at the time didn't want her to be told because she couldn't do nothing, laying there as an invalid. She was going through enough. That's the one thing that bears on my mind, that she was told. I didn't want it in order to protect her. I wanted her to know, of course; I knew she had to know but at the same time I didn't want her to know. It broke my heart. Her laying there so sickly. She couldn't get well. There was nothing you could do for her.'

Straight in front of bedridden Cecil at that time sat her favourite photograph of Larry, taken when he was a teenager. It was placed on top of an old wooden chest. Now her youngest boy was gone for ever.

Cousin Judy, who looked upon Larry as a brother she never had, came down to the white house: 'I just couldn't believe it for a very long time. The only way I could bear it was to not believe it was really Larry who had been killed. I told myself it was a mistake. I remember my dad telling me to go home and cry it all out. I knew it was true but I didn't want to believe it. It hurt so badly. I knew I was in denial but I couldn't accept it. It was so devastating. When you walked down to the house, it was very, very quiet. The brothers and sisters all together. Very quiet.'

On Monday, the day after Fate and Cecil had received the news, Tommy Murphy (Sangie's son and one of Larry's very best friends) was out on his postal round: 'I was a city mail carrier at that time. I was delivering to the Mangum Funeral Home and a friend of mine worked there. As I walked up the steps to go in the office and deliver the mail, Tommy Hayley stopped me and said, "Hey, have you heard about Larry Byford? He's been killed in Vietnam." I shook my head, and I tell you, it knocked me off my feet. I couldn't complete my deliveries. I had to go home.'

y County) Texas, Wednesday, June 28, 1967 26

Shelby County Man Was Viet Nam Victim

Resident Of Short Community Was Fourth County Fatality To Loose Life

The Viet Nam conflict has taken the life of the fourth Shelby County soldier.

Mr. and Mrs. Fate Byford, of Strong Community near Center, received word Sunday of the death of their son, Pfc. Larry Byford, 22 years of age.

Larry started his service duty in October of last year and had been in Viet Nam since April 9.

The telegram stated that he was investigating a cave when hit by hostile small arm fire.

His body will be returned to Center for burial.

Survivors include his parents, Mr. and Mrs. Fate Byford, three brothers, Harold of Port Nectes, David of Baytown and Huey of Mansfield, La.; three sisters, Debra Lynn Byford of Strong; Mrs. Benny Bradshaw of Center and Mrs. Herbert McMellon of New Orleans, La.

Pfc. Larry Byford

East Texas Light newspaper front page, 28 June 1967

Two days later, the local weekly newspaper, the *East Texas Light*, was published. Below the masthead was the usual strap line: '*Covering Shelby County Like The Pine Straws Cover The Ground*'. Larry's death was the main story on the front page. The headline read: '*Shelby County Man Was Viet Nam Victim.*' Next to the photograph of Larry in uniform and peaked cap was the caption: '*Resident of Short Community Was Fourth County Fatality To Loose* [*sic*] *Life.*'

Other papers in the east Texas area followed up the story: '*Pfc. Larry Byford Killed In Viet Nam Fighting*'; '*Etex Soldier Loses Life In Vietnam*'; '*Byford Killed In Vietnam War*'; '*Services Pending For Center Army Man*'.

By now, the whole community was aware of the Byfords' loss and messages of condolence began flooding into their home.

On Thursday, six days after he was killed, Larry's body arrived back in Center, escorted by Sgt Billy E. Dixon from the HQ department of the 2nd Training Brigade at Fort Polk. Nancy's husband, Herbert, together with Cecil's brother in law, Gene Samford, went to identify the body. Herbert recalled: 'He had an escort with him, an army sergeant. He asked me to identify the body so the family would be satisfied, knowing they didn't have some other body in there. He was in a bag all zipped up. I identified him by his hair, his hands and his face. It was very hard for me but you took things as they were.'

That night, a vigil was mounted. A card shows that from midnight until 2 a.m. Fred Johnson and C.B. Gilchrist kept watch over the casket; they were replaced from 2 a.m. to 4 a.m. by Tommy Murphy and William Holt; then, as dawn broke, Jack Murphy and William Holt stayed with the body until 6 a.m.

Friday, 30 June was the day of the funeral. The Rev. Lewis Johnson, assisted by Dr Carrol Chadwick, officiated at the service that afternoon in the chapel at the Mangum Funeral Home in Center. Two hundred and three people signed the remembrance book of condolences. From there, the casket slowly made its six-mile journey to Mt Pleasant, winding its way through the woods and pastureland of his childhood. The casket, draped in the Stars and Stripes, was carried to the graveside by six pallbearers. There, a military service was conducted, accompanied by a unit from the Barksdale Airforce base.

As they made their way over the bumpy ground from the cemetery entrance to the graveside, the pallbearers – Melva Lee Tomlin, Delbert Graves, Bill Rushing, Tommy Murphy, Jimmy Bradshaw and Herbert Langford – walked in step, gingerly carrying the casket to its final place of rest. For the family and for those friends, the memories of the military funeral will remain for ever.

'It was hell. The 21-gun salute, that was bad,' David remembered. 'And she could hear it two miles away.'

'It was so loud. So piercing,' Mary June added. 'Everybody was just falling apart at that moment.'

Hughie held tightly to his chest the neatly folded American flag that had been draped over his brother's casket as he recalled: 'When they fired the rifles, that's what did it for me. When he blowed those Taps, I almost went in shock. It was so hard, buddy. When the Taps sounded, it pulled everything out of you. Larry was inside me that day. I mean, I knew he was in the box, because that's what they told me. I knew he was in there. But it felt he was still with me.'

'It was the saddest day of all,' Nancy sighed. 'All the family, all our friends, all the people in the local community were there. I remember the 21-gun salute. In a small community, every person who died in the war would receive the same thing. But this was us. The military man then took the flag and folded it as they do in that special way. I can see it now.'

'You feel like the war is useless and all that,' her husband Herbert – the last person to see the body – reflected. 'But what are you going to do? You wished it hadn't happened. I wasn't angry at no particular person or anything. It was just so sad.'

'She didn't even go to the funeral to say goodbye,' Pat sighed, tears filling her eyes. 'It was desperate.'

'I remember the dress I wore. It was a simple little dress – red, white and blue. I just remember all the sadness,' recalled Debbie, the beloved sister, the one closest to Larry. 'I remember the person playing the Taps. When you heard that, it was just an awesome feeling. I don't remember feeling anger at the time. It was just the enormous sense of loss. The sadness of it all.'

Cousin Judy had been in regular correspondence with Larry during his time in Vietnam: 'We were all out there in that little cemetery. Everything was greened up. It was approaching high summer. It was such a quiet, peaceful day. The cows were out in the pasture; it was just a very pastoral scene. When they did the 21-gun salute, I thought that's just so out of place in this peaceful scene with the land, the grazing, the cows. That's when I first realised how bad war is. That we could have a 21-gun salute in this peaceful little cemetery. And I was in tears, thinking Larry was not even in the prime of his life and yet it was over.'

The military men folded the flag precisely 12 times, leaving the stars on the top: a reminder of the national motto: In God We Trust. Melva Lee Tomlin, the best friend who had driven him to Dallas airport, the last person to wave goodbye, and a pallbearer on that day, remembered the casket descending into the grave: 'It was so hard to take. My best friend. Unbelievable. You just couldn't believe that he wouldn't make it back.'

Alongside him was Delbert Graves, the boy who'd hunted in the woods with Larry and travelled on the school bus with him every morning: 'I cried like a baby. Like all of us did who knew him well. My brother-in-law, Shorty Andrews, buried on one side, killed in Vietnam. Now Larry being buried on the other side of the same cemetery. It was so bad, so crap.'

Bill Rushing, another pall bearer and a domino-playing friend at the local store, recalled the moment looking down the newly dug hole: 'We were all broken-hearted. When you lose such a good friend, it's like losing a part of your own life. You feel touched deep down inside. A feeling of real loneliness.'

Tommy Murphy was the friend who had known him the longest: 'When they did the 21-gun salute, all the birds flew out of the trees. Then they passed the flag to Nancy. Well, it just tears your heart into pieces. I was so desperately mournful. Thinking about the past. I said to myself, "Goodbye, my friend. Goodbye."'

The saddest element of the whole day was that Larry's parents were not even there. Bedridden, disabled, unable to move, Cecil could not make it to the chapel or to the graveside. She was too ill to witness the final farewell. Faced with an impossible choice, her husband stayed at home to comfort her. Fate later told his children how he clasped her hand as they heard the distant sound of the gun salute, fired from two miles away, filling the room.

Five days later, a 'card of thanks' was published in the *East Light* newspaper:

> We are deeply grateful to our relatives and friends for all the deeds of kindness, the words of sympathy, beautiful flowers and prayers at the death of Larry. We especially appreciate the many thoughtful and loving acts of kindness done for him during his entire lifetime. Mr and Mrs Fate Byford and family.

Hughie and Tommye stayed at the family home for a week before Debbie went to live temporarily with her grandfather Lent and his second wife who resided just down the road. When Tommye returned home to Mansfield, she learned that she'd been sacked by her employer, the Western Electric Company, based in Shreveport, for taking the week off. Although she pleaded that she had been away to help organise her brother-in-law's funeral, it was to no avail. She was ordered to leave.

Eight days after the funeral, an envelope arrived addressed to Larry's parents and marked 'Department of the Army, Official Business'. It was sent direct from the battlefield of Vietnam by Larry's Company Commander, Captain Don Markham:

> Dear Mr and Mrs Byford,
> I extend my most profound sympathy to you on the recent loss of your son, Private First Class Larry S Byford who died in the service of his country, on June 23rd 1967. Larry was a rifleman, accompanying his unit on a search and destroy operation along the coast East North East of the town of Phu My in Binh Dinh Province, Republic of Vietnam, where he was mortally wounded by enemy small-arms fire while attempting to retrieve a critically wounded soldier from a cave. It may afford you some comfort to know that death came quickly and he was not subjected to any unnecessary suffering.
>
> Your son's death came as a shock to all who knew him, and his loss will be felt keenly in this organization. I sincerely hope the knowledge that Larry was an exemplary soldier and died whilst serving his country will comfort you in this hour of great sorrow.
>
> Larry's enthusiasm and devotion to duty, no matter how difficult the mission was, identified him as an outstanding soldier. He displayed the finest example of military bearing, discipline and conduct. I am proud to have served with him.
>
> Your son's personal effects have been collected and have been forwarded. I hope you receive them with no undue delay.
>
> We would like you to know the entire company paid homage to Larry in a memorial service conducted by Chaplain Perkins, the battalion Chaplain.
>
> Once again, personally and for the officers and enlisted men of this unit, our sincere sympathy is extended to you in your bereavement.
>
> Respectfully,
> Don Markham
> CPT Infantry, Commanding

'Death came quickly'; 'An exemplary soldier'; 'Devotion to duty'; 'The finest example . . .' However hard it was to digest, those sensitive phrases used in Markham's letter must have provided Larry's parents with some degree of pride and comfort.

A week later, the family heard more dreadful news. Jerry Hughes, a good friend of Larry who lived on the other side of the creek, was also killed in Vietnam. Twenty years of age, he died from small-arms fire in Pleiku.

In August, a letter arrived for Fate and Cecil containing a cheque to compensate them for the loss of their son. Like nearly all grunts serving in Vietnam, Larry had paid $2 a month in subs, regularly deducted from his pay, as part of the government-sponsored Service Group Life Insurance scheme. The scheme had been established two years earlier because so many American soldiers were being killed. The maximum pay out was $10,000.

The family are unsure how much was received or whether Cecil even knew of the payment, so ill had she become by this time. Ten thousand dollars. The maximum monetary value of a life lost while serving one's country. An actuarial calculation made for the value of five lost decades.

On 13 January 1968, less than seven months later, Cecil Byford died, broken-hearted. She was 56.

CHAPTER 13

FAREWELL TO THE LONE STAR STATE

I was back in Debbie's kitchen. I'd come to see Larry's medals. I was holding them in the palm of my hand. I traced their indentations and edges with my fingertips. Felt their weight. Larry had never seen them; had never had the chance to wear them with pride.

One was a five-pointed design with a raised star in the centre. An inch and a half wide, it was dark, plain and tarnished. The other was heart-shaped with a gold border surrounding a pale-blue background on which was mounted a cameo of George Washington. Above the heart, a shield of the coat of arms of Washington was laid between two sprays of laurel leaves. It was an intricate and striking design.

At the beginning of August 1967, the Bronze Star and the Purple Heart were sent to Larry's parents as posthumous awards. The Bronze Star medal, the fourth-highest combat award, was awarded for outstanding bravery and valour. The accompanying citation read:

> For heroism in connection with military operations against a hostile force. PFC Byford distinguished himself by heroism in action. When his company came under enemy fire and trapped a group of enemy soldiers in a cave, an officer was critically wounded attempting to talk the enemy soldiers into surrendering. PFC Byford, a member of the rescue element, attempted to retrieve the wounded officer. With complete disregard for his own safety, he exposed himself to the enemy trapped in the cave as he

> approached the wounded soldier. When PFC Byford reached the mouth of the cave, he was mortally wounded by the accurate enemy fire. PFC Byford's personal bravery and concern for his fellow soldiers were in keeping with the highest traditions of the military service, and reflect great credit upon himself, his unit and the United States Army.

'With complete disregard for his own safety' was, for me, a highly significant phrase to use in the context of his 'heroism'. His Purple Heart was awarded in recognition of the wounds he'd suffered on that same day. He was one of 351,794 who received that particular medal during service in Vietnam. Originally, the medals were on display at his grave. Then both of them had been wrapped in cotton wool, put in a small cardboard box and hidden away for safekeeping. Until that morning.

As the new year began in January 1968, Larry's parents received two more medals, which were also in Debbie's possession. The Military Merit Medal and the Gallantry Cross with Palm were both awarded posthumously by the government of the Republic of South Vietnam. Accompanying the medals their citation read:

> A courageous combatant, well known for his sacrifice, who always exhibited a spirit of goodwill and cooperation. He assisted the Republic of Vietnam Armed Forces in blocking the Red Wave of aggression from engulfing South Vietnam and South East Asia.
>
> With his enthusiasm and exemplary devoted manner, he willingly executed all of his entrusted missions and set a brilliant example for his comrades in arms. He died in the performance of his mission. His loss is greatly mourned by both his American and Vietnamese comrades in arms.

A covering letter concluded:

> I sincerely regret the sorrow that has come to your home and hope these tokens of appreciation will help console you for this great sacrifice you have given in the defence of freedom.

'Died in the performance of his mission.' But was it really *his* mission? He was carrying out orders from on high. From Tolson to General Westmoreland right up to LBJ in the Oval Office. While the official position was for the defence of freedom, blocking the so-called 'Red Wave of aggression', I was reminded of what Jo Anne Barbee, Debbie's childhood friend, had said to me the day before: 'I call it a rich man's game. Poor man fights. Rich man gains. Most of those who sat in the White House, they weren't in harm's way. It was a meaningless war.'

And the words of Melva Lee Tomlin, Larry's best friend, chimed too: 'He would have been the first one on the line whatever it took. But it was a useless war. We lost such a lot of good people for no reason, for no purpose.'

Next to the medals lay a metal badge. The horse's head and the diagonal slash were instantly recognisable as the First Team. Alongside were two metal rings, displayed next to the medals. I asked Debbie what they were.

'I remember him saying in one of his letters from Vietnam, "I'm sending you these earrings", and that he'd traded them with a little Vietnamese girl for some C rations,' she explained. 'Very simple earrings. I've never worn them. They're very large. But, of course, I've kept them.'

They were Larry's final gift.

Next to the earrings Debbie had placed two small black-and-white passport-sized pictures of him, displayed in a small, intricate metal frame. They had been taken in 1952 and 1953 at Center elementary school.

'These two photos of him as a kid are on the nightstand next to my bed with his dog-tag hanging over them. So last thing at night I see him and first thing every morning. Don't he look cute? I don't feel cheated for myself . . . OK . . . but I do feel cheated for him. He didn't have a true shot at life. Don't get me wrong. He loved to have a good time. To party. Stuff like that. He enjoyed life. But he would have made a super father and husband.'

Sitting alongside Debbie was her elder sister Pat. Delicate, fragile and frail, wearing an open checked shirt over a white T-shirt, she'd suffered a slight stroke only the previous weekend but was determined to be there. She was holding a copy of the *East Texas Light* newspaper from 28 June 1967. She stared at the headline:

'*Shelby County Man Was Viet Nam Victim*'. I could see a tear trickling down her cheek as she scanned through the article again.

'It was God's will. God took Larry at a young age because he knew best. It was just his time. God knows where he is. We may not understand a lot of it but it's God's will. You never get over it. You just have to carry it with you for the rest of your life.'

She passed me a Christmas card with a simple snow-covered forest scene on the front. It was sent to her the previous December by Gene Ashcraft, Larry's best friend at Fort Polk boot camp. They'd promised each other 45 years ago that if one of them was killed, the other would keep in touch with their family. Gene was keeping the promise. He sends Pat a card every Christmas. She treasures each one. I looked inside and read Gene's latest message:

> I think of Larry ever so often. I wonder what he would have turned out to be. A very fine person I do know that. I hate it so much that he missed out on life and his own family. Believe me we would have stayed in contact and saw each other over the many years.
>
> Gene

'Don't you think that's wonderful that Larry's war friend still keeps in touch with me all these years later?' she smiled wistfully.

*

There's been a local newspaper in the Center area since the late nineteenth century. Originally it was called the *Laborer's Champion*. Then the *East Texas Light* came along to compete with the *Champion* and eventually they merged in the late 1970s to form *The Light and Champion*. The offices of the paper look out on to Center's main square, facing the old courthouse. The pace of its news reflects the pace of life: slow, gentle, almost sleepy. The little newsroom harks back to the early days of the community press in America. The publisher today is JoAnna Martin: 'It's a community of hard-working individuals believing in giving to others. They are people very much about helping their neighbour when in need. Faith plays a central role here. Loving our neighbour. Strong values of faith, family and friendship are the pillars of this generous, peaceful community.

'If Larry was still here today he'd recognise that. The things that we have been in the past still carry forth today. We love our home, our state, our country, with a strong sense of pride. We know we are going to raise up a group of young men and women who are going to stand for their home and its protection.

'He'd still find his heart here at home. He should be remembered as one of our own. That puts him in a very high ranking. He may be a name somewhere on a wall but here he's our own. He stood tall.'

That strong sense of patriotism was in evidence wherever I went in Center. The American flag flew from shops, houses and in gardens. At the entrances to the post office and the large hypermarket in the town, I'd noticed large collages on display of present-day soldiers serving in Iraq and Afghanistan, with prayers, messages of goodwill and thanks festooned around the frames.

As well as the Stars and Stripes, the other sign I'd kept seeing everywhere in the little town were red, white and blue campaign posters seeking to re-elect the County Sheriff, Newton Johnson. As a teenager, he'd attended church services at Short every Sunday alongside Larry and played volleyball with him afterwards. I decided to call in on him.

The security button buzzed to open the thick-steel security door. In front of me appeared the silver-moustached, gun-carrying sheriff. Cigar in mouth, he shook my hand with the firmest of grips in the manner you'd expect of a sheriff. Behind his desk was a large picture of a soldier stalking through the jungle, clasping an M16 rifle. Underneath were the words: 'Newton Johnson, Republic of Vietnam, Hill 881, 1967'.

'I feel lucky, not just blessed, that I was able to come back,' Sheriff Johnson declared. 'It's being in the right place at the right time or the wrong place at the wrong time. You never knew what was going to happen from one minute to the next.

'There's more we could have done as a country, as a government, to end the war with a victory. It puts a bitter taste in your mouth. When we came home, we didn't have any ticker-tape parades. No congressmen and people of prestige saying what a great job we'd done and we're glad you are home. You walked through the airport and people spat at you and called you baby killers. Vietnam Vets were the forgotten warriors. When we were in Vietnam, we used to say that when we died we knew we're going to heaven because we've already been to hell.'

One man in Center who was determined to put that right was Larry Hume. As the Post Quartermaster of the local branch of the Veterans of Foreign Wars Association, he'd recently organised a Victory in Europe day in Center to remember those who served in the Second World War and, for the first time ever, a Welcome Home Vietnam Veterans parade. Those who'd served in the war and had come back paraded through the town centre and congregated at the main square, where a special service was held, including a rifle salute and the Taps, honouring those who were killed in Vietnam. The names of the eight men from Shelby County who lost their lives were read out, including Shorty Andrews, Jerry Hughes and Larry Byford. The occasion was warm, emotional and memorable, but the turnout by the community was disappointing.

I sat on a marble bench in the square, by the side of the old courthouse, and gazed at a new war memorial built recently 'as a tribute to the men and women who have served with pride and honor in the Armed Forces of the United States of America'. Prominently carved on the smooth, shiny grey marble were the words:

Center's new war memorial

It was the first time I'd ever seen a memorial honouring the dead of the future.

Charlotte Allen's office in the courthouse looked out to the memorial and those words had a special poignance for her. She'd lost her son, Corey, aged 18, in 2008 in Afghanistan. Killed when his armoured vehicle was blown up by an improvised explosive device, he was the latest Shelby County soldier to die in a foreign land. He represented the present. Today, Charlotte volunteers in the Veterans Welfare office advising on benefits: her personal way of honouring her son's duty and loss: 'For Larry, he was forced to go, so even though it was for the greater good, it was harder for him and his family. I know in my heart my son was doing what he loved, what he wanted to do, what he chose.

'When I look out through the window at the new memorial, obviously I think about my son but now I'll think about Larry too. It's a debt we can't repay – what they both did. There's a lot of glory, honour and pride. The people of Center must remember them for their service. For their commitment to their country. As long as the country is grateful to them, then they didn't die in vain.'

I was about to leave Center, Shelby County and Texas but there were two more places I had to visit before I bid a final farewell to the Lone Star State.

*

I dug the small spoon into the side of the clay bank and scooped up several samples, which I tipped into a plastic container. Then, as carefully as an archaeologist sifting for fragments of artefacts, I removed the dead leaves, tree bark and small chunks of rock, checked it was as smooth and fine grained as possible, then shook the mix of yellow and red soil into a paper cup. Once filled to the brim, I pressed down the lid and tucked away the cup in my shoulder bag for safekeeping. It was a symbol of Larry's childhood. And I wanted a sample for myself. I knew where I wanted to take this clay but that would involve another journey to be taken in the near future.

Just before I left, I pulled myself halfway up the bank, using the spindly tree roots to support me, and, when I'd reached a high enough point, I looked towards the white house for the very last time.

I drove away from Center, noticing as I did so the creation of several new roads and housing developments. The focus of the local industry remains poultry, agriculture and timber, but changes are clearly afoot. Recent successful drilling for natural gas and oil, locked in the Haynesville Shale below Shelby County, means that new motels are being built and new hypermarkets have opened to support the new industry's expansion. People searching for the next fortune. Just like the oil pioneers in Texas 80 years ago.

My final destination that day was as far removed from any noise and bustle as you could imagine. I went to the heart of the Sabine forest, to a remote place tucked away deep in the piney woods. There were no road signs, no names or references guiding me how to get there. Indeed, I'd had to ask a local store owner outside Huxley where it was and he'd kindly driven in his own pick-up to escort me to the spot. 'You'll never know you are there,' Tim laughed. Minutes later, he pushed his left hand out of his car window, pointed to the ground, then put his thumb up. 'You're here,' his lips mouthed.

Possum Trot

There was not one person to be seen. I was surrounded by trees and a ramshackle collection of old RV trailers, caravans, shacks and small wooden cabins looking out on to a bare open patch of grass. An abandoned pick-up truck with its front bonnet raised up was shaded under the branches of a pine tree.

The nearby Bennet chapel appeared to be the only fixed focal point in the place. This was Possum Trot. Nestled in silence and solitude, it's a poor black community of around 200 people, most of them out of work. The Bennet Chapel website described the place as 'common ordinary people living life one day at a time and having a burden for their community as well as for the world'.

I spoke later to the charismatic local Baptist pastor, W.C. Martin, and his wife, Donna. She was born in Possum Trot in 1961 and was a six year old living there when Larry left for Vietnam.

'It was a very loving black community of around 100 people then. Everybody knew everybody. Very close. Very warm. If you weren't a brother or a sister, you were a cousin or an uncle. There were two churches, Bennet and a Caucasian one, and a little store run by John Cruses,' Donna remembered affectionately. 'People lived in little wooden houses. Most who worked were in the logging industry out in the woods.'

How did the place get its name? I asked her.

'Way back in the old days the roads were dirty rough clay tracks and the possums would come out at night and trot across the track. Possums are still here. I wonder if calling himself Possum Trot had anything to do with the possum itself,' she speculated. 'Like them, maybe he wanted no trouble; he was warm, slow moving as far as life is concerned. The community then was very slow paced too. He had some connection with the place,' she laughed, 'Very, very rarely would a white boy come here then. Maybe he had a friend here. We'll never know.'

Why had Larry decided, apparently out of the blue, to call himself after this place while he was in Vietnam? I wandered around the small grass clearing, looking for any suggestion, any clue. I found nothing. Like his family and close friends, I remained none the wiser. I looked around again at the trees and the trailers. I knew he liked the sound of the name. Presumably that was the reason. But had he ever been here? Had something happened in this very place some 45, 50 years ago that made it special to him? What exactly was its resonance? As I said my final farewell to Possum Trot, I concluded that Larry was the only person who knew the answer for sure and he took that insight to his grave.

I prepared to depart from east Texas, aware that the events of Friday, 23 June 1967 would stay with me for ever. Having discovered so much about Larry's movements on that day, it seemed important to discover next what President Johnson was doing on that same day, and whether there were any meaningful links to be found. Larry in Vietnam: commanded to do his duty. LBJ in America: the Commander in Chief.

CHAPTER 14

LBJ'S LONGEST DAY

President Lyndon Baines Johnson was used to working long hours, but even by his own exacting standards, Friday, 23 June 1967 turned out to be one of the longest, most intensive and memorable days of his presidency.

LBJ was a workaholic who was on the go from dawn to midnight. 'I seldom think of politics more than 18 hours a day,' he once joked. Johnson was a man who pushed himself to the extreme. Although he'd suffered a massive heart attack more than 20 years earlier aged 46, he remained a man in a hurry. He was restless and relentless: on the phone from morning to night. An extraordinarily talented politician, he'd previously led the Senate with an unmatched wily skill and an unrivalled reputation as a masterful wheeler-dealer. The so-called 'Johnson treatment' was legendary within Washington – he'd pushed controversial legislation through by badgering, cajoling, coercing and promising future favours. Tall, domineering, demanding and, at times, bullying, the Texan was a deep patriot who possessed an intense social conscience. He was also strong willed and could be stubborn as a mule. He once described himself as a cross between a Baptist preacher and a cowboy.

'There are few who knew LBJ who wouldn't describe him as great. Flawed, yes, and not always good, but great,' Mark Updegrove, the Director of the LBJ Presidential Library in Austin, Texas, told me. 'He was a great, great man and he was capable of triumphant things but had feet of clay with monumental flaws.

People talk about the Machiavellian character but LBJ got things done nine times out of ten because he was accommodating, he was a master at knowing what people wanted, what the hot buttons to press were. He knew people and what drove them. He was a master psychologist. He was too smart to be ruthless.'

Four years before, he had been the 'Veep' (Vice President), the President's right-hand man. But the assassination of JFK on 22 November 1963 not only shocked the nation to its core but changed Johnson's life for ever. Just two hours and eight minutes after Kennedy's horrific death in Dallas, Lyndon Baines Johnson was sworn in as the President of the United States on his home ground of Texas, taking the oath during a hastily arranged ceremony on Air Force One, just before the plane took off from Love Field airport in Dallas to return to Washington. The photograph of him inside the plane, standing in front of local judge Sarah Hughes, holding up his right hand as his left one was placed on a missal, became one of the most iconic images of the twentieth century. To his left stood Jackie Kennedy, her face white with shock, wearing a pink Chanel suit spattered with her dead husband's blood. To his right was his wife Lady Bird, the new First Lady. At the back of the plane, inside a casket, was the body of the 35th President. Suddenly catapulted into the position of America's 36th leader, LBJ found himself heading the most powerful nation on earth. A year later he was elected President in his own right, with one of the largest landslide victories ever, and in 1967 he was Commander-in-Chief at a time of war. Responsible for the future course of the Vietnam conflict as well as for the destiny of world peace and stability, LBJ faced a heavy load indeed.

June 1967 was a tense period in the world. At the start of the month, the Six Day Israeli–Arab War had shattered the fragile peace across the Middle East. The arms race between the US and the Soviet Union showed no signs of relenting. The Vietnam War was intensifying, with hundreds of American soldiers being killed every month and the American nation becoming increasingly polarised. LBJ once claimed that before he went to sleep at night he'd ask: 'Have I done everything to unite the world, to bring peace to all the world? Have I done enough?' Anxious to fulfil his pledge 'to seek peace any time, any place', he was acutely aware on that morning of Friday, 23 June that the day ahead was of monumental importance.

At 6.35 p.m. the previous Thursday evening, the White House announced unexpectedly, and with only 16 hours' notice, that the President would meet the Soviet Premier, Prime Minister Aleksei Kosygin, at eleven o'clock that Friday morning. It was to be the first time that an American President and a Soviet Premier were to come face to face in five years. Relations between the two countries were fragile and icy. The likely summit agenda of the Middle East, the arms race and the Vietnam War were subjects of profound importance to both men, their nations and the whole world. The stakes were high. The goal would be to find, in Johnson's words, 'a common language' and 'to narrow our differences where they can be narrowed and thus help to secure peace in the world for future generations'.

Prime Minister Kosygin had arrived in New York earlier that week to address the United Nations General Assembly as part of its emergency debate on the situation in the Middle East. A meeting of the two men sometime during his visit to the US was contemplated but was by no means certain. Kosygin refused to go to Washington and insisted that any meeting should take place in New York. However, LBJ was wary of encountering large protests against the Vietnam War in the city and felt strongly that Kosygin should come to the White House. After all, Mr Kosygin was on American soil. They were like two petulant children, each refusing to give an inch. Eventually it was agreed they'd meet halfway so that neither was seen to lose face. A location was identified at the Glassboro State College campus in New Jersey, which was almost equidistant: 135 miles from Washington DC, 125 miles from New York City.

The talks were to be held inside a nineteenth-century mansion on the Glassboro campus called Hollybush. The building was an elegant 22-roomed brownstone house on Whitney Avenue, built in 1849, and the home of the college president, Dr Tom Robinson, who was given less than 24 hours' notice about the temporary change of use of his premises. As the White House spokesman described it, quiet, sleepy Glassboro was about 'to become the focal point of a troubled world's hopes and prayers'.

Hollybush mansion, Glassboro

Forty-five years on, I was standing outside the same Hollybush mansion. I'd gone to the campus to try to relive the proceedings of that summit, step by step, hour by hour. For there, on the same day that Larry had died, Lyndon Johnson, as President and Commander in Chief, took part in a critical summit in the hope of nudging open the door towards securing long-term peace in Vietnam.

Today, Glassboro State College is known as Rowan University. The Italianate villa design of Hollybush, with its distinctive South Jersey ironstone, decorative railings and tower, still looks exactly as it did in 1967.

A small brass plate outside the main porch declares:

> Hollybush is best known as the site of the 1967 summit between United States President Lyndon Johnson and Soviet Premier Alexei Kosygin, the first summit between the Cold War superpowers.

The President was up at 4.30 a.m. in the White House that Friday morning, preparing for the meeting. Four hours later, he was chairing a working breakfast with his senior advisors.

At that time, 8.30 a.m. in Washington, it was 7.30 p.m. in Vietnam. Larry's body was lying outside the cave at the Rockpile. He'd been shot while the President had lain asleep during that Thursday night. The Major lay nearby. The heat was intense and the members of the Company were waiting until it was deemed safe to recover the bodies. The President, of course, had no knowledge of Larry's death, not even as a raw statistic hidden in a morning update on casualty figures.

One of LBJ's key aims for the summit that day was to begin a dialogue with the Soviet leader about the terms of a potential settlement in Vietnam but, at the same time, be determined not to show signs of weakness or any lack of resolve. As the President and his advisors ate and talked in the White House, Kosygin was leaving New York in a motorcade heading for Glassboro via the New Jersey Turnpike.

Before setting out, the Soviet Prime Minister had ensured that he had a hotline to Hanoi in the unlikely event of a breakthrough at the session. But on that Friday morning, Ho Chi Minh, who was 77 years of age, extremely frail and having difficulty breathing, wasn't even in North Vietnam. He'd gone to Guandong in south-east China, where he was receiving specialist medical treatment. In his absence, the North Vietnamese leadership in Hanoi were arguing among themselves about whether to plan for the launch of an all-out offensive in the South in the near future or continue to play it long. But all of Ho's team remained united about achieving the same end goal: reunification and 'liberation', whatever the cost. In that context, Kosygin, like Johnson, was pessimistic that any significant progress on Vietnam could be made at that morning's session.

Just before ten o'clock, the President left the White House by helicopter and within an hour his motorcade was pulling up at Hollybush to prepare for the arrival of the Soviet delegation.

Meanwhile, as darkness began to fall on the coastal plain of Binh Dinh, the bodies of Larry and the Major remained unrecovered on the Rockpile, lying in the open near the entrance to the cave.

I looked around at the neat grounds of Hollybush, filled with mature trees and bushes. It was there on that Friday morning that a crowd of around 2,000 LBJ supporters had gathered, some carrying posters of the President's face, others lifting placards declaring, 'LBJ: All the Way', 'Back LBJ in Vietnam', 'Work for Peace' and 'Congratulations Grandpa'. Eight hundred accredited press had also descended on Hollybush. The weather was grey and humid, and the newly installed air-conditioning machines were on full blast, cooling the meeting rooms.

Outside the mansion, I read a copy of the President's official diary for that day. At that moment, at eleven o'clock, '*there was a great air of excitement*' but '*the President's face was tense and his hands would open and close, clenching them into a fist and then releasing them*'. Reporters, too, noted his strained expression.

Kosygin's motorcade was running 20 minutes late. The President walked across to the assembled crowd then went inside Hollybush for a glass of water and a Titralac (calcium carbonate) tablet before retiring to the bathroom for a second time.

At the Rockpile, it was 10 p.m. It was still too dangerous to retrieve the bodies; no one was sure how many enemy combatants remained hidden among the rocks and caves. Charlie Company's platoons were playing a waiting game in the dark, trying to monitor the gaps among the boulders and hoping to outwit the enemy and secure the area at first light.

At 11.25 a.m., the President came out of the front door of Hollybush to greet Mr Kosygin as his limousine pulled up. Both men were suited smartly and soberly.

Forty-five years on, I was standing outside that same mansion, viewing the black-and-white newsreel taken of that greeting, captured by a news cameraman at the exact spot where I was standing. It felt like I was there in the moment.

The crowds opposite Hollybush cheered ecstatically. As they

stood side by side, the difference in height between the two men was striking: Kosygin was four inches shorter than LBJ who, at 6 ft 3 in., was the tallest president in US history. The President leaned forward as he walked. Both men looked serious. 'You chose a nice place,' Kosygin declared, as the two men posed for photos. Kosygin came to the microphone and saluted the friendship between the Soviet and American peoples. Again, the crowd cheered rapturously. President Johnson responded that they were on a search for peace for the benefit of all mankind. They proceeded indoors, where the main parties congregated in a makeshift conference room.

I followed in their footsteps, accompanied by Christine Deehan, Director of Events at Rowan University and my Hollybush guide for the afternoon. 'All the President's men were gathered right here,' she told me enthusiastically. Rusk and McNamara were among them, together with Soviet Foreign Secretary Gromyko.

Kosygin opened the conversations by congratulating the President on becoming a grandfather for the first time. Patrick Lyndon Nugent had been born to Johnson's daughter, Luci, only two days earlier. 'I've been a grandfather for 18 years,' Kosygin proclaimed, 'and have no regrets.' They smiled, shook hands and the two men entered the small, green-walled library next door for the start of their one-to-one session. Both knew that neither side was likely to offer up a major initiative that would break the deadlock on Vietnam. Indeed, LBJ expected the Soviet stance to be firm: peace could only be secured if and when the US left Vietnam. The summit, therefore, would be a 'holding action', a chance for a dialogue and, hopefully, an opportunity to develop a personal relationship.

The original furniture they had used that day was requisitioned later by the President for his own museum, but two chairs and a small table were set out in the middle of the intimate room, in a similar position as they had been that morning. I looked around the walls, which were filled with photographs, newspaper cuttings and other memorabilia recalling the day, including the covers of *Time*, *Newsweek* and *Life*, all showing photographs of the two men at Hollybush. I sat down next to Christine and imagined that proceedings were underway.

Prime Minister Kosygin face to face with President Johnson
(Courtesy LBJ Library. Photo by Yoichi Okamoto)

Together with their two interpreters, William Krimer and Victor Sukhodrev, the two men got down to business. Sitting together beneath an ornate chandelier, Kosygin in an upholstered armchair, LBJ in a Victorian pedestal rocking chair, they leaned towards each other and started to talk earnestly. Two glasses of water had been placed on the small table between them. At times, the two men's faces were less than a foot apart. President Johnson's official diary noted that Mr Kosygin used his hands a lot 'to emote' throughout the morning session.

The theme of grandchildren continued as an opening subject of common ground. 'You don't want my grandson fighting yours and I don't want yours shooting at him,' LBJ declared. He hoped the grandsons would grow up to know each other. He said that both of them had lived through the horrors of war and did not wish their grandchildren to share that kind of experience. Kosygin reminded the President that during the Second World War he was in Leningrad and he would never forget the American help at that time.

After discussing the Middle East and the arms race at some length, the subject of Vietnam was finally raised towards the end of the session. The President took his pen and a piece of paper and drew a map of North Vietnam and South Vietnam, separated by the demilitarised zone. He sketched an impression of the North Vietnamese Army going below the DMZ to attack South Vietnam. LBJ explained that the US bombing of the North was aimed at stopping that military deployment and that although some of his advisors wanted him to invade the North, he had no desire to conquer North Vietnam. What he wanted was self-determination for the South and to allow free elections in which they could choose the kind of government they wanted. He emphasised that he was willing to consider a peace settlement only if it recognised the separation of the North and South: one country communist, the other a democracy. If the North stopped its infiltration of the South, the Americans would stop bombing the North. Kosygin, who LBJ described later as 'reserved, contained but jolly', did not reply.

At 1.30 p.m., the two men joined the waiting delegations for lunch in Hollybush's dining room. I walked through to the same room, noticing the elegant three-part bay window that flooded the area with light. That day, drapes had covered the window to provide secrecy and security. The President asked Kosygin what he wanted to drink. 'Whatever you are having,' came the reply. The President called for vodka and the two men downed the drink quickly, Russian style. They sat together and began a meal of shrimp cocktail, a main course of roast beef and rice pilaff, followed by pineapple sorbet. The President made light conversation about his own birth date with the Soviet Foreign Minister Andrei Gromyko, who told him that 1908 was a very good year for wine. The President smiled and said he wished the two countries 'could agree on everything like they agreed on that'. At the end of the lunch, with a glass of Californian Cabernet Sauvignon in his hand, the President stood and proposed a toast to Mr Kosygin and to peace in the world: 'We both have special responsibilities for the security of our families and over and beyond all our families is the security of the entire human family inhabiting this earth. There is a special place however in this world and a special responsibility placed upon our two countries because of our strength and resources. I want to emphasise that the results of today's meeting will be judged by what we can achieve in the future in order to achieve peace.'

By then, it was 2.40 p.m. on a balmy Friday.

On the Rockpile it was 1.40 a.m., Saturday, and the area was still in darkness. Occasionally, a flare was set off, providing a sudden explosion of light. The Major and Larry Byford remained lying by the caves. Charlie Company was still waiting anxiously for dawn to arrive.

At ten past three, when lunch had ended, a short adjournment was called so each leader could consult with his team. The two men then met again in the library for forty minutes.

Kosygin began the afternoon session by informing the President that two days before he had been in contact with Pham Van Dong, the Prime Minister of North Vietnam. Kosygin had asked Pham what he could do to help bring the war to an end. Pham Van Dong's reply had just been received while they were having lunch: stop the bombing and they would immediately go to the conference table. Kosygin strongly advised LBJ to take up the offer. He compared Vietnam to the Algerian War in which Charles de Gaulle's France eventually had to sign a peace treaty signifying the end of the French colonisation of Algeria. He then stated his belief that the same outcome would happen to the US if the war continued. He reiterated his belief that the North Vietnamese would never give up their goal of a unified Vietnam and that sooner or later American forces would have to withdraw. Kosygin advised it would be better to do that sooner rather than later. If not, the President would carry on the war for ten years or more, killing off the best of his nation's young people in the process.

Responding, LBJ warned of the potential of a North Vietnamese betrayal. He said he would be crucified politically at home in the United States if the North Vietnamese continued to send troops into South Vietnam once the US had stopped the bombing of the North.

Kosygin said if the bombing stopped immediately, representatives of the US and North Vietnam could meet the following day in Hanoi, New York, Moscow or Paris. From there, the negotiators would work out what was to follow. It would save hundreds of thousands of lives, Kosygin emphasised. If no such direct contact was made, no solution could be found, he said.

The President asked Kosygin if he could help personally to ensure that self-determination for the South Vietnamese people was secured at the conference table. Kosygin replied he couldn't answer that without consulting the North Vietnamese.

As the session drew to a close, the two leaders agreed to extend their talks and to meet again at the same place two days later.

'It was just conversation, pleasant, no vitriolic stuff,' LBJ would later tell former President Eisenhower. They left the study and headed through to the front porch of Hollybush to address the waiting cameras and crowds.

'Our meeting gave us the opportunity to get acquainted with each other,' the President proclaimed. The talks had been 'very good and useful'. He revealed the unexpected news that they would be coming back to the same place the following Sunday at 1.30 p.m. to resume talks. Mr Kosygin said that he had nothing to add and hoped the waiting press would not be offended that they hadn't been told much.

They had not reached any agreements, but the 'Spirit of Glassboro' had been amicable. The Cold War warriors had greeted each other face to face and defused the overall tension just a little. That in itself was progress. In the President's own words: 'It does help to sit down and look a man in the eye all day long and reason with him, particularly if he is trying to reason with you.'

Mr Kosygin climbed into his limousine. As he did so he declared: 'There are many beautiful and wonderful things to be done. War should be a thing of the past.'

The talks were headline news on every bulletin and in every newspaper across the US and the western world. In stark contrast, Russia's *Pravda* treated it as a brief 37-word down-page story with the simple headline: 'Meeting of A. Kosygin and L. Johnson'. Radio Moscow didn't even mention the Glassboro summit until hours later.

Meanwhile, the war in Vietnam continued. There was no let-up in the fighting. No breakthrough whatsoever in the possible journey to peace. The meeting had been useful. But in the end it was just talk.

By then, it was 5 p.m. on the Friday at Glassboro. In Vietnam it was 4 a.m. on Saturday. As soon as dawn broke, Larry's body was retrieved and taken down the slope on a makeshift poncho stretcher. At the beach it had been placed in a body bag. It was still there, waiting to be collected by the medevac chopper.

I sat down on the grass opposite Hollybush and reflected on the state of the war at that time. Hundreds of people dying every month. No let-up in the fighting. A stalemate both politically and militarily. America divided. Passionate views either side of a ferocious internal debate. Each and everyone believing they were right.

Was LBJ right or wrong to pursue his goals in Vietnam? Which side would I have been on then without the benefit of hindsight? One thing was for sure – by then it had become the most divisive war in the history of the modern American nation.

Although the summit sessions were over, and it was late afternoon, the President was still less than halfway through his schedule for the day. The subject of Vietnam was to cling to him like poison ivy for the remaining hours.

At 5.17 p.m., he boarded his helicopter and headed for Philadelphia, where he transferred to Air Force One. Waiting on board was his eldest daughter, Lynda, and various Democratic Party members of Congress with their partners. They were all heading for a Party fundraising dinner to be held that same evening more than 2,000 miles away in Los Angeles. At 7.39 p.m. local time, Air Force One was landing at LA's international airport.

At 8 p.m., the President, in black bow tie and white tuxedo, arrived at the Century Plaza Hotel, entering via a side door to avoid waiting protesters. The hotel was completely sealed off. The Presidential Ball was the first such dinner to be held to raise funds for the Party's 1968 Presidential election campaign. Each guest had paid $500 to be there and the Banqueting Room was packed full with over 1,000 supporters. After listening to comedian Jack Benny – the Master of Ceremonies – open the proceedings, LBJ settled down for a meal of La Salade Johann Strauss, followed by Le Filet de Boeuf Forestiere, then Rochers de Glaces Assortis. Wine and champagne were served throughout the evening.

By then, over at the Rockpile it was 8 a.m. on Saturday. Larry's body was being flown to the Grave Registration Centre to be processed before being sent home.

Anti-war poster publicising the Los Angeles rally
(Photo courtesy of The Center for the Study of Political Graphics)

Outside the Century Plaza hotel, an anti-war demonstration was starting to turn into a violent confrontation with the Los Angeles Police. A protest that in the words of the *Los Angeles Times* would become 'The Bloody March That Shook LA', a clash 'between anti-war protesters and the LAPD which injured dozens, irrevocably changed the city and its politics, and foreshadowed a coming national upheaval'.

Earlier that evening, to coincide with the President's visit, some 80 anti-war groups had gathered a mile away at the nearby Cheviot Hills playground. They were joined by thousands of members of the public for a rally to protest at US involvement in the war. The boxer Muhammad Ali, who'd recently been convicted for refusing the draft, was there signing hundreds of draft cards brought by demonstrators. H. Rap Brown, the student activist leader, declared to the gathering crowd, 'Ours is not to do or die; ours is but to reason why; hell no, we won't go!' The protest singer Phil Ochs gave his first public performance of his new song 'The War Is Over' later described as 'one of the most potent anti war songs ever written' and 'the greatest act of bravery by a topical song writer.' His words resonated with the growing crowd as he sang:

So do your duty, boys, and join with pride
Serve your country in her suicide
Find the flags so you can wave goodbye
But just before the end even treason might be worth a try
This country is too young to die
I declare the war is over
It's over, it's over.

The plan was for the rally to move off as a peaceful march down Avenue of the Stars, passing in front of the Century Plaza hotel before continuing round the block.

The local KPFK radio station's live coverage from that evening described the crowd as varied – young and old, rich and poor, workers from all walks of life; 'ordinary citizens representative of the type of crowd on an LA street corner . . . the electorate'.

However, earlier in the week, the main organising group for the event had been secretly infiltrated and the police were fearful that a portion of the crowd might 'rush' the hotel and try to storm the Presidential Ball. That intelligence persuaded police and security chiefs to mount a massive force of some 1,300 officers, who were waiting for the march to descend on Century Plaza. The number of protesters far exceeded the LAPD's original estimate of 1,000. By the evening, 10,000 had turned up and the police believed the situation was potentially serious.

As the protesters began their march down Motor Avenue, they raised placards exclaiming: 'Get out of Vietnam' ,'We Want Peace', 'Hell No We Won't Go', 'Negotiate Now' and even 'LBJ: How

Many Kids Have You Killed Today?' Some shouted out 'Fascist' and 'Worse than Hitler' but they were a small minority.

Protester clashes with LAPD officers during the Century Plaza rally, Los Angeles, Friday, 23 June 1967 (Photo courtesy *Los Angeles Times* Photographic Archive, Young Research Library, UCLA)

When a section of the demonstrators sat down in front of the hotel building, they were ordered by the police to keep marching and 'to disperse in an orderly parade or be arrested for an unlawful assembly'. But many of the protesters later claimed they couldn't hear the police above the crowd noise and the music. The officers moved in, forcibly dispersing the protestors, using batons to beat those who refused to move on. The violence escalated, leaving many in the crowd injured and bloodied. Several lay unconscious in the street.

KPFK's broadcast highlighted eyewitness reports of police hitting women with 'billy clubs and night sticks'. One man said he'd seen a man being attacked to police shouts of 'Beat him, beat him.' The police counterclaimed that they were subjected to attacks with rocks and pieces of wood. Chaos, confusion and brutality reigned. Fifty-one people were arrested. Scores were injured.

The LAPD later justified its actions by citing a clear violation of the permit orders that allowed the march to go ahead only if it kept moving, and the police claimed that the violence by some protesters was pre-planned. Whatever the rights and wrongs, this was the most violent confrontation in LA since the Watts Riots two years earlier. The event prompted outrage and widespread complaints about the excessive use of force by the police.

The following day, the *Los Angeles Times* carried the headline: '10,000 In Melee: War Protest Mars LBJ Visit', but some of its journalists complained to their editors about the paper's biased pro-police reporting of the event and demanded that more balanced articles be published during the following week.

As the *Los Angeles Times* would report subsequently, the violence marked a turning point for LA, a city not known up to then for attracting large demonstrations. No other presidential visit had sparked such unrest in the history of the city. Moreover, the paper claimed, the Century Plaza protests foreshadowed the rapid growth of the national anti-war movement through the rest of that year and its growing militancy. As the LAPD field commander, John McAllister, reflected later: 'The importance of this demonstration cannot be underestimated in terms of its relevance to the LAPD, to the magnitude and effectiveness of the anti-war movement, and to what kind of public appearances President Johnson would risk in the future.'

Back inside the hotel ballroom, away from the chaos outside, the President rose to his feet at 10.30 p.m. and addressed his supporters. As his speech drew to a close, he turned to Vietnam and to the growing protests around the country: 'Those who do not smell the powder or are near the blast of the cannon, who enjoy the luxury and freedom of free speech and the right to exercise it most freely, at times really do not understand the burdens that our military are carrying there tonight, who are dying for their country, or the burdens that their commanders are carrying, who wish they were all here asleep in bed or even carrying a placard of some kind.'

Little was he aware that Larry Byford had died for his country that very day. Then LBJ reflected on the war itself: 'I just say this to you. There is no human being in this world who wants to avoid war more than I do. There is no human being in this world who wants peace in Vietnam more than I do. When they tell me to negotiate, I say "Amen". I have been ready to negotiate and sit down at a conference table every hour of every day that I have been President of this country. But I just cannot negotiate with myself. And these protesters haven't been able to deliver Ho Chi Minh any place yet. I was not elected your president to liquidate our agreements in South-East Asia. If that is what you want, you will have to get another president. But I am going – as I have said so many times – any time, any place, anywhere, if, in my judgement, it can possibly, conceivably, serve the cause of peace. That is why I went to that little farmhouse way up on the New Jersey Pike today to spend the day, and that is why I am going to get over to see my grandson by daylight in the morning. I have been up since 4.30 a.m. – 1.30 a.m. this time. I have been almost 24 hours on the go. Give me your confidence and your prayers. God knows, I need them.'

The President enjoyed a standing ovation that lasted several minutes. He listened to The Supremes give a live performance on the ballroom stage before departing the hotel by helicopter at 11.35 p.m. Twenty-five minutes later, Air Force One was taking off from LA international airport, heading for his home state of Texas. At 4.08 a.m., he transferred to his Stonewall ranch. 'It had been a long day,' he reflected later in his diary.

Within five hours, LBJ was up and taking phone calls from senators and his Press Secretary. That Saturday afternoon, there was a short time to relax, to tour his ranch and, most importantly, to go to Seton Hospital in nearby Austin to see his grandson for the very first time. There, dressed in a white hospital gown, LBJ went to welcome the latest addition to his family, to marvel at the perfection of a brand-new life and to witness the start of a new generation. Innocent and pure, untroubled by conflict, negativity or strife, the baby lay cradled in his mother's arms.

By then, Larry had arrived at the Grave Registration Centre. His details had been recorded then his body had been placed in a casket that was stacked up, ready to be flown home to Texas.

I looked at the official photograph taken by Yoichi Okamoto that afternoon. It showed LBJ putting a protective arm around his daughter Luci and gazing tenderly into the eyes of his newborn grandson, who was staring up at him and yawning. The photograph adorned the front cover of the following week's *Life* magazine and was published in newspapers across America and the world. LBJ left baby Patrick a set of six gold cups that had been given to him as a welcome gift by Alexei Kosygin.

Less than 24 hours later, LBJ was back at Hollybush, face to face with the experienced Russian grandfather. The talks that Sunday afternoon continued to be amicable but firm. Once again in the green-walled study but now with interpreters Alexander Akalousky and Sukhodrev, the President began by telling Kosygin that his own military expenditure on Vietnam could only be reduced if the Soviet Union ended its supply of military equipment to the North. Outside, the heavens opened with a torrential downpour.

LBJ said he'd studied Hanoi's message carefully. If the US bombing of the North was to stop and direct peace talks were to begin, the US must expect North Vietnamese forces not to advance any further into the South and US forces, in turn, would not advance north. Kosygin replied that he would transmit the message to the North Vietnamese leadership. But no response to the proposal ever came back either directly from Hanoi or via Moscow. The President realised Kosygin had no mandate. 'The door to peace was still tightly barred,' LBJ wrote later in his memoirs, *The Vantage Point*.

Later that evening at the White House, LBJ briefed that the summit had made the world 'a little less dangerous' and said that ways had been discussed to move the conflict from the battlefield to the conference table. Arriving back in New York, Kosygin announced that any improvement in relations between the Soviet Union and the United States was dependent on the US ceasing its bombing of the North and pulling troops out of the South.

The 'Spirit of Glassboro' had enabled the two Cold War leaders to meet face to face and to talk candidly. That was progress in itself. They'd got to know each other a little and had squared up to the problems facing them in a spirit of mutual respect. But, as expected, there had been no resolution on Vietnam and the stalemate would continue. The American bombing and combat deployments would persist. The war would go on in earnest.

Standing inside the front porch of Hollybush, the two men shook hands and bid farewell.

The Glassboro summit and LBJ becoming a grandfather dominate the front pages of the news magazines, June 1967

By then, more than a thousand miles away from Glassboro, the two military men had arrived at the modest wooden front porch in Short, east Texas, to inform Fate that his beloved son was dead.

*

During the same month, the Politburo and Central Military Party Committee in Hanoi approved a secret resolution to start planning for the so-called 'General Offensive and General Uprising' initiative, better known as the Tet Offensive.

Some months later, Johnson reflected: 'Until the men in Hanoi face the problem of ending the war, we have to stand firm and fast. Thus far since Glassboro we have met with little more than bellicose statements and evasions.'

I stood outside the main door of Hollybush, trying to imagine those final scenes at the summit. As I walked away, a party of Moldovan academics was entering the house for the next tour. In 1967, Moldova was part of the Soviet Union. Today, following the dissolution of the USSR, this landlocked region, nestled between Romania and Ukraine, is an independent nation, a member of the Council of Europe and aspiring to join the European Union. History teaches you that anything can happen, even the most unimaginable of outcomes. If only at Glassboro that day . . .

CHAPTER 15

THE DIVISIONAL COMMANDER

It was the happiest of times. We'd moved to the Yorkshire mill town of Huddersfield in April 1966 when I was eight years old. Our home, 10 Occupation Road, was a three-bedroomed detached red-brick house in Lindley, a smart northern suburb. Located on a leafy road of detached houses opposite the town's new hospital, the home we nicknamed 'the Palace' had a mature garden at the front full of shrubs, trees and rose bushes, and a garden at the back that was big enough to play football. My family couldn't believe their luck, having moved there from a tiny two-bedroomed flat. We didn't own the property; it was a police house that came with my dad's job.

I sat outside the driveway 44 years on, looking and remembering. I'd not been there since we'd left in 1968. But I had to come back. The house had taken on a greater significance to me because it was the place where we were living at the time when Larry Byford died in Vietnam.

What had happened to my dad, Lawry Byford, in those intervening years since he'd returned from the Second World War? His life had certainly changed beyond recognition and he'd become a successful police officer. By 1967, aged 41, he had risen to the rank of superintendent and was the Huddersfield Divisional Commander of the West Riding Constabulary in his native Yorkshire. It was his first substantive leadership role.

After being in Reims on the day of the unconditional surrender of the Germans back in May 1945, my dad returned to Bletchley, the signals training centre north of London. From there he transferred to India, first to Delhi then to Calcutta, handling signals messages relating to the early stages of the partition of India and East Bengal. There he met up again with his colleague Norman Ashdown, who'd joined up with him that same first day at Bletchley back in August 1944. Lawry was about to be transferred from Calcutta to Peking, to work in the Diplomatic Wireless service, when he received the news that his father George was terminally ill with cancer. So in 1946, he was given compassionate leave and demobbed. He returned to Normanton to say farewell to his father and support his mother.

The last thing he wanted to do after the experiences of that past year was to go back down the coalmine as an apprentice electrician. He'd seen the world. He'd experienced a totally different way of life. He'd witnessed leadership at the highest level and close at hand. In his own words: 'World War Two changed my concept of leadership completely. Having come from this small mining town with not much scope at all and then rubbing shoulders with people like Lieutenant General Gerow and others under his command, they were wonderful examples to me of how a leader should act. If you can imagine me at 19. Here's a chap, Gerow, who'd had the most extraordinarily difficult time on the battlefield, Omaha Beach, the first Major General into Paris, the Battle of the Bulge, who, when I joined him, had done just about everything. And yet he would walk by, and in a way I suppose he realised I was only on secondment as a Brit to the Americans, but he always had that smile and twinkle and didn't give a formal salute like you'd expect in the British Army. Instead, he'd offer a lovely smile, saying, "Hiya, fella." Now, that sounds unimportant but it was the opposite to me. My concept of leadership came right there from the Americans, no question about that. When I was with them, I learnt such a great deal that stayed with me for life. They were fantastic to me.'

Lawry realised then that he wanted a better life and the chance to take on a leadership role in the future. Coming out of the war, the idea of working in a command environment appealed to him. So, too, did public service and law and order. With that in mind, he decided to join his local police force in 1947. Starting at the bottom as a constable, he filled that role for almost ten years.

His ambition grew steadily and, as a driven man, he was determined to progress in his chosen career.

However, he soon realised that he'd need to attain some academic qualifications to ensure his advancement. But there was a problem: he hadn't one qualification to his name and was not used to the discipline of study. Aiming high, he contacted his local university in Leeds, who advised him to take a correspondence course in three subjects, equivalent to today's A levels, which would qualify him to apply to university. Accordingly, while working as a policeman in the day, he studied in the evenings and at weekends for two years. When he passed his subjects, he applied to study law at the University of Leeds and was accepted as a mature student.

So in 1953, he arranged a punishing schedule: to work nightshifts in the police force, attend university during the daytime, and do extra study at weekends. By then he was married to my mother, Muriel, and by 1955, Jeremy, his firstborn had arrived. My mother loyally supported his endeavours all the way, although it can't have been easy, seeing so little of her husband and raising Jeremy almost single-handedly at times. Lawry Byford graduated with an Honours degree in Law in 1956 but his studies were far from over. He then decided to qualify as a barrister, studying at night and weekends on top of his day job in the police. By 1958, I had been born and he had been called to the Bar: 'I just felt, having left school as a young teenager with no academic qualifications and having just come back from the war, that the first thing I had to do was to acquire those academic attainments, because without them I wouldn't stand a chance in any interviews for senior positions in any sort of profession. That's why I worked all those nights on a very regular basis for three years so that I was able to go to university in the daytime. And studying those long hours on top of the day job, reading for the Bar, getting those qualifications, was a real slog but, coupled with the instructive things I'd learned in the army from the Americans, they gave me the framework for my professional life.'

The boy who'd been snubbed and rejected at the time of his 11-plus exam, and who'd left school at 13 with no academic qualifications, was now a rising star. Of the thirty-three senior officers in the West Riding force, he was the only one who'd joined after the war had ended. His senior colleagues looked upon him as the coming man and he relished it. The hard work and sacrifice was proving to be worth it. His career had taken off. He'd risen quickly through the ranks as a detective, working at the Criminal Investigations Department (CID) headquarters in Wakefield and then as an instructor at the Detective Training School. By 1964, he was seconded to the National Police College in Hampshire, where he joined the Senior Command Course. He then returned to his beloved Yorkshire in the summer of 1966 to be the Commander in charge of the Huddersfield Division of the West Riding Constabulary.

'It was something I was hoping for and had been looking forward to for a long time. It was the first time I'd been in command of something,' he recalled.

Denis O'Toole was my father's Administration Sergeant, his personal assistant within the ranks, throughout his time in Huddersfield: 'Your dad was quite unique at that time in that he was the only senior officer with a baby. All the others were too old. He was most impressive: tall with black hair that needed Brylcreem to keep it tidy. His leadership style was firm but consensual. He knew what he wanted but preferred to take people with him amicably. I learnt a great deal myself from working so closely with him, such as not to take decisions too quickly. There's almost always time to reflect if only for a few moments and he taught me never to make a decision when you're angry.

'My strongest memory of him at that time was his personality was such that you never wanted to let him down. He inspired you to "put in that little bit extra" every time.

'He was a hell of a grafter: he went on and on. I used to joke with him that he led from the front and left chaos at the back. He'd never stop. He'd usually go home at five o'clock for an hour to see the family, have a knockaround with you, and then be back in the office for a couple of hours until around eight-thirty. He was relentless.'

That sounded to me like the work ethic of Lyndon Johnson – on and on, non-stop, obsessed.

By the summer of 1967 he'd been married to my mother, Muriel, for 16 years. He'd met her as a young 22-year-old policeman while on the beat. Wintertime in Normanton was usually wet, windy and cold, so most policemen used to find a place to rest for a while to escape the rigours of the weather. One of his sanctuaries was the local Empire cinema, where he used to shelter in the lobby. He'd sit on the radiator to warm up and would have a cup of tea and a chat to the cashier, Margaret Massey, who was impressed by his manners and liked his *joie de vivre*. Margaret had one child, 16-year-old daughter Muriel, who was her parents' pride and joy. She was still attending school at that time and used to walk to the cinema regularly to wait for her mother to finish her shift. She was a striking-looking girl with thick, wavy, dark-brown hair, large brown eyes and a very slender figure. Well mannered, intelligent and proper, she was a good catch. Before long, Lawry and Muriel's paths had crossed in the cinema lobby and they struck up a first tentative conversation. Shortly afterwards, he went to see a film on his own and found her sitting directly in front of him. Grabbing the opportunity to talk to her without her mother's presence, he offered to walk her home, after which they started going out together on a regular basis. Three years later, they were married. By June 1967, they'd created a family of three children: Jeremy, myself and baby Jill who was seven months old.

Lawry Byford with his son Mark in the mid-1960s

'It was a very happy time domestically. Life was fantastic,' my father recalled. 'Two sons aged twelve and nine and then we'd just had a daughter. Our social outgoings had to cover the wishes of the three. Football and speedway for the boys. Walks in the park looking at the birds with the baby. It was a wonderful time.'

My mother remembered the summer of 1967 rather differently: 'I felt like a prisoner at that time. I was already pregnant when we arrived in Huddersfield and soon after I had the baby. I couldn't drive and therefore spent nearly all of my time at the house looking after her and bringing up you boys. I felt trapped and rather lonely then. Your dad was working very hard, striving, putting in very long hours. He didn't know any different.'

Although Britain was not involved directly in the Vietnam War, my father took more than a passing interest in its progression, and by the summer of 1967 he was increasingly troubled by what he saw on the television, heard on the radio and read in his newspapers: 'I just felt at that time, when I looked back at my own experience 20 years before in World War Two with the Americans, all of us knew what we were doing and why – defeating a dictator, a fascist who was creating so much unhappiness, killing so many innocent people, directly challenging the security and future of our own freedom. We had a clear and common goal. But with Vietnam at that time I felt so sorry for the guys. Perhaps if I hadn't served with the Americans I wouldn't have given it much thought, but seeing the stark nature of the television pictures, in particular, and thinking of the soldiers I had been with, I was thinking, "How do they feel about why they are there? Who is the common enemy? What are they fighting for?" I felt frustrated for those American soldiers and looked at it despairingly. I just couldn't see the reason for it. I just felt for them.'

The Vietnam War was the first war in which television news coverage had a profound effect. Named the 'living-room war' it made a huge impact, especially in America but also to a significant level in the United Kingdom. Vivid scenes of the fighting were shown night after night on the news bulletins. The military didn't restrict the access of the film crews to the war zones, nor did it censor coverage before transmission. The stark pictures of American soldiers dying on the battlefield, grunts setting fire to people's straw homes, napalm and Agent Orange destroying much of the countryside, all led to increasing levels of scepticism and concern about the role played by the Americans. A steadily increasing wave of opposition swept across the United Kingdom as well as in the United States.

Vietnam presented Harold Wilson, Huddersfield's homegrown British Prime Minister, with a dilemma. In 1965 and 1966, he'd come under strong pressure from President Johnson and his administration to send a token British Army contingent to Vietnam so that the President could claim it was a truly worldwide multinational force, fighting on behalf of the free world and not involving America alone. 'If you want to help us in Vietnam, send us some men and send us some folks to deal with those guerrillas,' Johnson stated clearly. Australia, New Zealand, South Korea, the Philippines and Thailand all agreed to send soldiers to fight the cause against communism. Britain, alongside France, refused. The UK was sceptical about the war and its aims, and Wilson recognised that his electorate wanted to stay clear of direct engagement. My father strongly supported that stance at the time.

But Wilson had a delicate path to tread. He wanted to maintain the close relationship between the US and Britain. Indeed, the fragile state of the pound at that time meant that he needed US economic support more than ever. The UK and the US had been joined at the hip in the battlefields of Europe 25 years earlier and then subsequently in Korea. But Wilson believed that Vietnam was different.

Along with his Labour Party Cabinet colleagues, including Foreign Secretary George Brown and Defence Secretary Denis Healey, Wilson remained steadfast in refusing to send British troops to Vietnam, to the frustration of Johnson. He cited Britain's ongoing military commitment in Malaysia and the British co-chairmanship of the 1954 Geneva Conference that had agreed to the cessation of hostilities across Vietnam and to the holding of internationally supervised elections. Wilson saw himself in the role of potential peacemaker in the conflict, helping to bring the warring sides together in pursuit of a negotiated settlement. But that brought its own tensions. Johnson once told him: 'I won't teach you how to run Malaysia and you don't tell me how to run Vietnam.'

Prime Minister Harold Wilson and President Lyndon B. Johnson meet at the White House (Courtesy LBJ Library. Photo by Yoichi Okamoto)

Although Britain historically had a close, indeed 'special', relationship with the United States, Wilson had also travelled to Moscow many times and knew Kosygin relatively well. In February 1967, while Kosygin was visiting Britain, Wilson thought he could use that unique position to help bring the two sides together to secure a solution. The initiative was called the Sunflower plan. It wasn't the first time such a third-party initiative had been attempted. The French, the Poles and the Italians had all tried exploring different options and had all failed.

But Wilson was determined to give it his best shot. The plan was focused on a Plan A and Plan B framework. Plan A involved the Americans first unilaterally stopping their bombing of the North, on the clear but private understanding of a Plan B then being enacted in which the North Vietnamese Army deployments into South Vietnam would end.

However, at the 11th hour, during Wilson's discussions with Kosygin, the Americans hardened their stance and changed the wording of the proposal, insisting that the words 'have stopped' should replace 'will stop'. The North Vietnamese ending of its deployments into the South would be a precondition before the Americans stopped their bombing.

The White House gave the North Vietnamese 12 hours to agree. The result was that the Sunflower plan collapsed, apparently on the strength of two words. The fighting continued. Wilson was furious and cabled Johnson to say the change had put him in a 'hell of a situation'. Johnson claimed the original language used had been a misunderstanding and that the planned deal was a phoney one anyway that was never going to work. One diplomat later told Wilson that if he'd pulled it off, it would have been 'the diplomatic coup of the century'.

However, under Wilson's direction, British troops never entered Vietnam and Britain never lost a single life in the war. For that, my father believes, Huddersfield's most famous son should be given the credit he deserves.

A television current-affairs programme my parents particularly enjoyed at that time in the summer of 1967 was *24 Hours* on the BBC. Broadcast at 9.55 p.m. each weekday evening, the programme was presented by Cliff Michelmore and Kenneth Allsop. It investigated and analysed the main news stories of the moment. One of the programme's outstanding journalists was 32-year-old Julian Pettifer, who'd reported from Vietnam for the BBC for the past year. Recently, he'd transferred to the US to report on the impact of the war in America. My parents were both great admirers of his work. In the 17–23 June 1967 edition of the *Radio Times*, the main radio and television listings magazine in Britain, delivered every week to the Byford home, Pettifer wrote an insightful article about his new posting to America:

> What's happening in Asia is the turbulent backcloth for the American drama or perhaps the American tragedy. Before I arrived here I knew that the Vietnam War dominated the American news media, that casualty figures filled the headlines. But I never realised to what extent the war dominates the daily lives of the people here. So much has been written about the schizophrenia of American society, of the bitter divisions caused by the war, that I hesitate to mention them here. But the fact remains that almost every report we send you from the United States will reflect in some way the reaction of the American people to the strife in Vietnam. There is on the one hand a sense of national paranoia born of frustration, a yearning to finish the war whatever that means; and on the other hand a retreat from

> thought, a collapse into clichés like 'my country right or wrong'. Having written this much I'm tempted to tear it up and start again, fearful that the impression I give is 'anti-American', that our report will be filled with condemnation and gloom. Nothing could be further from the truth. If my time in Asia taught me anything at all, it was an awareness of the vast potential for good that the United States has in the international field. My time in the United States has only confirmed that view.

I still have a clear recollection of viewing a particular television programme on the BBC in that same week. On Sunday, 25 June 1967, the day that Larry's family were informed of his death, my brother and I were allowed a special treat to stay up until 10 p.m. to watch a programme called *Our World*. It was a unique and ambitious production, a first-time-ever live international satellite link-up involving America, Britain, Mexico, Tunisia, Japan and Australia among others. The US input included a live report from Glassboro fronted by Dick McCutcheon standing outside Hollybush.

Britain's contribution to the programme was a live performance at 9 p.m. by The Beatles, direct from Abbey Road studios. The world's most famous pop group unveiled a brand-new song, primarily written by John Lennon, entitled 'All You Need is Love'. Lennon, a strong pacifist who was totally opposed to the Vietnam War, had been determined to write a universal, simple, positive message. Studio One at Abbey Road was decked out with balloons, flowers and placards proclaiming 'All You Need Is Love' in many different languages. The Fab Four sat on stools singing harmoniously 'Love is all you need'. Four hundred million people watched the broadcast around the world – at that time, the biggest television audience ever. The Beatles' new album, *Sgt Pepper's Lonely Hearts Club Band*, was number one in the UK and the US charts that week. The message of peace and love had been clearly received and understood, and the so-called 'summer of love' was well underway.

At the same time that my family and I were watching The Beatles perform, over in east Texas Larry's siblings were heading to the old white house in Short, shocked to the core, having just heard the news that their brother had been killed and that his body was on its way home.

*

I left Occupation Road and drove to Greenhead Park on the northern edge of Huddersfield town centre. Standing on Belvedere Terrace, I took in the panoramic view. The old clock cafe still there on my left, where we used to buy ice cream, and the bandstand, paddling pool and Italian gardens in the distance. Remembering Sunday afternoons when my mum pushed the pram along the boulevards as my dad kicked a football with me on the wide-open spaces of grass, I watched a grandfather flying a radio-controlled helicopter as his fascinated grandson ran around excitedly.

In June 1967, the broad avenue straight ahead was lined with magnificent elm trees right down to the park gates. Since then, Dutch elm disease had claimed them all, thereby exposing the magnificent Victorian villas at the edge of the park.

I looked behind at the huge war memorial commemorating both the First and Second World Wars. When I was nine, it seemed so foreboding, even scary. It was then the largest monument I'd ever seen. Designed by Sir Charles Nicholson, the wide, semi-circular colonnade of yellow sandstone faced on to a tall stone column of victory, topped by a shining gilt bronze sacrificial cross. I still found it extraordinarily impressive. On the column was the simple inscription:

1914 – 1918 IN MEMORIAM
1939 – 1945

Originally dedicated in 1921, it was built to commemorate the 4,500 Huddersfield men who lost their lives in the First War. The 1939–1945 inscription was added at the end of the Second War. There were no names.

I then walked slowly down the park avenue and past Fitzwilliam Street towards St Patrick's Catholic Church. I hadn't been inside for decades. In 1967, I was a young altar boy there, regularly assisting Father Magee at Mass. As I entered the main door, I recognised instantly the statue of the Sacred Heart, the bronze friezes of the Stations of the Cross and the stained-glass window above the altar with Christ's crucifixion depicted in the centre.

I lit two candles: one for Larry and all those who lost their lives in the Vietnam War; and one for all those who perished in the Second World War. I sat quietly in the pew, appreciating the tranquillity. I thought about Vietnam and Larry. It all seemed so heroic and yet so pointless. His own courage and sense of duty was beyond doubt. But for what? I still couldn't find a convincing answer.

I came back to my car and drove into the town centre. I switched on the car radio and soon realised that an extended news report had displaced the scheduled programme. Three soldiers from Huddersfield had just been killed among a team of six in the single worst attack on British troops in the Afghanistan campaign. The bulletin said they had died in Helmand province when their Warrior armoured vehicle was blown up by an improvised explosive device, an IED. Privates Jake Hartley 20, Anthony Frampton 20, and Danny Wilford 21, all from the town, were killed instantly. The family of Private Wilford had issued a statement saying how proud they were 'of their hero'. The report brought the past abruptly into the present. I pondered. Had nothing changed in the last 45 years? Had no lessons been learned from the past? Young soldiers were continuing to die in a far-off land, fighting for a controversial cause. Mourned by families, friends and colleagues, and leaving behind them a legacy of 'heroism'. And in both the United States and the United Kingdom, the nations were deeply divided about the conduct of a war thousands of miles away and its aims.

I ambled down John William Street and noticed a display in a travel agent's window:

> Vietnam: a beautiful country with an extraordinary history and a fascinating future. A country of startling contrasts from high terraced mountains to pristine coconut fringed beaches. From dynamic cities to remote summer palaces. Mesmerisingly beautiful.

I walked up the stone steps of the town's library, a place I'd visited every week in 1967 as a child, and headed to the local history section on the first floor. Scanning through microfiche tapes, I tracked down the editions of the local newspaper, the *Huddersfield Daily Examiner*, for the week beginning Monday, 19 June 1967. On the front page of the Thursday evening paper, 22 June, the death of a local councillor was highlighted alongside the wedding of a local couple. There was also a latest dispatch from Vietnam. It was a small agency report, tucked away towards the right-hand side. It looked inconsequential. The paragraph contained the following words:

> REUTERS REPORT
> Saigon: In South Vietnam, American troops reported killing at least ninety Viet Cong in two fierce clashes in the coastal regions about two hundred miles north east of Saigon.

Just 29 words. The troops referred to in that report were the Second Battalion of the Fifth Cavalry, 1st Cavalry Division (Airmobile). Among those American soldiers was a certain Larry Byford, fighting alongside his Charlie Company colleagues. The report was about the bloody battle at Van Thien that had taken place two days before his death.

Back then, my parents were avid readers of the *Huddersfield Daily Examiner* every evening. I sat back and contemplated. On that Thursday evening, they'd probably read the report in the *Daily Examiner* just as Larry was landing at the Rockpile.

Minutes later, I arrived at St George's Square in front of Huddersfield's splendid Victorian railway station entrance. A bronze statue of Harold Wilson, the town's most famous son, took pride of place in the centre. I reflected. If only Wilson had been able to secure that peace agreement in February 1967. If only President Johnson had been more flexible. If only the North Vietnamese had been more willing to compromise and been more trustworthy. If only . . .

CHAPTER 16

AN HONORABLE PEACE?

By the end of 1967, polls showed for the first time that the majority of the American people thought that their country's involvement in the Vietnam War was a mistake.

Three months later, on 31 March 1968, President Johnson stunned the nation when he announced in a live prime-time television address that he would not run for re-election later that year: 'With America's sons in the fields far away, with our hopes and the world's hopes for peace in the balance every day, I do not believe I should devote one hour or one day of my time to any personal partisan cause or to any duties other than the awesome duties of this office – the presidency of your country. Accordingly, I shall not seek, and I will not accept the nomination of my Party for another term as your President. But let everyone know, however, that a strong, confident and a vigilant America stands ready tonight to seek an honorable peace – and stands ready tonight to defend an honored cause – whatever the price, whatever the burden, whatever the sacrifice that duty may require.'

Mark Updegrove, the current Director of the LBJ Presidential Library, told me that Johnson's primary motive for stepping down was his health: 'His decision not to stand again was not brought on by the Tet Offensive. By then, he'd already more or less said to his internal advisors that because of the state of his health, the heavy weight on his heart, he felt he had to go. 1967 was where the heat really got turned up on the war. He felt the losses acutely. If you see how much he aged in office, you see how greatly he felt the individual losses. He'd seen what had happened to Roosevelt and Truman, and also to Woodrow Wilson with his stroke. He didn't want to do that to his country. The primary driver was his health.'

But the state of the war in Vietnam had eroded any realistic hope Johnson had of securing a second term. In November 1968, the Democrats lost the election and the Republican candidate, Richard Nixon, became America's 37th President. The war continued to involve American combat troops for another five years but a priority of Nixon was to reduce the American military presence and to establish peace talks. Nixon, like the majority of the American people, wanted to get out as fast as politically possible.

On 2 September 1969, Ho Chi Minh died from heart failure, aged 79. On 22 January 1973, Lyndon Johnson died after suffering a massive heart attack. He was 64. Neither man saw the war's outcome resolved.

'He did feel to the very end of his life that he was preventing World War Three from breaking out by keeping the communists in Vietnam in check,' Mark Updegrove told me. 'He'd said if you let them in your porch, then they'd be in your bedroom, then they'd be raping your wife. But there's no question Vietnam was a failure, an example of failed leadership. But one has to understand it in the context of the Cold War. There were so many nuances. But LBJ remains a towering figure in American history because of his domestic policies, his enormous courage on civil rights, in health care, the environment, the arts. It's remarkable what he left. But then there's Vietnam. He longed to be considered in the pantheon of great presidents, alongside Washington, Jefferson, Lincoln, FDR. Vietnam was the great tragedy of that era but when you look more objectively at the man's vision, he becomes a more significant figure and his domestic achievements were utterly remarkable.'

Ironically, LBJ's death came just five days before the ceasefire was signed in Paris, ending America's combat presence in Vietnam: the so-called 'Peace With Honor'. By March 1973, the last American troops had left.

Despite the ceasefire being signed, fighting soon broke out

again between North and South Vietnamese forces. On 30 April 1975, Saigon, the capital of South Vietnam, was captured by the NVA, marking the end of the Vietnam War. Within months, the formal reunification of Vietnam was established and North and South were one communist state. For the United States, that represented defeat in the longest and most divisive overseas war in its history.

The same month that Saigon fell, the new post-Watergate President, Gerald Ford, spoke at Tulane University: 'Today, America can regain the sense of pride that existed before Vietnam. But it cannot be achieved by re-fighting a war that is finished as far as America is concerned. As I see it, the time has come to look forward to an agenda for the future, to unify, to bind up the nation's wounds, and to restore its health and its optimistic self-confidence . . .

'We, of course are saddened indeed by the events in Indochina. But these events, tragic as they are, portend neither the end of the world nor of America's leadership of the world. Let me put it this way, if I might. Some tend to feel that if we don't succeed in everything, everywhere, then we have succeeded in nothing anywhere. I reject categorically such polarised thinking. We can and should help others to help themselves. But the fate of responsible men and women everywhere, in the final decision, rests in their own hands, not in ours.'

A total of 58,282 Americans, 250,000 South Vietnamese soldiers and more than 1,000,000 NVA/VC military were killed in the Vietnam War. Around a further one million North and South Vietnamese civilians are thought to have died in the conflict. On the basis of those stark statistics, the Americans lost less than 6 per cent of the total deaths suffered by its enemy . . . and yet the enemy won.

Why did the United States, then as now the world's leading superpower, lose the war in Vietnam? Was it poor military tactics? The failure of attrition and the success of enervation? Was it the President's cautious, compromised stance, unwilling to allow his military to secure victory at all cost? Was it the American military's own failure to understand the history, culture and mindset of the Vietnamese people? Was it the weakening of team spirit in the field as the drafted American soldiers were replaced on rota every year? Was it the corruption, endemic in the South Vietnamese government, that failed to win over its own people? Was it the passionate will of the North Vietnamese who pursued the goal of independence and reunification with a singular and relentless iron will? Was it the protests across America, which were the catalyst to the loss of support for the war across the country? Was it the open, honest but highly critical US media coverage? Was it the Tet offensive? Even though the North Vietnamese may not have won the individual battles, did the overall impact of Tet provide the knockdown blow enabling the North to eventually win the war?

In reality, it was a combination of all of these factors – a potent mixture of mistakes, confusion, caution, arrogance, corruption and division. Many military strategists have argued that the way the US fought the war, it was never winnable.

In retirement, General Westmoreland would emphasise how the US never lost a major battle in Vietnam but were forced to deploy a defensive strategy rather than an offensive one, which compromised his army's capability. 'I didn't have the political authority to extend the battlefield,' he said. He liked to make reference to the words of Sun Tzu, the old Chinese warrior-philosopher from 2,500 years ago, to explain what happened to the United States in Vietnam: '*Break the will of the enemy to fight and you accomplish the true objective of war. Cover with ridicule the enemy's tradition. Exploit and aggravate the inherent frictions within the enemy country.*'

I was also struck by the words of Ken Burington, the Tall Comanche archivist, who was a 20-year-old volunteer when he arrived in the field with Charlie Company in June 1967, joining the Second Platoon a week before Larry died. He told me: 'The war was not well managed at a senior level. We had an effective army but Westmoreland won his reputation in logistics and McNamara had come in from the Ford Motor Company. He dominated the generals. If you fight a war, it should be fought to win or you're wasting your own men's lives. I used to have a T-shirt saying: "Participant South East Asia War Games: Second Place". That's my feeling.

'We kept Russia out of Cam Ranh Bay. They didn't have a Pacific presence. If they'd got a deep-water port there, that would have complicated things. People in the Philippines and elsewhere are grateful about the domino theory and not spreading communism further.

'For us it was our longest war. For them it was their shortest. You have to look at history. It was worth it. Look at Vietnam today. We set the hardcore communists back. What we did was establish the legitimacy of a lot more relaxed society down South to the old grey men from the North who were unable to impose their will on the South. Vietnam today is very different to how it could have been. It could have been like Albania.' He went on: ''67 was the turning point. There were more than 500,000 Americans there. After that, there was a holding action to keep the campuses back at home stable. The middle classes turned against the war. Too many sons were being lost without a legitimate return. The goal kept moving. The sacrifice became too expensive. They became disillusioned and support evaporated such that it was time to wave goodbye and come home.'

The more I read, listened and reflected, the more I realised that the summer of 1967 had been a hugely important turning point in the war: the time the North Vietnamese gave the go-ahead to plan for the Tet Offensive; the time President Johnson recognised he was unable to secure either the crossover point or a viable political settlement in the immediate future; the time America's divisions broke out significantly on to the streets across the country. It was then, in effect, that the seeds of the US defeat were planted. And it was then that the Byford family from Short, Texas, lost their beloved son and brother.

I decided to track down 'four wise men' who were intimately involved with the war at that time to hear their reflections, forty-five years on. First I contacted Lord Healey, aged 94, for his thoughts. Between 1964 and 1970, he was a member of Harold Wilson's Cabinet, serving as Defence Secretary throughout that Labour government and, therefore, hugely involved in shaping Britain's stance on Vietnam.

'It was a fine balance. We didn't want to put troops ourselves in there but the price was not to oppose the US policy itself. But I told McNamara personally that it was a disaster,' Healey told me in a brief conversation on the phone from his home in Sussex. 'We were strongly pressed by the President to put troops there but we said they were fighting it in a way that would be a disaster for them. We were asked to intervene but Wilson had no intention to take part and he was absolutely right. No one can deny that it damaged the US reputation across the world so badly because they lost it. They lost the war with millions of casualties. I never thought they'd win it. Bombing makes more enemies than it kills and that proved to be the case. It was a tragedy. The American soldiers did their duty doing a job their government told them to do. But it was a disaster from start to finish.'

He didn't want to speak any more.

'Read my book, *The Time Of My Life*. It's all in there. I have nothing to add.'

I turned to page 225 of his memoirs:

> My next stop was the scene of the greatest political tragedy and military debacle suffered by the United States in its whole history – Vietnam . . .
> In the event, the United States got the worst of both worlds – the odium which its military methods were bound to attract, plus the humiliation of ultimate defeat.

Healey's view could not have been clearer.

Harry Middleton joined the White House staff back in 1967 as a speechwriter to President Johnson. He helped craft many of Johnson's speeches during his final months in office, including those setting out the Administration's policies on Vietnam. He told me from his home in Austin, Texas, what it felt like in the White House at that time: 'The President was as much a Cold War warrior as Kennedy and Eisenhower before him. There's no question about that. He believed in the policy that had been followed from Truman: to check the advance of communism. Early in his presidency, he was greatly concerned about being involved in a land war in Asia. He was worried about what he was getting the country into. But he felt strongly too about the need to stand up against the aggression of the Soviet Union. His decision to sanction ground troops was in effect an Americanisation of the war,' he explained.

'When Secretary of State Dean Rusk said that if we do not do this we are running the risk of World War Three, it had a profound effect on the President. We'd been through World War Two, through appeasement. When Rusk said that, it sent a chill through the President. In my view, that was the determining factor. He saw no way out. No way back. He could not relinquish the role he'd assumed of using military force to stop what he saw as the aggression of the Soviet Union in South-East Asia.

'I was very much a Cold War warrior at that time too. I believed the policy was the correct one. I was in full agreement on it. Looking back now, I agree the summer of 1967 was the turning point. I don't doubt that. But of course I do not remember us thinking that at the time. Nor was there any indication when I was working with him on his memoirs that the President thought it was the turning point.'

When Lyndon Johnson left office, Harry Middleton spent many hours with LBJ at his ranch in Texas working on the President's memoirs, *The Vantage Point*. He was then invited by Johnson to be the first Director of the LBJ Presidential Library and Museum at the University of Texas in Austin, a role he fulfilled for more than 20 years.

'The President never expressed any kind of feeling that the policy was wrong. In the LBJ ranch, when we were working on his memoirs, he'd go over the policy over and over again and say: "What could we have done differently?" He never ever said we were wrong,' he told me. 'I changed my own mind in the course of the succeeding years when it became clear that all of Vietnam was communist but we were not threatened. The domino theory hadn't worked. Little by little I realised the policy had been wrong all along but that was in retrospect. I felt very sad for President Johnson. I had the feeling if any of us, if some of us, had had that conviction at the time, we could have turned him around. That, of course, was totally unrealistic.'

I asked Harry Middleton about the thousands of American losses that had been suffered while LBJ was in office.

'He agonised over every death, every loss. They weighed very heavily on him. Every one. He never accepted them simply as a price that had to be paid. They all personally were a real pain to him.'

Now 90 years old, Harry Middleton still lectures at the university about the Johnson years.

'The legacy of Vietnam has disordered, clouded what should be his soaring legacy domestically. They [his years in office] were a transformation in American life. They changed the way we live for the better and for ever. I hope that will be understood in history. I'm hopeful, little by little, that the tragedy of Vietnam will recede in importance in history. I think it's just possible that his domestic achievements will be paramount.'

Stanley Karnow, the Pulitzer Prize-winning author and historian, covered South-East Asia as a foreign correspondent from 1959 to 1974. He wrote throughout the entire duration of the Vietnam War for *Time*, *Life* and the *Washington Post* as well as reporting on *NBC News*. He was in Vietnam when the first two Americans named on The Wall were killed in July 1959. At the end of the war, he wrote the definitive history of the conflict: *Vietnam: A History*, which was published in 1983 and sold more than a million copies. I went to meet him in a nursing home in Potomac, just outside Washington DC, where he was recovering from pneumonia. He launched immediately into a well-worn anecdote: 'The commanding general in Afghanistan, General McChrystal, called me up on the telephone from Kabul some years back and he said, "What did we learn in Vietnam that we can use in Afghanistan?" and I said to him, "What we learnt was that we should never have been there in the first place." The phone conversation pretty much ended right there and then.'

Stanley Karnow, 87 years old, was full of stories, revelations and insights about his time in Vietnam 50 years ago.

'Vietnam was a futile adventure for the United States. You have all this stuff about how all the journalists were against the war. That was nonsense. What they disagreed with was the way the war was being conducted. The South Vietnamese were ill equipped to deal with guerrilla warfare. The idea Walter Cronkite changed the nation's attitude to the war after Tet was baloney. In fact, by the fall of '67 more people thought the war was a mistake.'

He took a sip of water from a straw. I noticed that on his bedcover lay the *Washington Post*. The crossword had been completed. This was a man who loved words and who, I soon discovered, was not afraid to express his opinions forcefully.

'The key mistake was getting involved in the first place. It was futile. Stupid. World War Two, the Korean War, they were different. When you really come down to it, more than 80 per cent of the American public today still think the war was a mistake. It will never go away. It will go on forever, people still debating Vietnam. Hawks, revisionists saying how they could have won it. That's mythology. It was a disaster.'

I told him about my experience at The Wall. He said he'd visited it many times since it was first built.

'When the people look at The Wall, they don't know what to make of it. It's very touching. Very simple. Very moving.'

Recognising his physical frailty, I was conscious not to outstay my welcome. As we said our farewells, he reflected: 'People say my book is the definitive work but I'm always learning about the war.'

Three months later, Stanley Karnow died.

The BBC correspondent Julian Pettifer reported from Vietnam throughout 1966 and from the home front in the United States during 1967, giving him a unique opportunity to see the war from both angles. In 1968, he received the British Academy of Film and Television Arts (BAFTA) Reporter of the Year award for his coverage of Vietnam. In Britain, his name remains synonymous with the reporting of the war. I went to west London, to visit him in his elegant basement flat filled with artefacts and art from his travels around the world.

'Wars are not won by ideology. Nationalism is much more important,' he told me. 'You'll never win a war where ideology is pursued over nationality. They were never going to win it. They couldn't win it. Moreover, you cannot win a war with a conscript army. Those poor guys out there in Vietnam, their heart wasn't in it. They didn't know what they were fighting for. The one thing they wanted to do was serve the year, get through it and get home.'

He took a sip of his tea as he went on reflecting: 'The summer of 1967 was the turning point in my view. I knew then that the Americans were not able to stay there and they couldn't win it politically or on the battlefield.

'The Vietnam War means great sadness to me – despair. It was a war that shouldn't have happened and lots of innocent people died for no reason. They were never going to win it. I'd hoped from the Vietnam experience that America could have learnt the lesson but they haven't with Iraq and Afghanistan. I was totally appalled by that; I was disgusted. If those young men on The Wall had died and a lesson had been learnt from their sacrifice, then I would feel something less than despair, but nothing has been learnt. You shouldn't get involved in foreign wars unless there's a clear objective and that's not been the case.'

Pettifer is now 77 years of age but his mind is still laser sharp and his deep feelings about the war have not diminished at all. He took hold of my arm.

'It's the biggest thing professionally that has affected my life, more than anything. It was so unnecessary. People should not have died. It should not have happened. The domino theory – what absolute nonsense. No one was brave enough to say, "Let's get out of it." No one dared. They were scared of betraying that macho culture. It angers me. So much suffering. So much hurt. For so little reason.'

He shook his head mournfully and, from his armchair, stared into the distance, silent, spent.

CHAPTER 17

TO WATERMELON HILL

I wanted to recreate Larry's experience of Vietnam as far as I could. I knew that I needed to go there in May or June, when I would feel the same heat, see the same landscapes, experience the same colours and detect the same smells of early summer.

Several of Larry's colleagues had told me about the wall of heat that hit them as they stepped out of the plane. Crossing the tarmac at Ho Chi Minh City's Tan Son Nhat airport in 80 per cent humidity, I soon understood exactly what they meant. The air was a heavy, stifling blanket that made breathing difficult and caused sweat to stream from every pore, drenching my clothing within seconds. It was to become an all-too-familiar sensation in the days to come.

Exactly 45 years after Larry Byford, I'd landed in the Socialist Republic of Vietnam, the 13th most populous country on the planet with 90 million people. His arrival must have been full of trepidation and fear but, in contrast, I felt excited and energised. I'd read so much about the place. Now, at last, I could experience it for myself.

As I was about to discover, Vietnam is a country of contrasts. The intense bustle, energy and vibrancy of Saigon, renamed Ho Chi Minh City since reunification, contrasts starkly with the sedate, gentle, traditional rural life of the Binh Dinh countryside. There's no one Vietnam, in the same way as there's no one United States or Great Britain. It's a country rich in diversity.

But there is one glue that binds the whole country together:

the Communist Party. It remains firmly in control and continues to have a monopoly on political power within a one-party state. The press, the flow of information and national and local decision making all come under its grip. Loyalty to the Party remains paramount.

At the end of the war, when North and South became one, the Communist Party propaganda machine promised a reunified country of stability and prosperity. But for almost two decades it was a place inflicted with desperate poverty and strife. Thousands of South Vietnamese were executed. Hundreds of thousands were sent off to re-education camps. The economic prospects of the country looked grim. The Leninist collectivism model, a Soviet-style state-controlled central-planning system, showed itself to be utterly inefficient and Vietnam collapsed into a dead economy with famine just around the corner.

But in the late 1980s and '90s, the Communist Party in Vietnam developed a new economic model of so-called socially responsible capitalism, whereby the Party remained in firm control but opened up the country to free enterprise and the market. It was called 'Doi Moi', meaning renewal, restoration. This change from a command economy to competition was similar to the revolutionary recipe that was being introduced at the same time by Deng Xiaoping in China.

Consequently, the economy took off. Liberalising the regulatory framework, selling stakes in publicly owned companies and opening up trade generated a remarkable average GDP growth rate of 7.5 per cent over a ten-year period. In 1994, the United States lifted its economic embargo. By 2006, Vietnam was hosting the Asia Pacific summit, welcoming Presidents Bush, Putin and Hu to Hanoi. By 2007, it was a member of the World Trade Organisation and the following year it became a non-permanent member of the United Nations Security Council. In the past decade, it has enjoyed one of the fastest-growing economies in the world. Nearly all children now attend primary school and literacy levels are high. English is growing rapidly in the cities as a key language.

Vietnam is still a major producer of rice, maize, peanuts and coffee. Its fishing industry still plays a vital part in feeding its own people. But it's also a place that's moving on and moving up. A growing exporter of oil, textiles, garments, shoes and wooden furniture, its leading export market today is, ironically, the United States. Moreover, the former enemy is crucial in generating inward investment too. The US corporate giant Intel recently invested a billion dollars building a leading-edge microchip plant on the outskirts of the city in Saigon High Tech Park. It's Intel's largest facility in the world. The unique blend of a thriving market economy with omnipresent socialist oversight is based on the Communist Party still remaining firmly in control.

Communist Party banners in Ho Chi Minh City, 2012

As I walked the streets of Ho Chi Minh City, that potent mixture of market capitalism with the Party's overall control was clear to see: the frenetic energy of the fish and poultry stalls in Ben Thanh market; the vibrancy of the younger generation, texting and surfing on their mobile phones; the serenity of the new middle class as they performed graceful t'ai chi exercises in Tao Dan park; new fashion houses in Dong Khoi Street with the same high-end brands seen on Seventh Avenue in New York or along Avenue Montaigne in Paris; and street traders on every corner hustling for business. At the same time, red banners were displayed everywhere, emblazoned with the hammer and sickle, the Vietnamese Star and the face of Uncle Ho. One enormous billboard, with a smiling Ho Chi Minh surrounded by lotus flowers, doves and stars, reminded the people that it was one hundred and twenty-two years since his birth. It was a remarkable sight: two political and economic philosophies merging together in a new order.

I passed the main gates to the Reunification Palace. On 30 April 1975, a tank had crashed through the entrance where I was standing and a soldier raced through to what was then the Independence Palace and hoisted the Viet Cong flag above the roof. At that moment, the Vietnam War, the American War, call it what you will, was over. A huge banner hanging next to me declared: '37 years. 30/4 1975–2012' with an image of that very tank pushing through the gates. The war may be history but one is never far away from it on the streets of central Saigon.

Although the economic prospects of Vietnam have greatly improved, the rapid growth has generated fresh challenges for the Party and the country. There's a widening disparity of wealth between city and country dwellers, and the migration from countryside to cities has put a huge strain on infrastructure and sanitation. When I arrived, the country was experiencing inflation of 20 per cent. Property prices were falling in the big cities and many nascent businesses were going bankrupt as the growth rate fell from 7.5 per cent to 6 per cent and was forecast to fall further. The state-owned enterprises are still run poorly and have a reputation for corruption. Whilst the big cities may be an oasis for smart phones, broadband and modern lifestyles, the countryside remains very much third world, with the majority of workers barely able to scratch a basic living.

The impressive growth rates of recent times, of course, began from a very low economic base. The country as a whole still remains comparatively poor in the world economic order. However, on present trends, Vietnam could reach 70 per cent of the UK's GDP by 2050. And in contrast to the stagnant state of the US and UK economies, Vietnam's current expansion is nothing less than phenomenal.

When I checked in at a hotel in the centre of Ho Chi Minh City for an overnight stay, I noticed that the newspaper rack next to the reception desk displayed a number of Vietnamese English-language newspapers, with all of the headlines reflecting the spirit of the age: 'VN Sees 22% Rise In Exports', 'Return To High Growth After Lull', 'Market Forces Should Prevail', 'European Factories Falter, Asia Flourishes', 'UK Faces Long Slump As Crisis Hits Factories'. On one of them, I noticed a photograph of Britain's Foreign Secretary, William Hague, meeting Vietnam's Prime Minister, Nguyen Tan Dung. The accompanying caption highlighted how ties were being strengthened between the two countries as tourism and education initiatives were to be developed. It seems that today Vietnam is a place with which other countries want to establish firm connections. The challenge for the Communist Party is to maintain that growth of its economy and open up the country further, without letting go of its power.

I'd been in many lively cities around the world – Cairo, Delhi, Beijing, Nairobi, Sao Paulo, New York – but as I walked outside the hotel nothing prepared me for this melting pot of commerce and human chaos. The streets of Ho Chi Minh have an electric atmosphere. They bustle with vitality, providing a riot of colour and a cacophony of noise. Streams of motorbikes and scooters flow in chaotic disarray down every artery, so that crossing the road is a near-death experience. I felt as if I were walking out onto a Formula One Grand Prix track in the middle of a race, dodging and swerving as horns, bells and hooters blasted as one in Saigon harmony.

I broke away from the chaos of the main thoroughfares and made my way through the relatively tranquil back streets to the reflective surroundings of the War Remnants Museum on Vo Van Tan Road. As I did so, I thought about the millions of Vietnamese killed in the war as well as the family members who are still mourning their loved ones. I worked out that if a wall was constructed in Hanoi with the names of the North Vietnamese soldiers killed in the war, it would be twenty times bigger than the one in Washington. And that's without the South Vietnamese casualties and all the civilians across both North and South who also perished.

It became clear almost immediately that this was no ordinary military museum but rather a propaganda collection, proclaiming the evils of 'the American invasion'. Established six months after Saigon fell in 1975, it openly declares that its aim is to exhibit '*the remnant proofs of Vietnam war crimes and their consequences*'. It felt right and proper that I saw the war from the perspective of the Vietnamese Communist Party and engaged with its narrative at first hand. Over 50 per cent of the population of Vietnam were born after the war, so do not have any memory of it. The museum fills in the 'official gaps' for the half a million people who visit each year. Captured Huey and Chinook helicopters are proudly displayed on the forecourt together with a variety of American guns and ordnance. An opening caption thanks: '*the communist parties and working class of the countries in the world together with peace loving countries and progressive human beings for their whole hearted support for our people's patriotic resistance against the US and our national salvation*'.

Photographs of American anti-war protesters burning themselves in front of the UN HQ in New York and the Pentagon in Washington were placed prominently on an entrance wall.

I walked into the first room, which was entitled 'Aggression War Crimes', and was struck immediately by how so many artefacts and displays focused on the 1st Cavalry Division. Large black-and-white photographs showed villagers being rounded up for interrogation; a little girl pleading with soldiers not to kill her father; and a peasant 'subjected to tortures'. A graphic photo depicted a soldier kicking the head of a man lying on the ground with the caption: '*GIs from the 1st Cavalry Division torturing a peasant in Binh Dinh Province*'. Another showed three US soldiers holding down a man and pouring a bottle of water over his face with the accompanying words: '*They decide on a water torture. A rag is placed over the man's face and water is poured on it, making breathing impossible. Members of the 1st Air Cavalry use water torture on a prisoner.*'

And so it went on. The next showed women and children apparently being frogmarched to a waiting Huey with the caption: '*GIs from the 1st Cavalry Division round up inhabitants, drive them out of their homes, and put them aboard helicopters, Binh Dinh province 1967.*'

A particularly memorable image was of a GI from the 25th Infantry Division holding the mutilated corpse of a 'liberation soldier'. I breathed in deeply, shocked to the core at the brutality of the photograph: probably the most violent image I'd seen in my life. Another photo showed an injured NVA soldier: '*being led from a bunker by soldiers of US First Cav. This soldier held up the US advance for one hour with machine gun fire from his position. He was wounded and captured. "If he was in the American army," said US Army Colonel John Moore at the time, "I would recommend him for a medal."*'

Inside a glass cabinet, the familiar gold and black 1st Cavalry Division insignia patch was prominently displayed. Next to it, a photograph of 16 Hueys flying in formation over the Kim Son valley in Binh Dinh was labelled with the words: '*the crackest unit of the US Army with 16,000 men. Its casualties totalled 30,000.*'

Another presentation cabinet and more photographs of American doom, despair and carnage matched by the courage, passion of North Vietnamese soldiers and the fear and innocence of the Vietnamese people. The bias was blatant but powerful all the same: '*Wounded and weary American soldiers lie in the grit of a sandy ditch. Two companies of the First Air Cavalry Division and Viet Cong-North Vietnamese forces had battled for over 24 hours across paddies and coastal villages.*'

A famous Dana Stone image taken for the UPI press agency in 1966 was described as: '*Bong Son Binh Dinh: Soldiers of the US First Air Cavalry Division point their weapons at Vietnamese villagers whom they flushed from the brush along the riverbank.*'

One particularly distressing display was in the room dedicated to 'Agent Orange Aftermath In The US Aggressive War In Vietnam'. A disturbing photo of Nguyen Van Dam, born in 1979 with severe physical disabilities, was due, according to the caption, to Agent Orange as: '*toxic rains poured down continuously. 44 million litres of Agent Orange chemical affected between 2.1 and 4.8 million Vietnamese people.*'

Another panel reminded the visitor that landmines and unexploded ordnance still kill thousands across Vietnam every year.

I went outside and sat in the garden. The museum had given me plenty of food for thought. I had always realised, of course, that there are at least two sides to every conflict. But this was the first time I had been faced with the official Vietnamese perspective on the war. It didn't really matter whose side, if any, I was on. If I looked past the propaganda, it was clear that atrocities had been carried out by both sides. The effect of the display highlighted to me the fact that all wars involve unimaginable brutality and devastating damage to land, to individuals, and to humanity itself.

'That was then, this is now' is today's official Party line. Remember and cherish 'Victory, Independence, Liberation'. But Vietnam's priority for the future, the country's leaders emphasise, must be to develop a mutually beneficial relationship between itself and the United States based on respect, peace and trade. The US, too, is increasingly looking ahead rather than remembering the past. President Clinton struck a powerful note when he declared on his historic visit to Hanoi back in 2000: 'The histories of our two nations are deeply intertwined in ways that are both a source of pain for generations that came before and a source of promise for generations to come.'

There was one other place I wanted to visit in Ho Chi Minh City: the impressive, towering neo-Romanesque Notre Dame Roman Catholic Cathedral, built more than a hundred years ago at a time of French colonialism. Most Vietnamese today believe in the worshipping of ancestors. Confucianism, Taoism, Buddhism and Christianity are the main formal religions. Catholicism, with six million members, is a significant but minority religion, rooted in the south. There's a kind of uneasy truce, a mutual tolerance that enables the Catholic Church to function inside the Communist state. The Vatican and the Party each believe they are ultimately in control of the Church's presence in Vietnam. Each is suspicious of the other but tolerant in the interests of harmony and stability.

Within the sacred atmosphere of the Basilica, as Mass was being held, the humidity was so intense that my shirt was soon soaking wet. I lit a candle for all who had suffered in the Vietnam War: North and South, Vietnamese and American. Anyone and everyone who had died, lost loved ones or suffered terrible physical or mental injury.

*

After an hour's flight, as I came in to land at Phu Cat airport in Binh Dinh, I looked out of the window and marvelled at the breathtaking beauty of the landscape. Mountain tops with rugged ridges covered in verdant forestation gave way to the lush vegetation of the patchwork of paddy fields on the coastal plains, and in the distance yellow sandy beaches traced the contours of the coastline, beyond which lay a sparkling mass of ocean. This was the same spectacular view that Larry would have seen day after day as the swarm of Hueys flew over the same terrain, heading for the next combat assault.

To my amazement, the weather on landing was even warmer than in Ho Chi Minh City. The temperature was approaching 100° Fahrenheit, with no prospect of rain for months; the four-month monsoon season would not arrive until September.

Binh Dinh, a narrow province set between the central highlands and the South China Sea, is steeped in history. A former Champa stronghold from the tenth to the fifteenth centuries, the area still has the Cham mark stamped on the landscape in the form of distinctive red-stone temple towers. Ferocious battles, sieges and rebellions featured in the region for centuries as foes fought to secure power, independence or survival. Today, the population consists of four main ethnic groups: the Kinh, Ba Na, H're and Cham. It remains an internationally renowned centre for martial arts, especially kung fu. Agriculture and fishing still underpin the local economy and life remains basic and poor.

The simple lifestyle of the Binh Dinh countryside could not be more of a contrast to the frenetic boulevards of Ho Chi Minh City. Few tourists head there: it's well away from the historic cultural centres of Hue and Hoi An to the north, and off the radar for the backpackers and sun lovers heading for the vitality of Nha Trang to the south. American and Australian entrepreneurs are looking to develop some of the most stunning cave inlets as spa resorts but poor infrastructure is a major barrier to serious development. Indeed, away from the busy provincial capital of Quy Nhon and the small towns inland that cling to the route of Highway One – the country's main thoroughfare linking north and south – most of the Binh Dinh countryside has remained pretty much unchanged since the war.

There have been some improvements. The straw hootches have been upgraded to basic concrete homes, and dust tracks have been replaced with potholed tarmac, single-lane roads. Nearly all villages and hamlets have been provided with electricity in the past decade, thanks to the 'Doi Moi' economic renewal programme, and new irrigation channels have transformed the supply of water to the fields. But the age-old familiar sights remain: workers tend their rice crops, bent almost double; fishermen mend their nets on the quaysides and lake shores; and cows and goats roam freely along dusty tracks. Everywhere, cyclists and moped riders display extraordinary skills, in age-old style, balancing huge, unwieldy loads of rice, salt and watermelons as they travel from village to market.

The countryside is fecund and lush: coconuts, mangoes and bananas grow in abundance and the flowers – red lotus, yellow sunflower and purple bougainvillea – are startlingly vibrant. The pace of life in Binh Dinh continues to be gentle and steady, grandparents, parents and children often working the land side by side in peaceful harmony. Several generations live under the same roof and the old people are revered for their experience and wisdom. Everyone has a smile and bows deferentially, although, to my amusement, many chuckled at my full frame and 6 ft 3 in. height as they are nearly all slim and comparatively small. 'Giant!' one exclaimed.

The daily routine for the labourers is shaped by sunrise and sunset. One woman told me she's up at 5 a.m. every day. A cooked meal of traditional pho – rice noodles – with cucumber and some watermelon gets her set for the morning. By 6 a.m. she's working in the fields and at 11 a.m. she has to stop because of the heat. She takes lunch at 12 p.m.: green bean noodles or a stew of shrimp, crab or cuttlefish; sleeps between 1 p.m. and 3 p.m. and then returns to work. Leaving the fields at 6 p.m., she has a meal at 7 p.m. and is asleep in bed by 9 p.m. If it's market day, she gets up at 4 a.m. to get her produce ready to sell in the nearest town.

Today, nothing feels as far removed from a war zone as the beauty, stillness and slow pace of the Binh Dinh countryside. It makes the events of half a century ago all the more tragic. I happened across several war memorials that lie dotted around the landscape. Some are huge and ostentatious, clearly funded by the Communist Party. Most are simple, modest affairs set in the village centres and are all the more powerful and poignant for that. One, for example, was a simple wall on which was inscribed: 'To Those Who Were Lost Fighting For The Cause'.

My base was the port of Quy Nhon, from where I picked up my navigator and translator, 33-year-old Tong Duy Phuoc. An English graduate from the local university, he is married and has two young children. Phuoc was enthused by my journey and determined to help in any way possible. His knowledge of the local environment, his cultural awareness and sensitivity as well as his excellent command of languages made him an invaluable colleague. He appreciated that I was travelling as a tourist and agreed to roam the area with me in search of Larry's story.

For the next five days, I followed my mapped-out itinerary, accompanied by Phuoc. A six-hour round trip west along Highway 19, climbing up the highlands into the Gia Lai province, took us to the present day An Khe military base. I peered through the security fence at the remnants of the old Camp Radcliff barracks, the first place Larry had stayed after being assigned to the 1st Cavalry Division back in April 1967. The perimeter fence was as near as I could get and I was anxious not to arouse suspicion. I could see the Hon Tan mountain in the distance with a large bare patch on its forward slope where the huge 1st Cavalry insignia had once been painted.

Next, we headed down to the Binh Dinh coastal plain, to the

Phu My district, and the Bong Son beaches. First we reached the Dam Tra O Lake. I watched the local fishermen tend their nets in the fading light of the afternoon, ready to trawl for their daily catch of fish, crabs, shrimps and shellfish, and marvelled at the timelessness of the scene that had been played out every day for hundreds of years or more. Forty-five years ago, this beautiful, tranquil setting had been shockingly disrupted by American and NVA soldiers, engaged in ferocious battle on the lake shore. With Phuoc translating, I fell into conversation with a fisherman from Phu Ninh who told me he makes the equivalent of $3 a day if he's lucky. In 1967, he was 20 years old, and remembered the battles clearly. He pointed to the sky as he described seeing American helicopters hovering above, and indicated where the tanks had pounded through the reed beds. He recalled how he and his family fled to safety to the nearby town of Phu My, before returning home three days later. Then he gestured in the direction of the Cay Giep or 'Giep tree' mountains, which were visible from where we were standing, and told me that tigers and bears used to live there before they were killed off by the war and hunters.

Walking in the nearby sleepy hamlet of An Hoa, I read a sign above the road, which Phuoc translated: '*Nothing More Important Than Independence. This Whole Village Unites Together.*'

A couple of miles further on and I was in An Quang, another hamlet that Larry had once helped to cordon off ready for another Third Platoon search mission. The sign there stated: '*Here On 28th–30th June 1967, The Year Of The Goat, American And South Vietnamese Soldiers Killed 154 VC Soldiers and General Villagers*'.

People in the area spoke about the 'puppet soldiers of the South', the success of the 'Resistance War against the American invaders', and the need to continue 'to follow the teachings of the great Uncle Ho'. Some who were children back then remembered being given candy by the American soldiers. One said: 'Some were pleasant, some were nasty.' But all repeated the same mantra: 'It was a long time ago. Time has moved on', and claimed that they didn't bear grudges.

One man living just over the district borderline in Hoai Nhon showed me the abandoned American ordnance left on his land that he still kept as a souvenir. Then he took me to a discreet bush area where he removed bracken and tangled branches to reveal the entrance to an old tunnel where, according to him, the locals had hidden members of the VC, protected by his own family.

When I arrived at Lo Dieu, I searched for any sight of a human presence but discovered that the spotless beach was completely deserted. I walked down to the edge of the sea and dabbled my hands in the water as the waves broke on the shoreline. I looked all around me and thought again about those words Larry wrote in that letter back home:

> The mountains are real pretty. We went swimming in the South China Sea. I have a pretty good tan. It sure gets hot over here. We eat bananas and drink coconut milk all the time.

The words sounded like a diary entry from a backpacker's trip rather than a despatch from a war zone. But I could now see what he meant. Indeed, a later scene at Van Thien could have been the cover shot for a tourist guidebook to Vietnam. Elderly women crouched down in paddy dykes tending their crops, dressed in conical hats and black labour suits; others gingerly lifted shoulder poles from which hung huge sacks of produce. It was hard to believe that this was the same place where carnage had scarred the landscape less than half a century ago.

Walking along the Bong Son and Lo Dieu beaches, I tried to imagine the conditions experienced by Larry and his unit. I trudged in the extreme heat of the afternoon sun, through the heavy, powdery sand to gauge its texture; to experience the level of exertion required when walking through it; to register the strain when scrambling up the towering sand dunes that sat back from the shoreline. I found the whole experience utterly exhausting. I consider myself to be quite fit, but within a few minutes my legs felt like jelly and my clothes were soaking with perspiration. To my relief, I had an endless supply of cold fresh water in the car and I wasn't carrying anything other than a camera, whereas I was acutely aware that Larry would have been humping a 50-lb pack on his back and had two pitifully small canisters of water to last him all day.

Each of the places I had visited in Vietnam so far had played an important part in Larry's military life. Seeing them for myself had helped me to imagine him being there; to experience some of the conditions in which he lived; to meet some of the local people; and to witness the extraordinary country for myself. They had enabled me to start to put flesh on the bones of this part of his story. But in reality, I knew that they were just a build-up: early paragraphs and chapters that were leading with a sense of inevitability to the ultimate destination. I was yet to arrive at that place I wanted to see above all others. The place I'd travelled more than 8,000 miles to reach. The place where it had all happened. The Rockpile.

*

Travelling along the minor coastal road from Quy Nhon was an adventure in itself. The narrow road was at times almost completely submerged in deep, drifting sand, making the route almost impassable. When the road was clear of debris, we were faced with the challenge of negotiating our way around huge potholes at regular intervals.

At one time, we turned a corner to be faced with a whole company of the Vietnamese Army. More than 200 young men wearing green fatigues and black boots marched in unison, many in single file, others in pairs. We calculated the length of the phalanx to be at least a mile. They were on a forced-march exercise.

All were carrying packs and rifles; some were heaving along the company's gear and rations on shoulder poles. The heat was utterly oppressive yet still they kept going. I looked at their faces. All seemed determined, concentrated, purposeful. 'No photos, no photos,' Phuoc warned anxiously.

Soon we'd overtaken them and were heading towards the fishing village of Tan Phung, located just south of the Rockpile. The village was clearly poor. Scores of small circular fishing boats bobbed up and down in the waters of the wide bay. Nets and fishing pots had been laid out on the beach. Several fishermen were sleeping under the shade of two trees by the water's edge and one hung suspended between two shrubs in a makeshift hammock. Children playing on the beach were dressed in a variety of well-worn and torn European soccer shirts, probably sent to the area by charities: Manchester United, Chelsea, Real Madrid, Barcelona and Bayern Munich.

The fisherman woke up and jumped out of his hammock. Seeing that I was a stranger, he started to talk to me, with Phuoc interpreting. He told me that he had been 14 years old in 1967 and remembered the American helicopters hovering above the nearby hill. He pointed northwards.

'The soldiers ran up the hill there,' he said. 'There were lots of VC and Vietnamese Army. We knew they were there. Everyone knew.'

We tried to walk round the beach to the central part of the Rockpile but the incoming tide prevented us from making progress. Instead, we made our way north up a narrow dusty track out of the village. Ken Burington had sent me the military reference details for the Rockpile's location taken from the official US Army charts: Map 6937-3, Coordinates 055747. He had also translated that reference to 14 14 30 50 North and 109 11 31 11 East in longitude and latitude terms. I got out my GPS and followed the course. We were very close. We came to a recently built cemetery at the foot of a hill. The slopes, facing inland, were filled with boulders and big rocks. I knew we were at the western foot of the Rockpile. But this was inland. I understood from Don Jensen and Mike Martin's testimonies that the actual cave I was searching for looked out to sea. We got back in the car and headed north to the hamlet of My An. A resident there told us how he remembered the VC regularly hiding in the local village.

'Two to three were in each group,' Phuoc translated. 'They'd come out at night. They'd come from the north and the west, from the mountains, or they'd land by boat. We'd hide them.'

He directed us along a remote single-track road, newly constructed, running alongside the beach. As we travelled along I realised this must have been the landing point for Charlie Company back on Thursday, 22 June. They'd walked south along the sand from there. To the left of the road, the beach was no longer in existence. It was now an industrial shrimp farm: a series of constructed pools, with electrically powered fans pumping oxygen into the water. To the right were sand dunes strengthened by marram grass and specially planted 'duong trees', small green bush-like conifers.

Suddenly, it came into view. It was about a mile away but I recognised it immediately from the photos sent by Ken Burington: a long slab of granite, its slopes strewn with huge boulders, stretching down to the edge of the sea. It was unmistakable. I knew we had found the Rockpile.

Although it looked completely black from a distance, close up the boulders were different shades of grey and were interspersed with dark-green grass. I could understand why Don Jensen had described the rocks as big as houses. Some of them truly were. One huge round boulder sat precipitously at the top of the cliff. It looked as though it would fall into the sea at any moment. I started to scramble up the rocks. The going was hard and I made slow progress. Squeezing through the boulders, I reached a grassy slope. The place was so isolated and peaceful, populated by butterflies, dragonflies and sea birds. The slopes were steep and in some places fell vertically into the sea. I had to be careful. I couldn't see any caves. I checked the temperature. Four o'clock in the afternoon and it was more than 100° Fahrenheit.

Lan at the Rockpile, 2012

I returned to Phuoc at the base of the rocks, where I noticed a group of women working at a nearby shrimp farm. We got talking. One of the women was wearing a hat and a cloth that completely covered her face, shielding her from the intense sun. She untied the mask to reveal a warm, friendly face. I towered over her tiny frame, so I crouched down to make her feel less intimidated. She was called Lan, lived locally and was the mother of four children. She smiled continuously. I asked her when she was born. April 1967, she replied. Had she lived in the local area all her life? Yes, came the reply. She went on to tell me how her father had told her that, soon after she was born, there was fighting on the hill and that people had been killed up by the boulders. She gestured in the direction of the rocks. I asked her to point to the part of the Rockpile where the fatalities had occurred. She said she didn't understand. 'The Rockpile, there,' I pointed.

She said they didn't call it the Rockpile.

'Nui Go Dua,' she exclaimed as she pointed to the rocks, 'Nui Go Dua.'

'They call it "Watermelon Hill",' Phuoc translated.

I stopped him in his tracks. What did she say again? She explained that when she was a little girl, her grandfather and father had been watermelon farmers at the foot of the hill, which had given rise to the local name of 'Go Dua' or 'Watermelon Hill'. She went on to tell me that when irrigation came to the area, they stopped farming watermelons and turned their hands to running a small shrimp farm. 'A better business.'

I couldn't contain my emotions. I went down to the beach and sat quietly, feeling confused and sad. The American boy who loved playing dominoes at Sim Holt's store had been sent there to help prevent the so-called domino effect of communism. The boy who had grown and sold watermelons in east Texas had travelled thousands of miles to a foreign war zone, ending up here in this beautiful, isolated spot, only to lose his life on Watermelon Hill. Among the boulders. Among 'Charlie'. Among the watermelons.

I wanted to climb to the top of the hill but couldn't get up through the rocks. Lan told us to take the sand track further north where there was an easier trail to the summit. As we approached the hill from further north, we could see a lighthouse on the top. We began our ascent trying to steer clear of the hundreds of cacti and thousands of ants. Coming across more shrimp-farm workers resting under the shade of a nearby bush, we got chatting again. Chot, a fifty-one-year-old boom operator, told us that he had been seven years old in 1967 and that he lived in the nearby fishing village of Tan Phun. He remembered the VC hiding on 'Nui Go Dua', or Watermelon Hill.

'The Americans came in helicopters and landed there near the hill and on the beach,' he spontaneously recounted. 'I remember there was gunfire and skirmishes. A helicopter with a red-coloured cross on it came in. There was rifle and machine-gun fire all the time. Then later another helicopter came in.'

Chot at the Rockpile, 2012

He said that he was told later that some Americans had been killed there. He went on to say the Americans came to his village regularly when he was a boy and shared sweets and C rations with them. His family were strong supporters of the VC and had lived in a hole under the house when there was fighting. They also let the VC hide there. He said the Americans were friendly. He remembered their dirty faces, their iron hats and their sweaty smell in the heat. 'They meant food and sweets to us at that age,' he said. He pointed to the top of the hill. The Vietnamese regularly used the caves to store food and guns and to hide, he told us.

We began to walk up the trail to the summit, enjoying the spectacular views. When we reached the lighthouse, built in 1997, one of the keepers came out and told us that he'd heard the stories about soldiers hiding in the caves on Watermelon Hill.

'Where are the caves?' I asked.

'Nui Da Dung,' he shouted.

He pointed to the slope and to the huge grey rocks piled on top of each other just above the beach. I made my descent alone. I soon realised that these were no natural inlets carved out by the pounding sea; they were more like holes that had been formed between and underneath the huge rocks.

Looking down to the cave, the Rockpile, 2012

I took my time. The slopes didn't offer much grip and the scree in places made the trek hazardous. But I was determined to find what I was looking for. Halfway down, just below an enormous flat rock, I could see a gap between some boulders which formed a dark cavernous space. The hole was anchor-shaped, forming a deep, dark slash that appeared to lead to infinite hidden depths below. It provided a stark contrast with the surrounding grey rocks, which appeared to have been sprinkled with orange lichen. I knew instantly that this was one of the caves and its size led me to suppose that it was the one I had been looking for. I was convinced by the location that this was the cave entrance where Larry and the Major had died. But to my intense frustration, I was too big to squeeze through.

I sat down and rummaged through my bag to find the small glass jar that I'd filled some months before with clay from the banks in Short: the banks near the white house that Larry had loved to climb as a young boy. I opened the lid, poured the dried clay into my hand, threw its powdery substance into the cave inlet and watched it drift away into the darkness. A symbol of his birthplace scattered in the place where he died. Then I scooped some sand from the front of the cave into the same jar, which I returned to my bag.

I had brought with me a book of First World War poems by Wilfred Owen. I turned to my favourite, which seemed remarkably appropriate, 'Anthem For Doomed Youth':

What passing-bells for these who die as cattle?
Only the monstrous anger of the guns.
Only the stuttering rifles' rapid rattle
Can patter out their hasty orisons.
No mockeries now for them; no prayers nor bells;
Nor any voice of mourning save the choirs, –
The shrill, demented choirs of wailing shells;
And bugles calling for them from sad shires.
What candles may be held to speed them all?
Not in the hands of boys but in their eyes
Shall shine the holy glimmers of goodbyes.
The pallor of girls' brows shall be their pall;
Their flowers the tenderness of patient minds,
And each slow dusk a drawing-down of blinds.

I looked out to sea, towards the deserted island of Hon Dun some miles off shore. Alone, pensive and immensely saddened. I returned to the cave entrance and stood in silence for two minutes. Just like I'd done at The Wall. And at the graveside. For Larry. For Possum Trot.

*

On the way back to Quy Nhon, we stopped for a short break next to a field where a group of women were gathering watermelons. Opposite the field stood an old woman leaning over a gate at the entrance to her home. She began to chat with Phuoc. I asked Phuoc to ask her if she remembered the war, upon which she invited us in for a cup of tea. Her husband appeared, introducing himself as Mr Tung and his wife as Mrs Trinh. They were 83 and 82 respectively. We sat down at a wooden table in their main room. The couple were tiny and looked fit and well. She had a beautiful, peaceful face with sculpted cheekbones, and emanated an aura of serenity. The tea was duly served 'in friendship'. After a time exchanging pleasantries, we began to talk about the war and a remarkable story unfolded. She looked adoringly across at her husband as he began to speak.

Mr Tung and Mrs Trinh, Binh Dinh, 2012

He told us he'd first fought against the French in the 1940s and '50s. He was imprisoned then released when the French left. In 1966, he was a local VC leader, living underground below a house when a spy reported him. He was captured at midnight, then imprisoned in Quy Nhon jail, where he remained until 1969. He told us it was very tough there and he thought he was going to die, but he remained strong and 'committed to the cause'. He told us how he'd pretended he was going mad and the South's authorities released him to a controlled area. He managed to escape and went to the mountains to find his team. He was told what had happened whilst he'd been inside and discovered that three hundred and thirty VC local supporters had died in the area during those three years. He was sent to a village to be a secret leader and to foster a 'good connection' between the villagers and the Viet Cong. After the 'victory', he became a local chair of the Farmers Union.

While Mr Tung was in jail, his wife had been held in a separate prison. They met up on their release and she looked after wounded soldiers in the family's tunnel. She pointed at the wall to the special award she had been given for her 'courage and contribution'. Her certificate, his medals and a picture of Ho Chi Minh were displayed prominently side by side. Mr Tung took them down and showed them to me, glowing with pride. I asked him to reflect on the war some 40 years on.

'All that time America was the enemy and the American soldier was there to be killed,' he began. 'They were the most powerful military country in the world but the soldiers didn't have the same spirit, passion, drive or belief for the cause, nor did their leaders have the right strategy to respond to the VC.'

He stared me in the eye and then spoke louder, with emphasis and conviction: 'I feel totally loyal to Uncle Ho and the communist cause. Loyalty at all costs. I admired Uncle Ho as our leader and listened carefully to all he said and taught. Uncle Ho said, "When the war is over and there is victory, there should be no revenge to the Americans." Today, America is our friend and a good partner. We are fellow human beings at peace. There is now no hatred between us. War is terrible, truly terrible. I was proud of what I did. I was loyal. We won. We should now each take care of our families.'

He took a sip from his tea and waited for Phuoc to finish translating. He went on: 'If an American comes here to meet me, I would welcome him in a spirit of peace and friendship. But I will remain loyal to my country, to my party and to the Communist cause.'

I asked him what was the most important thing he had learned in his life? He smiled: 'Remember your family always. Family is the centre. Family, peace and happiness are what matters most. It was a terrible, terrible time. Now let future generations enjoy and value peace.'

It was precisely the same reflection on life, almost word for word, as that made by my father when we'd spoken about his own war just a few weeks before.

CHAPTER 18

I WILL NEVER LEAVE A FALLEN COMRADE

The first thing I saw upon my arrival at the small, functional airport in Columbus, Georgia, was a large wax model of a US soldier dressed in jungle fatigues, an ammo belt strapped across his chest. Behind him in a glass cabinet were displayed a Combat Infantry badge and a Vietnam Service medal. Next to the model, a billboard declared:

> United States Infantry In Vietnam: The US Infantryman served for eight years in Vietnam. Today these combat veterans are honored for their service.

The exhibit in the entrance hall had stood there for years but the welcome felt appropriate. I'd come to attend the 'Charlie 2/5 Reunion', a gathering that has taken place in different locations across the United States every two to three years over the past decade. This was to be a gathering to experience brotherhood, friendship, acceptance and remembrance. I felt apprehensive and somewhat concerned, knowing I'd be the outsider. I was unsure of the reception I would receive: whether or not I would be an unwelcome presence. When I arrived, Jimmy 'Tree' Machin, one of the organisers of the reunion, explained: 'The guys are very protective of each other and of themselves. Many don't want to talk about it at all. Many can't. I couldn't for 30 years. The reunion process is part of that healing, that help which enables them to get it out, to release it all.'

More than 90 Vets had signed up to attend the reunion, all of them having served in the Company sometime between September 1965 and the summer of 1972. Ten of them had been there in Vietnam at the same time as Larry in 1967. They were the men I particularly wanted to meet. I'd exchanged emails or spoken on the phone to some of them already but hadn't yet met any in person. I knew I was touching on a highly sensitive subject, having already detected several degrees of vulnerability in some of the men who had offered accounts so far. I wanted to reactivate some memories that had been buried for a long time, to find out as much first-hand information as I could. I knew I needed to take it gently: to listen carefully and gauge the emotional temperature of the men involved.

The Hilton Garden hotel on the outskirts of the city, a pleasant but rather nondescript building, was decked out in 1st Cavalry memorabilia, flags, balloons and bunting. The car park was filled with trucks, cars and motorbikes, many proudly emblazoned with that famous gold-and-black insignia. Most of the Vets were wearing special Charlie Company reunion caps, Stetsons, T-shirts and badges. This was a club, a special inner circle of brothers. Many were accompanied by their wives. Others, designated as Gold Star families, were there to represent some of the fellow brothers who didn't make it home.

John McCorkle, the chief organiser, opened the proceedings by highlighting the event as 'the chance to be re-acquainted with brothers'. The atmosphere felt warm, good humoured and respectful. He went on: 'Whether the war was good or bad doesn't really matter. We were called to duty and we served as best as we could.'

Columbus was chosen as the venue as it is adjacent to the huge army base of Fort Benning, the home of the US Army Infantry School. Indeed, the first event on the schedule was to head there to attend the graduation ceremony of the army's latest recruits from the 198th Infantry Brigade and to visit the recently opened National Infantry Museum, 'the cultural and spiritual home of the US Infantryman'.

At their passing-out parade, the newly qualified recruits marched in step, took the salute and stood proud when the national anthem was sung. I thought of Larry at Fort Polk back in February 1967. They all looked so young. They would probably be on their way to Afghanistan within weeks, destined to be some of the last American soldiers to serve there before the final pull-out in 2014. Speeches addressed to them emphasised the importance of the seven Army values: Loyalty, Duty, Respect, Selfless Service, Honor, Integrity and Personal Courage. The Soldiers Creed was recited. I'd never heard it before. One line particularly chimed with me: 'I Will Never Leave A Fallen Comrade'.

At the National Infantry Museum, a special exhibit allowed the visitor to enter the tropical jungles of Vietnam; to hear mock gun fire, large explosions and a simulated rainstorm; to meander round booby traps under three-canopy darkness; as well as to listen to the recorded voices of veterans providing a commentary of oral testimonies. Some children attending as part of a school party screamed and laughed at the barrage of noise. They thought it was fun. But I noticed how some of the Vets in the reunion party had decided to give it a miss and guessed that the last thing they needed was to re-live the experience. It would be too intense, too vivid and too painful a reminder of what they'd spent the last 45 years trying to forget.

Back at the hotel, I wandered round making personal contact with the Vets of '67. To my delight, all were fully engaged, supportive and keen to help with my project. I wanted to hear first their thoughts on being drafted and especially that word: Duty.

Don Demchak was 20 years old when he joined up with the Fourth Platoon as a draftee in June 1967: 'It was my duty. Coming from my little town in Pennsylvania, there was no such thing as a conscientious objector. My country called on me, so I did my duty.'

Clinton Endres, at 19, was also a willing draftee: 'I was drafted with four of my classmates. I felt included. I didn't want to be singled out. I had no doubts. Uncle Sam had called. I didn't know anything about Vietnam really – the military, airmobile or anything like that. I just knew I'd be going. It was something I had to do.'

John Wnek was less sure: 'My initial reaction was one of fear. I thought, "This is a serious business here", but I had no options. It was a legal obligation. If I'd had a choice, I'll be honest: I would have taken the other choice. But there wasn't any other legal option for me. I had no views on the war. I was apolitical. I wasn't interested. I thought, "I've got a little bit of college behind me. They won't put me on the front line." I was so naive. Then when I got there I thought, "Oh my God, we've got teachers here; we've got everybody here. And I'm nothing special. We're all going to die."'

Don Jensen was a little older than most of his drafted colleagues: 'I was 25. Oh, Jesus, it was the end of the world. I was married to my second wife. We were buying a house and a car. Jeez, then you get drafted. It was horrible. I wasn't going to try and get out of it. I looked at it as a duty. Both my brothers had been in the services. I'd paid attention to the newsreels. I knew there was a high chance. I was looking for it but I was still devastated when I got the letter. I just had the idea that the US was doing the right thing. I still feel to this day that we were.'

It felt odd to be the man now introducing Don Jensen to Clinton Endres, after a period of 45 years. Both had been members of the Third Platoon. Both had served with Possum Trot. This was the first time they had seen each other since then. Before long, they were looking through Don's extensive photo album, alongside their colleague Jay Phillips: reminiscing, laughing, highlighting names and places. Don appeared larger than life, wearing a blue checked shirt and a smart Stetson hat festooned with metal badges and yellow braiding. Clinton, bald now, with a trim white moustache, had a face that exuded kindness and modesty. He was also dressed casually in a checked shirt and was wearing a FNG badge, indicating this was his first reunion. Jay was still slim with white hair and a heavy white moustache. He was wearing a green Charlie 2/5 baseball cap and T-shirt.

The photos acted as a trigger and the memories soon came flooding back. At times, the men were tearful. Often, they were reflective. Each of them pointed out individual photographs, reminiscing as they did so. Some depicted soldiers carrying out their daily tasks: digging foxholes on the beach; building hootches with bamboo poles; eating C rations by the Cay Giep mountains. One photo showed two dead enemy soldiers who had been tied together by the Americans. Another showed a huge explosion going off in the distance. And, of course, there were attempts to identify comrades in each photograph.

I was especially keen to talk to the men of '67 about the events at the Rockpile and to hear their thoughts about the war 45 years on. I'd read all those transcripts about the events of Friday, 23 June when I was sitting next to Larry's grave at Mt Pleasant, so I already had a strong understanding of what had happened. But these men had been there in person with Larry on that very day. It was a chance to hear not only from each of them individually but also to bring them round a table to enable them to share their personal perspectives. Some had brought photographs with them that they'd taken on the day Larry died.

Don Jensen began: 'We'd just been engaged with the enemy for several days before getting there. I remember we air assaulted to the north end. They put some on top of the hill. Some of us on the beach. We could smell 'em. I said, "There's gooks there." We fanned around. Look, that's me on the beach just as we'd arrived.'

He handed round a photo of himself. He was bespectacled, carrying his M16 and a radio, with 20 other grunts in the background taking their positions on the beach. The sky was cornflower blue, the sparkling South China Sea stretched out behind them and Hon Dun island, half a mile off the Rockpile, was clearly visible. Prompted by the photos, the memories, questions and clarifications came thick and fast.

'We'd just swept a village. The birds picked us up,' John Wnek recalled. 'I remember seeing the Rockpile ahead of us. I thought this would be a beautiful place if there wasn't a war going on. They'd already flown a propaganda bird overhead saying "Give yourself up." We thought it would be a piece of cake. We didn't think it was hot. We thought it was a straightforward mission.'

Clinton Endres examined Don's photos closely: 'I thought we'd humped on the sand, landing up to it, but apparently I'm wrong. Our squad took up a position over there, higher up.'

Don Jensen wondered why the enemy was hiding there: 'Maybe it was an R and R place for them.'

Don Demchak was looking at a photo of the rock formations. Draped over his chair was a jacket he'd had made up for himself in An Khe in May 1967. On the back, the following words were stitched prominently: 'When I Die I'll Go To Heaven Because I've Spent My Time In Hell'. I remembered Newton Johnson had recounted the same phrase in the Sheriff's office in Center some months before.

'It was a mile or two on the horizon when we first saw it, it was so isolated,' Don recalled. 'Then we hit the beach about 300 yards away. Set up the mortars first, then spread around the bottom of the hill. We were on full alert. The mission was to search for the enemy and kill them.'

Jay Phillips remembered: 'The first time we swept through, we weren't delving into every nook and cranny. Then we stayed for the night.'

'Some of the rocks were as big as houses. Some with holes underneath forming natural caves,' Don Jensen explained.

'How the hell did those rocks get there? It looked like a pile of boulders had just been dumped there,' Tom Rutten told me. 'I thought it was a curious structure. I was in the First Platoon looking for cover on the beach. We couldn't set up a perimeter because of the sea. Illumination flares were there overnight. Sometimes someone could see something and fired up. You'd see a lot of shadows. A bush could be a gook. A gook could be a bush. There were guys taking pop shots throughout the night.'

'When a flare popped up, there was a gook with a rifle but he disappeared before I could shoot him,' Don Jensen recalled.

'We walked over the Rockpile twice,' Jay Phillips explained. 'We got a message from the boats off the coast that there was radio noise. On the second search in the morning, we'd seen human faeces outside a cave. I went down there. There were some NVA packs. That made me think there were gooks there. I went down a narrow passageway to look further, entering sideways.'

'I think we roped you in,' Clinton Endres interjected.

'Markham was looking for a small guy, not a tunnel rat, but I was new and thin so I went in,' Jay Phillips continued. 'I went down a narrow crevasse between the boulders, into an anteroom. There were a couple of field packs. There was also a mortar and some weapons. I went through some boulders to another room. I had to put something down to get round so I put down my .45. I used the flashlight. It was only three feet high down there. I saw one of the gooks. He reached for his AK. I bailed out real quick. I was scared. I went up the crevasse and told Sgt Endres what I saw.'

'I remember you yelling that you'd seen someone in the cave,' Clinton Endres responded.

'They were pretty hush about the Major coming in,' Don Demchak told me. 'They said they'd found the enemy in a hole on the hill.'

John Wnek took up the next stage: 'I remember them saying a Psy-Ops officer was going to come in with the helicopter. I thought, "Here we go."'

'It could have been late morning. It was certainly bright daylight,' Tom Rutten recalled. 'It was very loud with his bullhorn. I thought he was dangling off a rope ladder or dropping a line from a chopper. I thought the Psy-Ops officer was shot off that line but apparently that was them trying to take Larry Byford off later. It was all very confusing. The idea of open arms, giving yourself up, was always unlikely. This was the NVA.'

'I remember he went to the caves with his bullhorn shouting, "Chieu Hoi". I think he'd arrived in the afternoon,' Don Jensen recalled.

'Sgt Lock came up to our position and said he needed two volunteers to go down below and help him,' Clinton Endres interjected. 'Possum Trot and Whitey Wilson went down.'

'I heard someone was asked to carry his radio. I knew the Third Platoon was up on the hill . . . all I remember is some shit hit the fan and we lost the Major,' John Wnek replied. 'Then I heard we'd lost another. We couldn't get them out.'

'The Major was yelling in Vietnamese but the Vietnamese weren't cooperative,' Don Demchak said. 'Then I heard a rat-a-tat-tat and wondered what the hell was going on. There weren't many shots. He'd poked his head out. Boom. Boom. Then went back in. Then we heard more shots.'

'I was manning the radio,' Don Jensen explained. 'The word was passed out that the Major had been shot. And Larry had gone to help him. Then he'd been hit. Then the medevac came over. The penetrator [a rescue seat] was passed down.'

'The next thing I heard was we'd taken some casualties,' John Wnek recounted. 'Then I heard we couldn't get the bodies out of there. That got me depressed. What the hell had happened? Then when the body was trying to be got out, it fell back in. I thought, "Who's going to tell his mother and father about all this?" Then I tried to get it out of my mind. A coping mechanism.'

'I didn't know the Major had been shot. Sgt Lock came back up,' Clinton Endres remembered. 'He said, "One of your men has been shot; it's Possum Trot." What I then heard was that Possum Trot was giving the Major cover and then he tried to get his body and was shot. There wasn't much to say. We were very quiet.'

'They got Larry in a sling,' Don Jensen continued. 'The helicopter made so much noise. They were shooting at him. The cable split. And he fell down. I was watching the chopper being shot at. It was a medevac with a red cross. He was shot at as the dust off [medevac helicopter] veered away. The cable snapped.'

'They raised him up on the cable. The cable broke. He was dead. There was no rescue attempt until later,' Tom Rutten explained to me. 'Thinking about it, the gunners in the chopper may have cut the cable rather than it was shot, knowing he was dead. It would have had to have been a pretty good shot to break the cable.'

I moved the conversation on to the retrieving of the body.

'They'd tied some gook and took him to the cave,' Don Jensen remembered.

Larry Byford's body is flown away from the Rockpile, Saturday, 24 June 1967 (Photo courtesy of Don Jensen)

At this point, he produced an extraordinary set of photographs that he'd taken on the beach that afternoon: colleagues carrying Larry's body on a stretcher to a waiting helicopter; the body bag being loaded into the hold through the side door; the body bag lying next to a gunner as the helicopter took off. Next to the photos were written the words 'Larry Byford KIA'. I felt conscious that I was being given special access to such intimate scenes. The experience was deeply moving but almost too raw.

The conversation continued.

Jay Phillips: 'I remember they then lowered a shape charger down where the gooks were. Into the cave. The gooks cut the wire and it didn't go off.'

Don Jensen: 'It was two, maybe three, days we were there.'

Jay Phillips: 'We definitely went to LZ Uplift on the Sunday, because I wrote to my mother from there on the 25th. She had the letter.'

Don Demchak: 'Larry was the first person to be killed in our Company since I'd arrived. It woke me up to the fact you really were fighting a war, not policing one.'

He began to show photographs he had taken on that day.

'This is the Commander who we pulled out with his weapons. We kept him in a cave so that no one could take a potshot at him. These were the weapons we pulled out of the hole.'

Don Demchak explained how one of the photos showed a Vietnamese soldier being questioned in front of a cave entrance. Another showed a small cache of weapons laid out on the floor next to a bull horn. The Company captured three Soviet SKS rifles, one AK-47, one Chinese machine gun, two mortars, ammunition and rice.

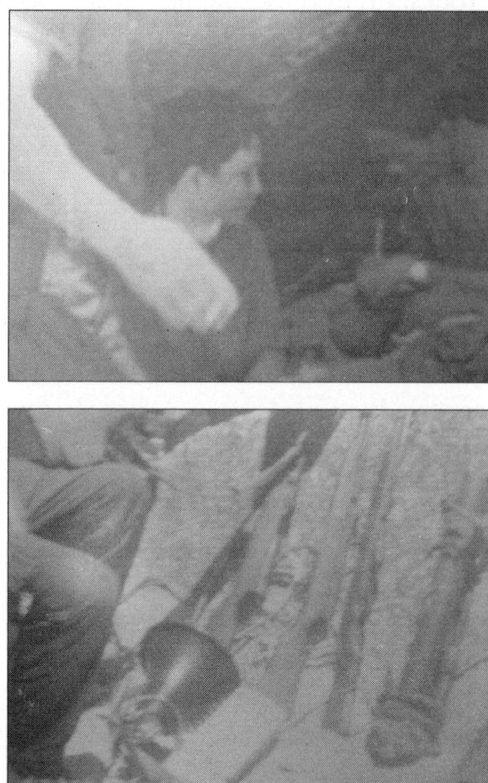

Captured soldier questioned. Cache of weapons recovered and the bullhorn, the Rockpile 1967. (Photos courtesy of Don Demchak)

'They put tear gas down after the deaths and one big guy came out of the caves,' Jay Phillips told me. 'There were a number of times in Vietnam I came very close to being killed. I asked myself each time, "Was my number up?" That was the first of six or seven times I nearly died. "Thank goodness it's not my day today," I thought.'

Charlie Company pulled off the mountain on Sunday, 25 June and turned it over to another company 'to finish the mopping up'. C Company moved to LZ Uplift to stand guard duty overnight.

I showed the men my own pictures that I had taken of the Rockpile only three months previously and shared with them that its name locally was Watermelon Hill. One photo showed Lan at the foot of the rocks. I told them she had been born there in April 1967. Another photograph introduced them to Chot. I explained how he was seven years of age at that time and could remember hearing the American helicopters hovering above the boulders.

'Well, I'll be damned,' Don Jensen exclaimed, 'Isn't that something?'

Later, both Jay Phillips and Don Jensen shared with me letters they'd written from the field at that very time, describing the events at the Rockpile. Jay Phillips' letter was written to his parents on 28 June from LZ Pony in the Kim Son valley:

> I know it's been nine days since I last wrote and I know this is entirely too long. However, the evening of the nineteenth, we made a helicopter assault back out near the coast and were very busy from then through to the twenty fifth.
>
> We swept a boulder-covered ridge located right next to the sea and about a mile long, hunting for an enemy radio transmitter detected in the area by Navy ships. We found nothing and moved back out in the sand inland and set up again for the night.
>
> That night, they reported more radio signals from the same area, so the next morning we began to sweep the ridge again from the opposite direction. This time, we detected many caves and hideaways hidden among the huge boulders, some fifty feet in diameter, and rock piles. The next several days and nights were spent searching and surrounding the cave areas and on the twenty fifth we moved back to LZ Uplift and let another company take over.

Jay explained that he didn't mention the deaths or his own escapade in the cave because he didn't want to worry his mother unduly. He was careful to censor his own correspondence.

Don Jensen wrote to his wife from the actual slopes of the Rockpile, in the middle of all the action, on the Saturday, 24 June:

> I couldn't write yesterday too many bulets flying around. The night before last NVA soldiers were crawling all over trying to get out. They got 4 then yesterday captured another yesterday in the morning. A NVA with a machine gun shot a few times, so this major went in the crevis that has a cave in the back (no weapon) to try to talk this NVA out. The gook cut him to shreds with his M. G. then some of our guys tried to get him out and the gook opened up on one of our guys. Knocked him down and just kept shooting. They put cover fire in on the gook and got the kid out. Then the medivack came in and droped a sling just as they were putting the kid in the sling the gook shot up the choper hiting one door guner. The ship got away ok but the kid they were picking up fell down into the deep crevis where the gook was. We couldnt get the bodies out yesterday. The gook would shoot everytime they tried.
>
> I knew the guy real well he was from texas posumtrot texas we called him possum. He was in our platoon. If we cant get the guys out the plans are to blow the whole works and bury them their. Its a sickning affair. The dead are smelling very strong now its a night mare. Its noon now and theyre going to try to recover the bodies.

I felt I'd pursued the events at the Rockpile enough. I knew what had happened. I was pretty clear on the timetable. All war is confusing and chaotic. It would be impossible to confirm or tie down every precise detail. But the testimonies, recollections, photographs and letters had given me a most detailed and graphic account of the tragedy. The desperate story had unfolded a little further and I felt incredibly sad. I went for a walk outside by the lake to gather my thoughts and to reflect on what I'd heard.

The men from Charlie Company 1967 remained together for a while as brothers in arms. They signed a 1st Cavalry Division flag that I'd brought with me, each leaving his own personal message for Larry.

That same evening, a banquet was held in the main room, preceded by a deeply moving ceremony to remember the 75 members of the Company who didn't make it home. The dress code was flexible, but most of the men were dressed smartly in special gold-and-black 1st Cavalry shirts, black trousers and black shoes, and wore Stetsons or caps. I saw one patch sewn on a shirt stating, 'Not all wounds are visible' with a sketch of a soldier holding his hands over his eyes. Another exclaimed, 'United Again Cavalry. In Brotherhood Forever.' Embroidered on a third were the words, 'In Memory 1959 to 1975: 58,282 Brothers And Sisters Who Never Returned'.

A table covered with a pristine white cloth was positioned in the centre of the room. Placed on it were a brass bell and a set of empty glasses. Donnie 'Bull' Bulloch, who in 1969 was a squad leader in the Second Platoon, stood in front of the table at a lecturn and began slowly, methodically, to read out the individual names of the 75 who had fallen. Each time his distinctive Louisiana drawl called out a name, a member of the Company came up to the table, placed a small American flag in one of the glasses, struck the bell and, as the sound chimed around the room, stood to attention in front of the glasses and saluted. It was an incredibly powerful and dignified ceremony.

About an hour in, when Freddie Robinson's name was called, I knew I'd be the next one up. John McCorkle had asked me earlier to take up the flag when Larry's name was called: 'LARRY STEPHEN BYFORD'.

I rose from the table, Jensen at my side and Demchak opposite, both watching my every step. I placed the small flag in the sixth glass, struck the bell firmly and stood to attention in silence. As I looked at the cluster of flags on the table and then closed my eyes, I thought about Larry's parents, his siblings, the old white house, the Rockpile, as well as Larry himself. I sat down feeling emotional but honoured. Clinton, sad and crestfallen, looked across and gave me a slow wink of approval.

When the last of the 75 had been remembered, everyone in the room stood up in solemn reverence. The roll call of names had lasted more than a hour and had felt like those first moments I'd experienced at The Wall. Name after name after name. Lonny Branch, a medic who served from 1969 to 1970, then came to the lectern to propose the loyal toast to them all: 'Seventy-five of our brothers did not come home. We were angry because of their death. But now we see it was their choice, not to die, but to be willing to. Their unconditional sacrifice was not easily understood by those of us left behind. Whether Vietnam was a bad war or a good war doesn't matter. It was *our* war. We fought first and foremost for each other. Seventy-five Charlie Company troopers fought and died valiantly, giving us the opportunity to come home. Our cause was just. We remember the dirt and the sweat. We remember the strength of our youth. We remember you.

'Tonight Charlie Company honours the courage, sacrifice and devotion of our fallen brothers. We give tribute to their families and their memories. We will never forget what they did for us. We will always have their faces to remind us of the times we spent together. Their laughter.

'The hardest part of losing our brothers, sons, fathers, husbands was trying to live without them. We still miss them. Their memories have become our treasures. To our fallen brothers, we offer this toast. Because of their bravery and heroic sacrifice, we are here today. We are kept free by better men than ourselves. Thank you, brothers. To us you will always be forever young.'

I almost expected Bob Dylan's evocative song 'Forever Young' to start up. Instead, rather strangely, 'Groovin' by the Young Rascals played out across the room: the same song that was number one in the charts on the day when Fate heard the news.

Had it been worth it? Was Larry a hero in their eyes? They were the two questions I wanted the men to answer before I left the reunion. I meandered amongst the community of '67, intrigued to hear their replies.

'For me personally, if I think of the war as a total unjustified war then that would be a waste,' Jay Phillips explained candidly, 'It's not helpful. Was the war winnable? My feeling now is probably not. I was going there to fight Communism but when you're there, you're fighting for your buddies. In 1967, I thought we were winning the war. By 1969, I was back home wounded and marching against the war. I wanted my buddies out before they got hurt.'

Jay was awarded three Purple Hearts.

'I question it. I don't know what we gained from it,' Clinton Endres reflected, 'As far as what the US got out of it officially: well, they say that we lost the war. I don't know. Maybe we gained some brotherhood. But was it worth it? All the lives we lost. In a sense you'd say it wasn't but in another sense I'd say it was.

All those guys who lost their lives, you can't say they did it for nothing. We lost the war but they did it for their brothers, for their fellow comrades. That's worth something, isn't it?'

'It was a waste of time. There should have been a political settlement,' Tom Rutten told me. 'For me, it was a lost year. I'll never get it back. Some say they'd never trade it for anything else. I'm not sure. I used to say that but I don't think that any more. You lose empathy. You never get rid of it.'

'We had the wrong tactics. Body count – that's not a plan,' Tom Blancett said. 'We didn't belong there. The government making us the world's police force. We didn't gain anything.'

'It wasn't worth it,' Don Jensen remarked. 'We should have finished it off. We shouldn't have abandoned those people. We never lost a battle but we lost the war.'

John Wnek looked out on the lake at the Canada geese who were honking loudly to each other in the shallows. He took hold of my arm: 'Now, knowing what we know, we should never have tried all that domino stuff, the cancer of communism. Maybe I did something to slow it down. But I don't know if it was right or wrong. For me, was it worth it? I had a tough time after I came back with survivor guilt. I felt depressed about it all. Me living and friends not coming back. I found it difficult to cope with my anger. With people who didn't understand why we'd gone. Once I was called a "fool" for going.'

'I didn't know about post-traumatic stress disorder, PTSD, but talking to the guys they said, "You have the symptoms,"' Don Jensen explained. 'You don't realise you have it. I estranged myself from my family, from my friends. No one came to visit me. I didn't go to visit them. Because of the war.'

This theme kept surfacing in many of the conversations I had with the Vets. Some talked about being unable to face crowds or go to ball games. Even supermarkets were a no-go area. Many talked about sleep deprivation, constant nightmares, flashbacks and acute depression. One revealed he couldn't sit at a table in a restaurant if someone was behind him. Many talked to me about anger issues as well as alcohol and drug abuse. 'You're scarred for life, do you understand?' one Vet said as he looked me in the eyes sorrowfully and grasped my hand.

Mike Kopaczewski was just 20 years old when he arrived as a lieutenant to lead the Second Platoon the month after Larry died. Universally known as 'Lieutenant K', he spoke emotionally about the impact of his time there: 'Morale was good at first but it began to tumble. I just loved my men. My men were number one to me. All I cared about was that I wanted my men to get home. I just wanted to get all of them back safely. I didn't lose anyone.

'I shut off everything for 35 years. Then I came to a reunion and the dam opened up. It all flooded back and I fell apart. But I come because I love my men. Even though some are as goofy as hell. I love them and they got home. That's why I'm here. The war was worth it to me. I did my job there. Larry's death was the ultimate tragedy. The country needed him to do something and he did it. He did his duty. The government wanted to stop us being overrun by communists. Every one who served, who fought, if they were in a bunker, if they were out in the field, they were a hero. But what he did makes him a special hero.'

There was that word again. Hero.

'He was definitely a hero,' Jay Phillips proclaimed. 'He was a draftee, he wasn't in Canada and what he did, in my book, he's a hero.'

Not surprisingly, Clinton Endres agreed. 'He did his job. He was a good friend. He was a hero to me.'

Tom Rutten reflected: 'Most of those 58,000 on The Wall were in the wrong place at the wrong time. They were unlucky. Maybe a thousand of them did something special, sacrificed themselves for someone else. He may have been the closest guy to the Lieutenant or the Sergeant and he was told, "Go and see if he's dead." Then the gook comes out and he's killed. Was he following orders or was it his own initiative, thinking he'd just go up and check it and try and rescue him? We don't do too many things spontaneously.'

'Maybe, fresh out of training, he clicked and went to rescue him,' Tom Blancett intervened. 'He didn't run the other way, did he? So, he's a hero.'

'He was definitely a hero. All 58,000 are heroes but he's a special one,' John Wnek told me. 'He did something extraordinary. He volunteered to rescue the Major's body. Something I don't think I would have done. Above and beyond the call of duty.

That's his legacy. It's guys like him who made the First Team what it is. He gave his blood. God rest his soul.'

Don Jensen grasped my arm firmly and stared into the distance: 'He was definitely a hero. I don't think all 58,000 on that Wall are heroes. Most were in the wrong place at the wrong time. They caught a bullet. But he took it upon himself to help the Major. He didn't have to. No one forced him to. It was his sense of patriotism, his sense of duty, to help another man. That showed true heroism. I don't think I would have done that.'

As I got up to leave the banquet and pack my bags, a couple came across to my table, seemingly anxious to make contact. 'I'd heard about your project. I'm the lucky one,' the man said quietly.

His name was Joe Roudebush and he told me his story. He arrived in the field with the Second Platoon in July 1969, two years after Larry was killed. His tour of duty lasted less than five hours. He was lying in a foxhole on the Cambodian border on his first night when it was mortared. He thought he was dying. Heavy bleeding and severe injuries to his neck, shoulder and back gave him every justification to think his time was up. He couldn't move. He lost consciousness. Minutes later, his squad leader, John Kortinos, came back to drag him out of the hole, and then called for the medevac. Joe was flown to Japan, where he stayed in hospital for three weeks, after which he was hospitalised in the US for three months. Even though he was only in combat for 300 minutes, Joe attends each reunion so that he can see John, give him a big hug and thank him for saving his life.

'I just had an angel above me. I was the luckiest guy,' he whispered, his eyes filling with tears. He'd got married only the week before he left for Vietnam. His girlfriend, Lana, had a premonition that he'd be wounded in action and so decided she must marry him before he departed. 'God has a plan and his plan was to help Joe,' she cried, squeezing Joe's hand tightly.

They've now been married forty-three years and have two children and five grandchildren.

'I realise I'm the luckiest guy,' he continued. 'Larry was one of the unluckiest. I've enjoyed all the joys of life. He didn't. That's the saddest thing.'

CHAPTER 19

A SPECIAL RELATIONSHIP

'That's where Bernard Flanagan lived – he was wounded on D-Day. A lovely, gentle lad,' he reminisced as we approached the Dalefield estate.

'There's the house, 44 Neville Street, brand new when we moved in.' He looked through the car window and peered up at the slate roof and red chimney stack. A little further on and he was bubbling again with enthusiasm.

'We swapped houses and moved here to 35 Dalefield Avenue. I can remember being brought out of that front door on a stretcher when my appendix burst. I was 13.'

I was back in Normanton with my father, enjoying a trip down memory lane. We were travelling around his birthplace – the coalmining town that had helped to shape his early life.

'Here's the site of my school on the left there, next to the Lane End Catholic Club. All gone now. Just a car park. And there's the entrance to St John's church. That's where your mum and I stood for photographs on our wedding day 62 years ago with snow on the ground. And that's the road that went up to the pit, just there,' he remembered with nostalgia.

Today, all the coalmines in and around Normanton are closed, and the vast network of railway sidings have been either turfed over or built upon. Normanton has changed dramatically over the past 40 years. The building of the M62 motorway, one mile north, has realigned its purpose, merging it with the extended commuter belt of the city of Leeds and turning it into a major road-freight depot. Everything today is so much cleaner: the buildings, the pavements and especially the air.

Lawry and Muriel Byford outside St John the Baptist Church, Normanton, 1950 and 2012

'Do you ever go inside St John's church these days, Dad?' I enquired.

'Yes, I go there more regularly than ever . . . to attend funerals.'

Just a few minutes later, as darkness fell, we drove past Haw Hill Park, its war memorial tucked out of sight behind the green metal gates. We were heading down Castleford Road to our destination, the New Wheatsheaf Banqueting Centre, 400 yards away from the technical college where he'd begun his metal work course, aged 13. My dad was there to be hailed by the townsfolk of Normanton as a Queen's Diamond Jubilee Honorary Citizen.

A letter had arrived four months earlier. '*The position of honorary citizen shall hold a place of high esteem in the minds and hearts of its people*,' the correspondence proclaimed. My father was to be one of four recipients. When he got the letter, he was so proud. The place that had shaped him in childhood was to recognise him in the twilight of his life. I felt strongly that, out of all the honours he had been awarded over the years, this was the one that mattered most.

After the event, we drove back to Pannal, less than an hour away. I wandered around the house and ended up in my dad's study, where I knew the certificate and trophy presented that night would soon be displayed. I scanned the walls, filled with photographs, certificates and memorabilia, many of them highlighting the achievements of his police career. One cartoon amusingly depicted him as Clark Kent flying over Buckingham Palace, the Queen hanging onto his cape, with the words 'SUPERCOP' emblazoned across the top.

What had happened to the Divisional Commander since he served in Huddersfield at the time when Larry died in Vietnam? In 1968, my father was promoted and moved to Lincolnshire and by 1973 had become Chief Constable of that county. In 1977, he joined the Inspectorate of Constabulary and in 1983 became Her Majesty's Chief Inspector of Constabulary, leading the independent assessment of all police forces across England and Wales, from neighbourhood watch schemes, through to serious crime, to the fight against terrorism. In that role, he was also the principal independent professional advisor to the government on all police issues. It had been an impressive rise. In the space of 15 years he'd gone from his first commanding role to the very top of the British police. In 1981, he led a highly publicised review of the Yorkshire Ripper serial murder case which introduced the revolutionary HOME computer system for future inquiries. In the mid 1980s, after the IRA had attempted to murder Margaret Thatcher and members of her cabinet at the Conservative Party conference in Brighton, he worked closely with American law-enforcement agencies on the development of counter-terrorism strategies. He was knighted by the Queen for his services to the police in 1984 and, on his retirement, he became President and Chairman of his beloved Yorkshire County Cricket Club.

I noticed two plaques hung on the study walls: one from the John Jay College of Criminal Justice in New York City, dated May 1976, and presented: '*in recognition for outstanding service to criminal justice education in the United States*', and another, dated March

1987, with the crest of the FBI prominently displayed: '*in recognition of your friendship and co-operation with the FBI*'.

Then I caught sight of a painting of Admiral Lord Nelson, of 'England expects every man will do his duty' fame. Above it hung another framed picture with the title: 'Be Ye Men of Valour', which quoted 'The Apocrypha' from the Book of Maccabees – used by Winston Churchill in his first prime ministerial broadcast address to the UK nation in May 1940 as the threat from Nazi Germany became acute:

Arm yourselves and be ye men of valour,
And be in readiness for the conflict,
For it is better for us to perish in battle
Than to look upon the outrage of our nations
And our altars.
As the will of GOD is in HEAVEN
even so let HIM do.

And there on his mahogany desk were three pieces of Second World War memorabilia. A copy of a black-and-white photograph, taken at SHAEF Forward HQ in Reims, of a smiling General Eisenhower, together with his deputy, Air Marshall Sir Arthur Tedder, announcing the ending of the war in Europe. In the background were the Stars and Stripes, the Union Jack and SHAEF's own flag. Next to it was another photograph, a copy of the actual surrender document, signed earlier by the German and Allies representatives at 02.41 a.m. precisely on 7 May 1945. Of course, my father wasn't present at the actual signing, nor at Eisenhower's press conference, but he'd been despatched to Reims to arrive in the town at the time of that historic moment to work on communications. Next to the photos was a copy of a SHAEF insignia badge. I laid it on the palm of my hand, examining its intricate design. I read subsequently that its design symbolised the flaming sword of avenging justice piercing the black Nazi oppression; the rainbow, a symbol of hope, represented all the colours of the national flags of the Allies; the crescent of sky blue represented the peace to come. It was a reminder to him of those extraordinary days he'd spent as a recently drafted

19 year old at the SHAEF HQ in Versailles, back in 1944.

I sat on the sofa in his study and reflected. I'd spent years trying to understand how this poor working-class boy, with such little early education and no formal qualifications, had risen to the top of the British police to become a respected and revered member of the British establishment. I had often wondered what had been the catalyst for such a rise. Had there been a specific moment that had changed him? I realised then that the search for Larry Byford's story had inadvertently revealed the answer to that long-standing question: it was the moment when my dad had been despatched to Versailles that had changed everything.

Watching Eisenhower and Gerow operate, and working alongside the Americans, he had been lifted out of a life of dull mediocrity and transported to a place where his eyes had been opened up to the infinite possibilities and myriad opportunities in life. He came back from those five months at war a changed person, determined not to go back to the pit as an apprentice electrician. The Americans had given him confidence, hope, ambition and a determination to succeed. He had been infected by the dream of meritocracy and knew that life would never be the same again. Once back home, he had set off on a journey to prove himself and to grab every opportunity.

That simple act of Gerow's at the Chateau D'Ardenne had left a deep, indelible mark that would remain with him. 'Hiya, fella,' coming from a Lieutenant General – and to him, the lowest rank of all. From that moment on, my dad realised that, however high up the ladder you climb, you had to be there for your troops: to treat everyone with the same respect, whatever their rank, whatever their status, whatever their background. It's what I have admired most about my dad for many years, and I realised that it had been instilled there and then. It was a profound revelation to me. It mattered. That powerful moment when I saw Larry's name on The Wall in Washington had driven me to discover not only his story of duty and heroism but also my own father's story of drive and success. And thankfully I'd embarked on the journey while he was still able to relate it to me.

The following day, I decided that the time had come to take my dad through Larry's story. I wanted to fulfil my promise, made at the Normanton memorial almost exactly one year earlier, to come back and tell him what I had discovered. I wanted to share the details of Larry's childhood and early adulthood, leading up to his time in Vietnam and the events that culminated in his death. I wanted to explain how his siblings, friends and Vet colleagues feel today. I wanted to take him through the photographs, the letters, the testimonies.

Having listened to me recount Larry's story in detail, he was ready to reflect. Hearing Larry's story of loss and bravery made him once again recognise and acknowledge his own good fortune in war. Fate, chance, God's will, call it what you want, had dealt him a good hand. His war had given him inspiration and opportunity; a stark contrast to Larry's, which had meant death. He summed it up: 'Larry drew the short straw, leading to his sad wartime experiences which compared sharply to my own renaissance. What a fascinating, poignant story,' he reflected. 'It pulls at the heartstrings. Such a human tragedy. He's like an unknown warrior. A simple country boy who faced an awful misfortune. But he was a definite hero. He did something extraordinary and unusual in trying to rescue the Major. He fulfilled the soldier's creed: "Never leave a fallen comrade". For that, his family and friends can feel proud. They should focus on their affection and pride for him, not dwell on what he was fighting for and the futility of it all.'

He looked through the photographs of Larry as a child and in uniform at Fort Polk, and then focused on the images at the Rockpile and the body bag being flown away. He sighed in anguish.

'For me, there are legitimate wars and there are wars like Vietnam, and then Iraq, and now Afghanistan, which, in my view, have no real purpose. Those in charge may have thought they had legitimate reasons but they were totally wrong, totally misconceived. So many people on all sides killed. And you think, "What was that all about?" People don't read their history books. Wilson was right on Vietnam. I just hope Tony Blair reads your book and reflects.'

'They would have been so much better leaving it all alone but they never learn,' my mum intervened.

'Johnson was a good bloke basically,' my dad continued, 'and I think he did what he thought was right but they were all enmeshed in this idealism about the evil of communism and the need to destroy it. But you then look at history and think, "Oh, dear!' It's the same with Iraq and Afghanistan now. Thirty years ago, the Russians thought they could sort out Afghanistan. Now if you asked them was it worth it, they'd say definitely not.

'Every day, it seems, the news comes in. Just like this morning, there were two more British soldiers killed. If you ask the average sharp-end soldier who has been to Iraq or Afghanistan, "Why are you there?", do you think they'd say, "To maintain the democratic tradition, to uphold freedom"? No, they'd say, "To honour my regiment, to support my colleagues." They've no real idea, politically, why they're still there. And all those people who line the streets at Wootton Bassett when the coffins come home, they're saluting the bravery, the duty, the sacrifice, not the cause.'

I could feel him getting angry, the force of his feelings and a growing sense of determination shaping the tone of his voice.

'Now, Tony Blair . . . if ever there's an example of a man enamoured by the red carpet at the White House, it's him. If you asked Blair now, if he was sitting here with us, and he was really honest with himself, he ought to say it was the biggest mistake of his life. If he's any conscience, he'd say that. If he looked at himself in the mirror and was truly honest, he would say, "Yes, I was wrong. I made a mistake." Blair has got a lot to answer for. Yes, the special relationship is crucial but you still do what is right. Wilson has never been given the proper credit that he deserved for keeping us out of Vietnam. It took some bottle. But the reality is he had more clout, more courage about him than Blair.'

*

I remember that throughout our childhood my dad had praised the Americans and emphasised to my brother and me the importance of the 'special relationship' between our countries. 'We'd have never won the war if the Yanks hadn't been there for us in our darkest hour,' was a favourite phrase of his. Now I realised that his love of the big band leader Glenn Miller and his music, his enthusiasm for the 1946 film *The Best Years Of Our Lives* and his strong encouragement for me to travel around the United States as a teenager in 1976, in America's bicentennial year, had all been firmly rooted in his own war experience and in his appreciation of the special relationship between the United States and Great Britain.

All recent US presidents and British prime ministers have referred to that phrase at one time or another. Winston Churchill first used the term in 1944: 'It is my deepest conviction that unless Britain and the United States are joined in a special relationship . . . another destructive war will come to pass.'

President Roosevelt and Churchill sealed such a bond, at their countries' critical time of need, through their special personal relationship based on mutual trust, respect and affection. After the Allies' victory, in his famous 'Sinews of Peace' address in Fulton, Missouri, in 1946, Churchill once again exclaimed: 'Neither the sure prevention of war nor the continuous rise of world organisation will be gained without what I have called the fraternal association of the English-speaking peoples. This means a special relationship between the British Commonwealth and Empire and the United States.'

In reality since then, the 'special relationship' has ranged from intense warmth and closeness to coolness and lack of rapport, depending on the leaders at the time. Kennedy and Macmillan, Reagan and Thatcher, Clinton and Blair, Bush and Blair were particularly close. Eisenhower and Eden, Clinton and Major, Bush and Brown were not. President Johnson and Prime Minister Harold Wilson never hit it off after Wilson took the firm stance not to send troops to Vietnam. But the phrase has endured for more than six decades.

Indeed, in his tribute message to Her Majesty The Queen on her Diamond Jubilee in 2012, President Obama emphasised it once again: 'In war and peace, in times of plenty and in times of hardship, the United States and the United Kingdom have shared a special relationship. As we work together to build a better future for the next generation, it is gratifying to know that the bonds between our nations remain indispensable to our two countries and the world.'

Following on the heels of that special relationship between the US and the UK was there, I wondered, also a special relationship between Larry and Lawry? Was there any evidence of a direct link between the two Byford families? So many times on my journey, people had asked me, 'Are you connected?' and I'd give the same answer each time, 'I don't know, I don't think so, it doesn't matter. It's not the point of the story.' I didn't want the mission to be rooted in genealogy, so I'd avoided investigating. But I was intrigued. Was there a blood link between the Byfords of east Texas and the Byfords of Yorkshire? I decided to take a look.

My father had never researched beyond his own grandfather in regard to his own lineage. The morning after he had received his honorary citizen award, we sat down together in his living room, opened my laptop and began the search.

Together, we traced our family back to my great-great-great-great-great-grandfather, Robert Byford. The earliest record showed that he was married in 1783 in the Wilford deanery in Suffolk. He was a comber, an ancient trade involving the cleaning and preparing of wool ready to be spun into worsted yarn. It was a shock to my father to learn that his Yorkshire roots went back only one generation and that his family, in reality, were from East Anglia, living in the counties of Suffolk and Essex.

Across the Atlantic Ocean, over the course of the last ten years, Larry's elder brother, David, and a fellow genealogy enthusiast, Linda Davenport, each have been separately trying to track back the relevant American Byford family line. I had already discovered that Larry's father, Fate, was the fourth child of Hugh Franklin Byford and Emma Wall. Also, that Hugh was born in 1874 in Texas, married Emma in 1902 and died in 1936 aged 62.

Larry's great-grandfather, John Wesley Byford, was born in 1835, probably in Tennessee. One census indicated Greenville, Texas, but that was possibly the place where he was working at the time. John married Catherine Parish Day, from Ohio, in Hopkins County, Texas, in 1858 when he was 23 and she was 18. David understands that John Byford served in the American Civil War and was deeply affected by shell shock and stress.

Precise details of Larry's great-great-grandfather's life are hard to pin down. Both David and Linda have spent a considerable length of time each trying to uncover who he was. It's thought that his name may have been William Byford. One record indicates that he was from Maryland. Another shows that at one time he lived in Tennessee.

I mentioned all this to a friend. 'You've heard of *Albion Seed*, haven't you?' he exclaimed. I didn't know what he was talking about but soon became engrossed. *Albion Seed* is a unique and breathtaking historical work that reveals the early cultural history of what is now the United States. Written by David Hackett Fischer, it was published in 1989. The book identifies four British 'folkways' – groups of people who moved from four distinct regions of England or 'Albion' to the area that became the United States. The first of these four migrations were English Puritans who moved from East Anglia to the New England or Massachusetts area between 1629 and 1640. Nearly all were Protestants who became the breeding stock for America's Yankee population. Within East Anglia, Fischer indicates, the Puritan movement was 'strongest in the small towns where so many migrants left for Massachusetts'. These included Colchester, Braintree and Woodbridge, all of which I now knew had connections with my own Byford heritage line.

Frustratingly, I found no mention of the name Byford anywhere in his book. I wondered whether an ancestor of Robert Byford, the comber, living a century before him somewhere in East Anglia, had travelled on one of those boats across the Atlantic in the early 1600s to New England. And if so, did the family move from there to Maryland, where they were relatives of William Byford, Larry's great-great-grandfather? It would be a huge leap of faith to believe that – pure speculation with no hard evidence whatsoever. But it was a possibility.

I contacted David Fischer directly. Today, he is a Professor of History at Brandeis University near Boston. What did he think? He was reluctant to commit and felt that I needed more hard evidence before I jumped to any conclusions. Clearly, he was right to be sceptical and it was understandable for him to be unwilling to say any more. But all the same, I thought to myself, you never know. One can only ponder, dream and speculate. The chances that the Byfords on both sides of the Atlantic are related seem low. But as Larry's brother David said to me: 'You never know, Mark. We could be very, very distant cousins. And you know, I'd like that very much.'

'I'd like that too, David,' I responded. And so would the 'honorary citizen'.

*

The exhibition at the Imperial War Museum in London was entitled 'War Story: Serving In Afghanistan'. Comprising a series of individual photographic portraits of armed forces personnel serving on the front line, the display was powerful, with each photograph taken against the same clean white background, throwing into sharp relief the detail of every feature. The frank, full-on stare of the soldiers invited the public to interpret their expressions, to imagine the shades of experience that lay behind their eyes.

An interactive showcase nearby played out oral testimonies of the soldier's lot in Afghanistan. I noted down their phrases such as 'pinned down' and 'horrendous'. One spoke graphically about a colleague losing his lower limbs. Another described 'shards of skin and bone hanging out'. A school party of multiracial young children stood beside me. One girl, aged about eight, spotted a Taliban flag and cheered. 'I love the Taliban,' she told her friend.

The conversation I'd had with my dad about the wars in Iraq and Afghanistan sprang to mind. He'd made it clear that, in his view, both wars should never have happened, that the lessons of Vietnam had not been learned.

The visit also triggered memories of Geoff Hoon, who had been one of my university law lecturers. In 1977, Geoff lived in my hall of residence, as did Stuart Walker, a PhD student. Very soon, the three of us became good friends and would often have heated debates lasting late into the night in which we would passionately try to put the world to rights. Little did Stuart and I know then that Geoff Hoon would go on to enter politics and that, 20 years later, he would become Secretary of State for Defence in Tony Blair's Labour government. With Blair, he was the man who, controversially, took Britain to war in Afghanistan and Iraq, alongside the Americans.

Geoff Hoon, UK Secretary of State for Defence, with Donald Rumsfeld, US Defense Secretary, Pentagon, February 2003

Bush and Blair. Rumsfeld and Hoon. The Afghanistan War began in October 2001 with the launch of 'Operation Enduring Freedom'. The Iraq War, in the spring of 2003, became the most divisive conflict involving the United Kingdom in living memory.

I contacted Geoff Hoon, told him about my journey and began asking him to explain the difference between Britain's lack of involvement in Vietnam and the active response in Iraq and Afghanistan. I made the point that Wilson's Labour government had refused to join the Americans in Vietnam and that, in contrast, Blair's Labour government had been joined at the hip with the US in Iraq and Afghanistan.

'I think it's a fair question,' he responded. 'The two impressions I would have are as follows. First, Denis Healey's generation were scarred by the Second World War. I think people like him were determined not to put people through what he'd been through. That generation wanted to move on, to not go through what they themselves had gone through. Second, I would draw a very strong distinction between Afghanistan and Iraq. With regard to Afghanistan, I am absolutely confident 9/11 was an attack on all of us and if we did not respond collectively then that would have been, in effect, an act of cowardice.

'I accept there is a more accurate analogy between Vietnam and Iraq in the sense that we did not have to do it. But I am absolutely certain that we had no choice but to go in to Afghanistan. With regard to Iraq, we had a choice but we didn't have a choice about Afghanistan.'

'So what is the difference between Vietnam and Iraq?' I asked.

'I think the difference is context,' he responded. 'I think maybe the Americans were slightly unlucky in Vietnam. The time was against them. They were in the wrong place at the wrong time. The war was unwinnable. Yet Korea a decade earlier was not the wrong thing to do. If you go to Seoul today and see how they halted the advance of totalitarianism and communism there, I think they thought they'd do the same in Vietnam but the time was against them. I think the tide of history will show that in Iraq we did the right thing because the Arab Spring, the movement to democracy, was ultimately a vindication of first getting rid of an evil dictator.'

I told him I could fully understand the purpose behind the Second World War and the Falklands War. They seemed to be clearly justified to me. But in Vietnam, the chance of an invasion of US sovereign land was nil. Yes, the Soviets were funding the North Vietnamese. And, yes, I understood it was all wrapped up in the Cold War. But how could Vietnam be justified?

'Well, would you not have gone into Korea in the '50s then?' he responded. 'Today, South Korea is a successful, independent capitalist democracy free from the horrors of the North. I just don't think it's straightforward. The Americans were unlucky in Vietnam and the real failure was not to understand the way the wind was blowing. The Americans think they can throw things at problems until they win.' He went on: 'For me, Afghanistan is like the Second World War and the Falklands – an absolute no-brainer that we needed to be there. I accept Iraq is more divisive. We didn't have to do it. We could have said if the Americans want to do it, then let them get on with it. To that extent, there is an analogy with Vietnam.'

I reminded him that five years after the Vietnam War ended, Robert McNamara, the former US Defence Secretary, had admitted, 'We were wrong, we were terribly wrong.' I went on to ask Geoff Hoon whether he still honestly feels that, in hindsight, Iraq was the right thing to do.

'Time will tell if it was right, in my view,' he replied. 'It's glib to talk about the tides of history but I think something crucial is now underway in the Arab world with regard to democracy, and Iraq is part of that.'

'What did the Iraq experience teach you?' I questioned.

'That it's easier not to do something,' he said. 'It's extraordinarily difficult to take these decisions and to live with them. To have that responsibility. I went to see my dad at that time. I used to see him every Sunday. I remember him saying, "I wouldn't like to be doing what you're doing." I thought, "Bloody hell, here's a man who spent six years in war and I'm never going to do that." You do bear that enormous responsibility.'

What about conscription, I wondered. Would it ever happen again?

'The one clear thing is you cannot send conscripts into war in the future. You couldn't conscript people. You'd have experienced soldiers looking after inexperienced ones. Conscription, in military terms, is a waste of space.' He continued: 'I think there is a distinction between a war of national survival, like the Second World War was for Britain, as against the kind of operation we conducted in Iraq or the Americans carried out in Vietnam. They were more about being a good international citizen and recognising that powerful countries have obligations for foreign-policy reasons, not for reasons of national survival. It follows you can use and maybe have to use conscripts in a war of national survival but, on the other hand, using people who've been conscripted for foreign-policy reasons I don't think could be managed now in a modern democracy.'

Following the conversation with Geoff Hoon, I recalled an interview on the BBC World Service's *Witness* programme, broadcast in December 2009, in which Denis Healey discussed the contrasting positions between Harold Wilson and Vietnam and Tony Blair and Iraq. Lord Healey, the former Defence Secretary in the two Labour governments between 1964 and 1970, said that if British troops had been sent to South Vietnam in the mid 1960s, he would have resigned. The case then against sending British troops to join with the Americans, he said, was 'overwhelming'. So what did he have to say of the American-led invasion of Iraq in 2003, in which British troops were involved?

> I think Tony Blair was very, very foolish. He believed very, very strongly in the special relationship. But after his first two years, nearly all his decisions were wrong, particularly the war in Iraq . . .
>
> It was a dreadful error. I warned two years beforehand that if we got involved in a war in Iraq, there'd be a big increase in Islamic terrorism and Iraq itself would dissolve into civil war.

In the same week that I had talked with Geoff Hoon in 2012, another full-time, professional UK soldier was killed in Afghanistan. Captain Walter Barrie from the Royal Scots Borderers, 1st Battalion The Royal Regiment of Scotland, was shot dead by a man wearing an Afghan army uniform in the Nadf-e Ali district of Helmand province. His was the 438th death to be suffered by UK forces in the Afghanistan War. By then the Americans had lost 1,955 personnel there. In the Iraq War of 2003, the United Kingdom lost 179 and the Americans lost 4,487. None of those deaths, in either war, involved any conscripts, in stark contrast to Vietnam.

Forty-five years on, echoing the Vietnam War opinion polls at the end of 1967, the American people in 2012 again declared a strong and growing opposition to the country's latest foreign war venture. By then, a decade after it had begun, polling showed that two-thirds opposed the war in Afghanistan and thought it was going badly. Similarly, in the United Kingdom, the vast majority believed the war had become pointless and more than half favoured an immediate withdrawal of British troops.

On a visit to Afghanistan in 2012, the Prime Minister, David Cameron, said: 'We have paid a heavy price but the reason for coming here in the first place was to stop Afghanistan being a haven for terror . . . I think it was the right decision.'

At the same time, the UK's Chief of the Defence Staff, Sir David Richards, emphasised: 'With our partners in NATO/ISAF we have been more successful than many, regrettably, recognise. Over the past decade, we have closed Al Qaeda's bolthole, helped underpin a more viable government, overseen elections, trained an army and police force, and put a country that suffered 30 years of war into a position where industry, education and the rule of law are beginning to grow. True, there is a long way to go. But we are heading in the right direction.'

But in that week I spoke to Geoff Hoon, *The Times* newspaper headlined a main story as: '*Afghanistan "not worth life of one more soldier"*.' The veteran British politician and former Royal Marine Lord Ashdown argued that there was no hope of victory:

> It is not worth wasting one more life in Afghanistan. All that we can achieve has now been achieved. All that we might have achieved had we done things differently has been lost. The only rational policy is to leave quickly, in good order and in the company of our allies. This is the only cause for which further lives should be risked. It is now crystal clear that we have lost in Afghanistan.

I rang my dad and read out Paddy Ashdown's article. 'I agree entirely,' he said. 'It's terrible. We haven't learnt anything.'

CHAPTER 20

RETURNING TO THE WALL

The sun was beginning to set on my project; the months of research, travel, conversations and contacts were drawing to a close. There was one place left to go. One place that would draw my journey full circle, taking me back to where it had begun.

Dragging my suitcase into the porch, I noticed an envelope with a US stamp lying on the floor. I had a flight to catch, so my first instinct was to leave it until my return, but I realised that it might be what I had been waiting eagerly for. I opened the envelope to find three photos and a short note in capital letters:

> MARK,
> I HOPE THESE WILL BE USEFUL
>
> DEWEY SMITH

Dewey Smith, known as 'Smitty', was a member of the 1967 band of the First Squad of the Third Platoon that included Possum Trot, Clinton Endres and Jay Phillips. Neither Clinton nor Jay had seen nor heard from him since Vietnam.

When Jay had met me six weeks earlier at the Charlie Company reunion, it had prompted him to try to find Smitty, partly to re-establish contact but also to see if he had any photos or memories of Larry that could help me. Jay remembered that he was a North Carolina boy, so, having looked up the name in the relevant directory, he drove the 550-mile round trip to try to track him down. Eventually, the two men met for the first time in forty-five years.

On his return home, Jay emailed me immediately:

> Smitty has spent his life in Jamestown (with a minor detour to the Orient) and has had a couple of auto repair shops and a bar, so apparently he provided more than one kind of lubrication. He does not recall Larry's real name but just knew him by the moniker he used. The best news is that Dewey seemed certain that he had a photo of Possum Trot (sitting on a tank?) although he needs to do some searching before he can lay his hands on it. He does not have a computer or email.

When I received Jay's message, I was touched at the effort he had made. I hoped that Dewey would uncover the photograph of Possum Trot in Vietnam. If so, it would mean that the Byford family finally would have a memento of his time there. They treasured the photo of him leaving boot camp at Fort Polk with Gene Ashcraft, believing it to be the last image taken of him. But that was all they had. There was no visual record of his time in Vietnam – just his two letters and his posthumous medals.

I rang Dewey immediately, using a telephone number provided by Jay. Initially, he was reticent, reluctant to share many details with me, but after a while he revealed that he'd arrived as a 19-year-old draftee in February 1967 and remembered Possum Trot coming on board at the beginning of May: 'He was a young country boy. Tough. Down to earth. Good as gold. Like me, the whole time you're out there, you're scared to death. He was going down that tunnel that day in those rocks. He didn't make it.'

Dewey told me that he had never attended a Charlie Company reunion. He wasn't even aware of their existence and, rather than keeping in touch with fellow Vets, had focused on trying to shut out all the memories of Vietnam since coming home.

'It was crazy,' he told me. 'But I'm proud of what I did.'

He said his memories were hazy. He'd tried to 'put it all away' in order to cope with his post-Vietnam life. But he thought he still had a photograph of Possum Trot somewhere in the house. I told him that it would mean so much to me and, more importantly, to Larry's family if he could send it to me in England. 'I can't promise,' he said, 'but I'll do my best.'

I'd not heard anything for weeks and thought that his search had been to no avail. But then the photos arrived, just as I was about to set off on the last lap of my journey. I looked closely at them: two coloured pictures, marked 'May '67', and a small black-and-white image; all of them still good quality, although the colour ones were somewhat faded. Those two had been taken on the beach at Lo Dieu on the morning of 10 May following the amphibious landing. One showed Concepcion Leon, in the foreground, walking with a fellow grunt along the beach, armed with his M16 rifle and looking toward the camera. The second colour image depicted four dead NVA soldiers lying sprawled on the beach, bare-legged with arms outstretched, and three American soldiers looking down on them, apparently checking for signs of life. I couldn't tell if one of them was Larry. The rest of the platoon were clustered together on top of the sand dunes nearby.

The final photograph of Larry Byford, Binh Dinh, South Vietnam, June 1967 (Photo courtesy of Dewey Smith)

The black-and-white photograph was taken, according to Dewey, 'maybe the day before or two days before his death'. Larry was pictured sitting on top of a US tank next to another armoured personnel carrier. It was clear that both vehicles were stationary and the men had stopped for a break. One bare-chested soldier was taking a drink; the others were sitting around chatting. Dewey remembered that Larry had wanted to pose on top of the tank. 'I remember we hitched a ride. It's definitely him. It's just before he was killed,' Dewey later told me.

The photo was taken either on the afternoon of Wednesday, 21 June, or on the morning of Thursday, 22 June, following the battle in Van Thien when the 1/69th Armor had assisted Charlie Company in sweeping through the village. Whilst holding it, I remembered that Reuters report about the same Van Thien battle published on the front of the *Huddersfield Daily Examiner* two days after it was over.

The final photograph had arrived unexpectedly on my doorstep just as I was setting out to end my journey. I felt a sense of both revelation and completion as I realised that I was looking at an image of Larry Byford just hours before he died. I returned the photographs to their envelope and put them in my bag.

*

From the very beginning of my journey, I'd always intended to return to The Wall. I wanted to revisit Panel 22E, look at line 52 and see Larry's name again, this time carrying the knowledge of his story. There was to be a special service on Veterans Day to commemorate the 30th anniversary of the Memorial's dedication in 1982. When President Reagan stood at The Wall two years later, he had declared: 'Those who fought in Vietnam are part of us, part of our history. They reflected the best in us. No number of wreaths, no amount of music and memorialising will ever do them justice, but it is good that we honour them and their sacrifice.

'The men of Vietnam answered the call of their country. They died uncomplaining. The men and women of Vietnam fought for freedom in a place where liberty was in danger. They put their lives in danger to help a people in a land far away from their own. Many sacrificed their lives in the name of duty, honour and country. All were patriots who lit the world with their fidelity and courage.

'They were both our children and our heroes. We will never, ever, forget them.'

I wanted to be there, alongside the thousands of Vets who were expected to attend. Importantly, I wanted to meet the man whose original vision and drive had resulted in the Vietnam Memorial. I wanted to find out more about him; tell him about the impact The Wall had had on me and thank him for inspiring my journey.

Washington DC was bathed in sunshine – unusual for mid-November. The temperature was over 70° Fahrenheit by midday and the sky was crystal clear. The leaves were falling fast, producing swirling carpets of orange, red and brown. My wife, Hilary, was with me to see for herself the black-granite chevron that had dominated my life for so many months.

We walked together down the full length of the National Mall, starting at the stunningly ornate Library of Congress in the east and passing the magnificent, gleaming white dome of the Capitol building. The Washington Monument stood proudly against the cloudless sky. Before long, we reached the national World War II memorial. Built and dedicated as recently as 2004, it honours the 16 million Americans who served and the 400,000 who died in that conflict. Carved on one plinth are the words: 'Americans came to liberate not to conquer, to restore freedom and to end tyranny'. We walked around the two triumphal arches; the fifty-six pillars; the dancing fountains; the wide pavilion and the 'Freedom Wall' engraved with four thousand and forty-eight gold stars each representing a hundred Americans who died in the war. The message in front of the wall stated boldly: 'Here we mark the price of freedom'. My father, I thought, would have loved that.

We moved on further west, past the tranquillity of the Reflecting Pool, towards the grandiose Lincoln Memorial. Standing on the steps, I tried to imagine the scene there on 21 October 1967 when more than a 100,000 gathered to protest against the Vietnam War – the climax to nationwide demonstrations held as part of 'Stop The Draft' week. It was the most dramatic sign that year of the waning support for the war.

I'd arranged to meet Jan Scruggs, the founding father of The Wall, on a site nearby that has been designated for a new Vietnam Veterans Memorial education centre. Jan Scruggs is a remarkable man who conceived the idea for the Vietnam Memorial more than 30 years ago. On his return from the war, he studied psychology at university in an attempt to understand the post-traumatic stress disorder from which he and many of his comrades were suffering.

'I was traumatised by my own service in Vietnam. I lost friends there. I became a recognised authority on PTSD. I suffered from it myself,' he told me.

I was keen to know the catalyst for his desire to build a monument to those who had lost their lives.

Jan told me, 'I saw *The Deer Hunter* at the movies. The very next day I said to myself, "I'm going to build a memorial on the Mall." I had no idea what I was doing but I said, "I'm going to do it." I didn't care what the memorial was. I just wanted societal recognition of the duty the people had given in Vietnam.'

The scenes from the film that resonated so strongly were those that depicted the soldiers returning from the war only to be abandoned by both the authorities and the American public. He was horrified to be reminded that a hatred of the war had, in effect, evolved into a hatred of those who had fought in it. I was reminded of the time I, too, saw *The Deer Hunter* with Hilary while at university. Its impact on us was also very deep.

Jan Scruggs led the campaign to raise money to fund the project entirely by voluntary public subscription. There was no government funding available. He didn't want it anyway. To start the ball rolling, he put in $2,800 of his own that he'd raised from the sale of some land given to him by his father. Against the odds, he persuaded the decision makers in DC that it was right to honour the Vietnam Vets and that the memorial should stand with the other national monuments on the Mall.

'It has brought a lot of attention about the public sacrifice of the veterans,' he explained. 'Let us separate the war from the warrior. It's a very interesting intellectual concept. Telling people you can be against the war but you are not against the warrior. You are not against your fellow citizen who was drafted or volunteered. You can respect their service and yet disagree with the war. Fast forward from 30 years ago and our government decided it was going to change the world again with Iraq and Afghanistan. It hasn't exactly worked out but when the veterans now come back from there no one blames them. They get a pat on the back. A thank-you. These two wars are extremely unpopular with the American public, with Congress, but no one now castigates the veterans. So people have now separated the war from the warrior. That's one of the great things that have come from this memorial.'

Before meeting Jan, I had read the book *To Heal A Nation*, which recounts his story. I asked him what he meant by the title.

'I wanted to tie people together for and against the war. To connect people and help heal some of the wounds of a nation that had faced the most divisive war in its history with the exception of the American Civil War.'

Had he done it? I asked. Had The Wall healed the nation?

'In as much as any piece of architecture can, it's done a pretty good job. It was very clear, even 30 years ago, that it had an enormous psychological impact on people when they saw all the names. It touched people. Grabbed their spirit, their soul. The combination of seeing your own reflection and the names. The fact they're not in alphabetical order but laid out chronologically. So when survivors come, for example, they see the private alongside the major who he tried to rescue, side by side. That's so powerful. And everyone is equal. We insisted on that. No titles. It's very egalitarian and the right thing to do. Don't give the general more status than the private. They both gave their lives equally for their country, right?'

We headed towards The Wall together as hundreds of Vets congregated on Henry Bacon Drive just above the memorial. He was greeted constantly by 'Hi, Jan', 'Good to see you, Jan' and 'Hey, thanks, Jan, how you doing?' His legendary status among many of the Vets as the founder and president of the Vietnam Veterans Memorial Fund was plain to see. We made our way through the crowds to the edifice that had changed his life.

'So what do you think about those people who say, "The Vietnam War was a waste of time but I admire the guys themselves for their bravery and courage?"' I asked.

'That's generally what people think. It's all very complicated. It's very easy to say something that didn't work out wasn't worth trying. But it was a major moment in American history that spun a tad out of control. The context was the height of the Cold War. The Russians and the US hoped it could be completed relatively quickly. There could be a North and South. A bad guy and a good guy. Just like Korea. But nothing really worked and it became a terrible event in American history.'

Why is every other major monument in Washington white and rising from the ground and yet the Vietnam Memorial is black, and cut into the ground, hidden from view, I wondered?

'There is a psychological dynamic here. As you descend into The Wall, all the distractions disappear. You become part of it. It's amazing.'

We began our own slow descent towards the intersection of the two walls. I noticed the veterans' jackets and caps, many of them customised with badges and sewn-on patches:

> For those who fought for it, Freedom has a taste the protected will never know.
> Jane Fonda: Traitor Bitch
> I wasn't there but I still care
> All gave some. Some gave all

'This is a really powerful piece of architecture. People robbed of their future at such a very young age. Forever young,' he said, his own reflection passing through the names.

Before accompanying him to The Wall, I had told Jan about my project. He headed straight for Panel 22E and sought out Larry S Byford. I motioned to the name of the Major – Edwin Woods Martin – and instinctively he touched both names, linking them together.

'We're all on some kind of spiritual journey in our lives, Mark. Sometimes I think there's some kind of God or some sort of force that guides us to do something. Metaphysical issues that can't be proved. But yours is an extraordinary experience like nothing ever done in America before that I know of. It's important. It matters.'

Vietnam Veterans Memorial Fund founder Jan C. Scruggs links Larry Byford's name with Major Edwin Woods Martin on The Wall, November 2012

As we stood together by the Panel, we could hear a succession of voices calling out names one by one in a regular, sombre rhythm. A podium had been erected in front of The Wall and hundreds of volunteers had been taking it in turns over the last three days, during light and darkness, to read out each of the 58,282 names as part of the 30th anniversary dedication ceremonies.

Spontaneously, Jan said to me, 'I want you to go up on the stage and read out Larry's name.' It was so unexpected and such a great privilege. I knew I had to do it. Jan led me to the queue, then, when it was my turn, I walked up to the microphone and read out a list of 30 names. I ended with the name Larry S Byford. He shook my hand as I left the stage and embraced me warmly.

'America is a great kind of meritocracy,' Jan reflected. 'As a poor boy, I was able to change the landscape of the Mall. Bring some honour to a bunch of people who died. Because of the Vietnam Memorial, they then decided they had to also build a World War Two memorial and a Korean memorial. So I've probably had more of an impact on the Mall than I should have. I don't gloat over it. It was just something I had to do.'

*

At The Wall's midpoint, as I put my left cheek close up against the panel and looked east, I could see the Washington Monument standing proud in the distance. I turned and did the same with my right cheek against the western side of The Wall and there was the Lincoln Memorial. Gleaming white monuments on the Mall, hailing two of America's greatest individuals, linked together through a black wall of 58,282 names.

I sat on the grass opposite and my mind focused on its designer, Maya Lin. In 1980, she was a 21-year-old architecture student at Yale University. As part of her course, she studied funereal architecture and a final design assignment was to prepare an entry for the Vietnam Veterans Memorial competition. Extraordinarily, and controversially, the young Ohio woman of Chinese parentage won.

Her original proposal described the Memorial:

> as a rift in the earth, a long polished black stone wall emerging from and receding into the earth. The names, seemingly infinite in number, convey the sense of overwhelming numbers, while unifying those individuals into a whole.
>
> The memorial is composed as a moving composition to be understood as we move into and out of it . . . we, the living, are brought to a concrete realization of these deaths.

Maya Lin has spoken powerfully and movingly about her desire to face the truth of war honestly and to focus on the people rather than on the politics. Memorials are usually not about individual loss but about the victor, she said, but this was different. In her own words, she described The Wall's impact: 'It's only when you accept the pain, the death, can you come away from it, can you overcome it. It's up to each individual to come to terms with the loss. You see a name, you touch a name, and the pain will come out.

'If you can't accept death, you'll never get over it. The monument is about honesty. You have to accept and admit the pain in order for it to heal, to be cathartic.'

She'd focused the memorial on being participatory, accessible – a place for personal reflection and personal reckoning:

'It's for the Veterans but there's a universalness to it, a psychological thing about how it's working. The names rise up and you become part of it. It doesn't overpower you. It's very intimate. It's a timeline of a specific war but it's also about the universal loss in a war.

'All I wanted to do was open a space in the landscape that would open up a space within us.'

*

By one o'clock on that 11 November afternoon, the Veterans Day ceremony was underway. It opened with the Presentation of Colours, appropriately carried out by five members of the 1st Cavalry Division, dressed in formal regalia. The National Anthem followed. Then the Pledge of Allegiance. The Keynote Address was delivered by the Secretary of Veteran Affairs, Eric Shinseki, in which he talked eloquently about the Memorial's 'power of connection,' the 'intimacy of The Wall,' how it was 'a time capsule of the heart' and 'a conversation between the living and the dead'. A bagpiper played 'Amazing Grace' before the Taps ended the ceremony. The chilling sound from the bugler impacted on everyone gathered there. I looked around at the thousands crammed into the specially designated area in front of The Wall. Many were in tears. Some were standing upright, holding their right hand against their chest. Others were embracing their partners. A sea of emotions flowing over a bedrock of patriotism.

I recalled the words of Ken Burington, the fellow Vet from C Company who arrived in the field in June 1967. Visiting him two months previously, just down the road in Annapolis, he'd told me: 'Patriotism is a very viable value with a real sense of love. This country succeeds on the contribution of its citizens. I believe all the riches I share in – there is a contribution from my part that should be equal. I'm a citizen and it's not a free ride. Wasn't it Jefferson who said, "The tree of liberty must be watered from time to time with the blood of patriots and tyrants"? Sometimes you die. Mostly you don't. I didn't want to die or lose a limb. But I was fortunate.'

After the ceremony, scores of relatives and Vets processed slowly in front of The Wall. I noticed that the immediate, typical reaction was to reach out and touch.

Hilary was surprised by such a tactile response but the shiny polished surface seemed to invite people to stroke it; to trace the grooves of the names; to register the temperature of the stone, which fluctuates throughout the day, imbuing it with a sense of life. This tactile connection between the living and the dead, emphasised further by the reflection of each onlooker overlaying the names of the deceased, lent an air of intimacy to a unique memorial.

As ever, many people were leaving objects in front of The Wall. We saw photographs, messages, medals, a favourite beer, a helmet, a pair of well-worn army boots, a flag, a teddy bear, flowers, a poem, a draft card. I had been planning this moment for some time and had come well prepared.

Directly opposite Panel 22E, I laid out my own special dedication to Larry. I had acquired a large 1st Cavalry Division flag, which formed the basis of my display. On it were signed messages from his colleagues from Charlie Company 67, collected whilst I was at the Vets reunion. 'Welcome Home', 'You're Not Forgotten', 'Goodbye to a Squad Mate', 'I Will Remember You Always', 'RIP', 'A Cav Brother Never Forgotten' were some of the messages they'd written in black marker pen over the famous yellow-and-black insignia.

To its left, laid out on the flag's white-cotton background, I positioned my own personal tributes. The original rubbing of his name that I'd made when I first visited The Wall. The grey 1st Cavalry insignia patch given to me by Ben Miller at Dallas airport as he arrived home from Iraq and I was starting out on my journey. My original 45rpm vinyl record of 'All You Need Is Love' by The Beatles, first performed by them on Sunday, 23 June 1967 – the date when Fate and the rest of his family were informed of Larry's death. Below it, the American flag that I'd placed in the wine glass at the reunion ceremony in Georgia after striking the bell and reading out his name.

To the right of the signed insignia I placed a pile of sand I'd collected by the cave at the Rockpile – from the place where he fell on 'Watermelon Hill'. Above it I positioned the original edition of the *East Texas Light* newspaper, headlining his death, with a message written above the masthead by his beloved sister Debbie on behalf of all his siblings: 'Larry Byford was our brother. Killed In Action June 23rd 1967. Today and everyday he remains our hero.' Below it was the photo of Larry taken at Fort Polk and a 1st Cavalry insignia patch together with my father's war photo and a SHAEF badge. Larry and Lawry linked together at The Wall. In between them, there was a special message from my dad written on a card:

LARRY
I AM SO PROUD OF YOU, DEAR COMRADE
LAWRY

The presentation soon began to attract attention. To my surprise, the organisers who began placing the various regimental wreaths into a formal line incorporated my own work into their official display, placing it on the grass directly in front of Larry's name. Hundreds of people started to walk past slowly, respectfully. Veterans. Gold Star families. Friends. Officials. Visitors. Children. Many crouched down to look carefully at the different pieces of memorabilia on the flag, intrigued to work out and understand the significance of each object.

'He must have loved The Beatles,' one man said. '"All You Need Is Love."'

'I couldn't put it better,' his companion replied.

An elderly man looked down at the sand and commented to his wife: 'I wonder if that's from a beach where he died?'

Two Vets dressed in 1st Cavalry formal attire stood to attention and saluted. A father knelt down with his young son. He took his son's hand, sniffed and said within clear earshot, 'That's what a hero is.'

I looked behind at The Wall. It was late afternoon. The sun was setting in the west and the light was fading fast. We walked towards Panel 22E, which by now was warm, having absorbed the full day's sun. It was time for the final farewell. Extraordinarily, the image of the sunset had settled directly beneath Larry's name.

I stared at those 12 letters engraved on The Wall and closed my eyes.

I recalled those words on that other wall in Normanton.

> At the going down of the sun and in the morning we will remember them.
>
> Greater love hath no man than this. That a man lay down his life for his friends.

LARRY S BYFORD

He did his duty. He served his country. A true hero who made the ultimate sacrifice.

No longer simply a name on a wall. From sunrise to sunset. My journey was over.

ACKNOWLEDGEMENTS

A big thank you to the following for their contributions, advice and encouragement in supporting *A Name on a Wall*:

All Larry Byford's family, especially his living siblings: David, Hughie, Nancy, Pat and Debbie; and his cousin Judy Hilton. With special gratitude to Tommye Byford.

Larry's friends: Tommy Murphy, Melva Lee Tomlin, Delbert Graves and Bill Rushing, together with Gene Ashcraft.

The Vets from Charlie Company 2nd/5th 1st Cavalry Division who served with Larry in Vietnam in 1967: Ken Burington, Don Jensen, Clinton Endres, Jay Phillips, Richard Bratton, Mike Martin, Don Demchak, Tom Rutten, Tom Blancett, John Wnek and Dewey Smith: 'The First Team'.

John McCorkle, Jimmy 'Tree' Machin and Bob Brace at the re-union.

The Vietnam Veterans Memorial Fund, especially Jan Scruggs.

Shelby County Historical Society; LBJ Presidential Library; Vietnam Center and Archive, Texas Tech University; Christine Deehan at Rowan University; Normanton Library Local Studies Collection; Huddersfield Local Studies Library; Stephen Carter at the Huddersfield Daily Examiner library; Nick Marcus in the Information and Archive department at BBC News.

Julie Casburn for transcriptions; Stuart and Helen Walker for honest, critical assessment; Phuoc Tong for guidance in Binh Dinh; Ken MacQuarrie for passionate interest and support; Isobel Neil for persuading me that the moment at The Wall and the subsequent journey could be a book.

Mark Stokes and Tom Marcinkowski from Winchester Photographic.

All at Mainstream Publishing, especially Bill Campbell for backing the book; Ailsa Bathgate as editor for excellent oversight, skill and advice; Graeme Blaikie and Fiona Brownlee.

And Hilary Bleiker, for her endless creativity, talent and ideas without whom . . . The writing of this book was very much a partnership and joint labour of love, and she provided extraordinary support, suggestions and guidance throughout the project.

The author's royalties from the sale of this book will be donated to the Vietnam Veterans Memorial Fund. The VVMF is a non-profit organisation, based in Washington DC, with a mission to preserve the legacy of The Wall. Currently, it is raising funds to build a new Education Centre near to The Wall.

BIBLIOGRAPHY

THE VIETNAM VETERANS MEMORIAL

Hass, Kristin Ann, *Carried To The Wall: American Memory and the Vietnam Veterans Memorial* (University of California Press, 1998)

Langmead, Donald, *Maya Lin: A Biography* (Greenwood Biographies, 2011)

Lark, Lisa A., *All They Left Behind: Legacies of the Men and Women on the Wall* (M.T. Publishing, 2012)

Lin, Maya, *Boundaries* (Simon & Schuster, 2000)

Lopes, Sal (ed.) *The Wall: Images and Offerings from the Vietnam Veterans Memorial* (Collins, 1987)

Murphy, Kim, *The Wall: 25 Years of Healing and Educating* (M.T. Publishing, 2007)

Scruggs, Jan C., *The Wall That Heals* (VVMF, 1992)

Scruggs, Jan C., *Writings on The Wall* (VVMF, 1994)

Scruggs, Jan C., *Why Vietnam Still Matters* (VVMF, 1996)

Scruggs, Jan C., *The War and The Wall* (VVMF, 2002)

Scruggs, Jan C. and Swerdlow, Joel L., *To Heal a Nation: The Vietnam Veterans Memorial* (Harper and Row, 1985)

LAWRY BYFORD IN THE SECOND WORLD WAR

Eisenhower, Dwight D., *Report By The Supreme Commander to the Combined Chiefs Of Staff on the Operations in Europe of the Allied Expeditionary Force 6th June 1944 to 8th May 1945* (His Majesty's Stationery Office, 1946)

Bibliography

LARRY BYFORD'S CHILDHOOD

Shelby County Historical Commission, *History Of Shelby County, Texas* (Curtis Media Corp, 1998)

HISTORY OF THE VIETNAM WAR

Ang Cheng, Guan, *The Vietnam War from the Other Side: The Vietnamese Communists' Perspective* (Routledge Curzon, 2002)

Anderson, David L., *The Vietnam War* (Palgrave Macmillan, 2005)

Appy, Christian G., *Vietnam: The Definitive Oral History, Told from All Sides* (Ebury Press, 2008)

Cawthorne, Nigel, *Vietnam: A War Lost and Won* (Arcturus, 2003)

Gibbons, William Conrad, *US Government and the Vietnam War: Executive and Legislative Roles and Relationships Part IV* (Princeton, 1995)

Karnow, Stanley, *Vietnam: A History* (Viking Press, 1983)

Katcher, Philip, *Armies of the Vietnam War 1962–75* (Osprey Publishing, 1980)

Langer, Howard J., *The Vietnam War: An Encyclopedia of Quotations* (Greenwood Press, 2005)

Lawrence, Mark Atwood, *The Vietnam War: A Concise International History* (Oxford University Press, 2008)

Rottman, Gordon, *US Army Infantryman In Vietnam 1965–1973* (Osprey Publishing, 2005)

Rottman, Gordon, *US Army In The Vietnam War 1965–1973* (Osprey Publishing, 2008)

Rottman, Gordon, *Vietnam Infantry Tactics* (Osprey Publishing, 2011)

Sanders, Vivienne, *USA and Vietnam 1945–1975* (Hodder & Stoughton, 2002)

Sieg, Kent, *Foreign Relations Of The United States 1964–1968 Volume V* (US Government Printing Office, 2002)

Wiest, Andrew, *The Vietnam War 1956–1975* (Osprey, 2002)

1ST CAVALRY DIVISION

Coleman, Major J.D., *Air Cav: History of 1st Cavalry Division In Vietnam 1965–1969* (Turner Publishing, 2011)

Stanton, Shelby L., *The 1st Cav in Vietnam: Anatomy of a Division* (Presidio, 1987)

ON THE BATTLEFIELD

Herr, Michael, *Dispatches* (Picador, 1978)

Maraniss, David, *They Marched into Sunlight: War and Peace, Vietnam and*

America (Simon & Schuster, 2003)
Marlantes, Karl, *Matterhorn: A Novel of the Vietnam War* (Corvus, 2010)
Marlantes, Karl, *What It Is Like to Go to War* (Corvus, 2012)
Mason, Robert, *Chickenhawk* (Corgi, 1984)

PRESIDENT LYNDON BAINES JOHNSON

Bole, Robert D., *Summit At Holly Bush* (Glassboro, 1989)
Johnson, Lyndon Baines, *The Vantage Point* (Holt and Rinehart Wilson, 1971)
Updegrove, Mark K., *Indomitable Will: LBJ in the Presidency* (Crown, 2012)

HO CHI MINH

Brocheux, Pierre, *Ho Chi Minh: A Biography* (Cambridge University Press, 2007)
Duiker, William J., *Ho Chi Minh: A Life* (Hyperion, 2000)

HAROLD WILSON

Baylis, John, *Anglo American Defence Relations 1939–1984* (Macmillan, 1981)
Healey, Denis, *The Time of My Life* (Michael Joseph, 1989)
Pimlott, Ben, *Harold Wilson* (HarperCollins, 1992)
Routledge, Paul, *Wilson* (Haus Publishing, 2006)
Wilson, Harold, *The Labour Government 1964–1970: A Personal Record* (Weidenfeld & Nicolson, 1971)

VIETNAM TODAY

Ashwill, Mark A., *Vietnam Today: A Guide to a Nation at a Crossroads* (Intercultural Press, 2005)
Hayton, Bill, *Vietnam: Rising Dragon* (Yale University Press, 2010)

EARLY AMERICAN MIGRATION HISTROY

Fischer, David Hackett, *Albion's Seed* (Oxford University Press, 1989)

KEY WEBSITES

Charlie Company 2nd/5th 1st Cavalry Division: www.tallcomanche.org
Find A Grave: www.findagrave.com
Lyndon Baines Johnson Library and Museum: www.lbjlibrary.com
Vietnam Veterans Memorial Fund: www.vvmf.org